CW00662617

CHRISTOPHER ADAMS.

✉ chris@christopheradams.com.au

Interest Rate Derivatives

Interest Rate Derivatives
A Practical Guide to Applications, Pricing and Modelling

By Todd James

Published by Risk Books, a Division of Incisive Financial Publishing Ltd

Haymarket House
28–29 Haymarket
London SW1Y 4RX
Tel: +44 (0)20 7484 9700
Fax: +44 (0)20 7484 9800
E-mail: books@incisivemedia.com
Sites: www.riskbooks.com
       www.incisivemedia.com

ISBN 1 904339 94 8

British Library Cataloguing in Publication Data
A catalogue record for this book is available from the British Library

Publisher: Laurie Donaldson
Assistant Editor: Steve Fairman
Designer: Rebecca Bramwell

Typeset by Mizpah Publishing Services Private Limited, Chennai, India

Printed and bound in Spain by Espacegrafic, Pamplona, Navarra

Contents

About the Author

Todd James is originally from Canada and has over 10 years of derivatives and debt capital markets experience. This includes trading, marketing and structuring derivative transactions. His past experience covers debt capital markets, interest rate and cross currency swaps trading and structuring, and structured products marketing and structuring.

After spending seven years in London, Todd moved to Asia where he has resided for the past five years, structuring and developing structured products. He also provides regular workshops and seminars for corporate and financial institutions on derivatives, risk management and structured products.

Todd holds a BBA in business and economics from WLU, Waterloo, Canada, and an MBA in finance from the University of Toronto.

Financial Mathematics

TIME VALUE OF MONEY

The time value of money (TVM) refers to the fact that the value of a dollar today is different to a dollar received or paid in the future. The concept of TVM is an essential component in the calculation of the value of financial instruments, valuing future and present cash-flows. It is an important consideration in derivative valuation where cash flows occur at different times and are require to be converted to an equivalent or present value amount.

The TVM takes into account the cost or benefit of borrowing or lending cash over a period of time.

Simple interest rates

Simple interest is the amount of cash that is earned over a period of time, and paid at maturity. Simple interest is expressed as a "flat" amount.

Formula:

$$I = PV \times r \times \frac{d}{basis} \tag{1}$$

where

I	Amount of interest;
PV	Present value;
r	Interest rate;
d	Number of days;
$basis$	Day count basis.

What is the simple interest (I) if:

$PV = \$100$
$R\quad = 5.00\%$
$d\quad = 180$
$basis = 360$

$$I = \$100 \times 5.00\% \times \frac{180}{360}$$

$$I = \text{US\$2.50}$$

If you invest US\$100 for 180 days at 5.00% you would earn US\$2.50 in simple interest.

If we know the cost of money we can use this concept in order to determine the value of money at any given point in time. We can calculate what a dollar paid or received today is worth in 12 months time, or its future value. We can also calculate the current value of US\$1 paid or received in 12 months time, or its present value.

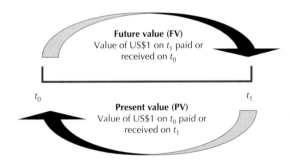

Future value (FV)

From the Equation (1) we can calculate the future value (FV) of any value, where the future value equals the present value (PV) of the original cash plus any interest earned over the period:

Formula:

$$FV = PV + I$$

or

$$FV = PV \times \left(1 + r \times \frac{d}{basis}\right) \qquad (2)$$

What is the future value (*FV*) if:

PV = \$100
r = 5.00%
d = 180
$basis$ = 360

$$FV = US\$100 \times \left(1 + 5.00\% \times \frac{180}{360}\right) = US\$102.50$$

If we invest US\$100 (*PV*) today for 180 days at an interest rate of 5.00% it would be worth at maturity (*FV*) US\$102.50.

Present value (PV)
Rearranging Equation (2) we can also calculate the present value of any future cashflow.
  Formula:

$$PV = \frac{FV}{1 + \left(r \times \dfrac{d}{basis}\right)} \qquad (3)$$

What is the present value (*PV*) if:

FV = \$100
r = 5.00%
d = 180
$basis$ = 360

$$PV = \frac{100}{1 + \left(5.00\% \times \dfrac{180}{360}\right)} = 97.561$$

US\$100 received in 180 days has a present value of US\$97.561. In other words, if we invested US\$97.561 for 180 days at an interest rate of 5.00% we would have US\$100 at maturity. The US\$97.561 is known as the present value or the discount amount.

Discount factors (DCF)
Formula 1–3 can be generalized to generate a discount factor for any given period derived from the simple interest rate. A discount

factor (DCF) can then be applied to any future cashflow in order to derive its present value.

Formula:

$$DCF = \frac{1}{1 + \left(r \times \dfrac{d}{basis} \right)} \tag{4}$$

where

DCF	Discount factor;
R	Interest rate;
d	Number of days;
basis	Day count basis.

What is the discount factor (DCF) if:

r	= 5.00%	Simple interest
d	= 180	Number of days from today to date of the rate
basis	= 360	Day count basis of the currency

$$DCF = \frac{1}{1 + \left(5.00\% \times \dfrac{180}{360} \right)} = 0.97561$$

For every US$1 we are to pay or receive in 180 days it is worth US$0.97561 in present value terms. We apply DCFs to value future cashflows in present value terms.

If we had to pay US$1 in 180 days we could invest US$0.97561 today, at 5.00% for 180 days and at maturity we would have the US$1, which is equal to the amount we need to pay. Therefore the present value of paying US$1 in 180 days is US$0.97561. In other words we are indifferent to paying US$0.97561 today or paying US$1 in 180 days.

If we were to receive US$1 in 180 days we could borrow US$0.97561 today at a cost of 5.00% for 180 and at maturity we would have to repay US$1, which is equal to the amount we would receive. Therefore the value of receiving US$1 in 180 days, in present value terms is US$0.97561. In other words we are indifferent to receiving US$0.97561 today or receiving US$1 in 180 days time.

EFFECTIVE AND NOMINAL INTEREST RATES

Not all interest rates are quoted equally. Interest can be calculated on a daily, monthly, quarterly, semi-annually or on an annual basis.

When you calculated interest on a term shorter than the payment period we say that the interest earns interest. We therefore must consider "interest on interest" or compound interest.

In order to compare interest rates with different payment frequencies we will need to convert the rates to a common term of reference. The nominal interest rate is the quoted or stated interest rate, while the effective interest rate is the equivalent annual interest rate. The effective annual interest rate is the equivalent interest rate if there was only one annual interest payment. The nominal interest rate (quoted or compound rate) is the interest rate, which is actually paid or received on a periodic frequency. We use the effective annual yields to compare rates, which are quoted or paid on a different payment frequency.

To calculate the effective (annual) yield from a given nominal or compound rate we use the following equation:

Formula:

$$r_e = \left[\left(1 + \frac{r}{p} \right)^{p} - 1 \right]$$
(5)

where

r_e Effective yield;
R Nominal (quoted or compound rate) interest rate;
P Number of interest payments per year.

What is the effective yield (r_e) if:

$r = 5.00\%$
$p = 2$

$$r_e = \left(1 + \frac{5.00\%}{2} \right)^{2} - 1$$

$$r_e = 5.0625\%$$

5.00% interest calculated and paid on a semi annual basis is equal to 5.0625% calculated and paid annually. We can also rearrange the formula to calculate the nominal or compound yield (r) from the effective annual yield (r_e):

Formula:

$$r = \left((1 + r_e)^{\frac{1}{p}} - 1 \right) \times p$$
(6)

What is the nominal (r) interest rate, payable semi-annual if:
r_e = 5.00%   Effective annual yield
$p = 2$ Number of payments per annum

$$r = \left((1+5.00\%)^{\frac{1}{2}} - 1 \right) \times 2$$

$$r = 4.939\%$$

We can use Equations 5 and 6 to convert between effective and nominal rates.

Formula:

Nominal to effective rate   Effective to nominal rate

$$r_e = \left(1 + \frac{r}{p} \right)^p - 1$$ $$r = \left((1+r_e)^{\frac{1}{p}} - 1 \right) \times p$$

Using the above formulae here are some common conversions:

Conversions	Formulae
Annual to semi-annual	$(\sqrt{(1+r_e)} - 1) \times 2$ or $((1 + r_e)^{1/2} - 1) \times 2$
Annual to quarterly	$(\sqrt[4]{(1+r_e)} - 1) \times 4$ or $((1 + r_e)^{1/4} - 1) \times 4$
Semi-annual to annual	$\left(\frac{r}{2} + 1 \right)^2 - 1$
Quarterly to annual	$\left(\frac{r}{4} + 1 \right)^4 - 1$
Quarterly to semi-annual	$\left(\left(\frac{r}{4} + 1 \right)^2 - 1 \right) \times 2$

Converting nominal interest rates

While we can always compare effective interest rates we may also want to compare the rates on a common nominal basis. Suppose an investment earns a nominal semi-annual interest rate of 6.00% pa and we want to compare the return of this investment with another one that pays interest on a quarterly basis. Rather than convert both rates to effective rates we can convert one nominal rate to another nominal interest rate.

The calculation can be broken into two steps:

1. Convert nominal semi-annual rate to an effective annual interest rate

$r = 6.0000\%$

$p = 2$

$$r_e = (1 + 0.06/2)^2 - 1$$
$$= 6.0900\%$$

2. Convert from an effective annual to a nominal quarterly interest rate

$r_e = 6.0900\%$

$p = 4$

$$r = ((0.06090+1)^{1/4} - 1) \times 4$$
$$= 5.9557\%$$

Example 1 Nominal, effective and continuous interest rates

	E × 1 (%)	E × 2 (%)	E × 3 (%)
Continuously compounded	4.000	6.000	12.000
Nominal monthly	4.007	6.015	12.060
Nominal quarterly	4.020	6.045	12.182
Nominal semi-annually	4.040	6.091	12.367
Effective annual	4.081	6.184	12.750

We will also need to consider the payment frequencies of the interest rates when we are calculating the present and future cashflows. Where there is periodic compounding we must adjust the *FV* (Equation (2)) and *PV* (Equation (3)) to take into account the more frequent interest payments.

Formula:

$$FV = PV \times \left(1 + \frac{r}{p}\right)^{p \times t} \tag{7}$$

$$PV = FV \times \frac{1}{\left(1 + \dfrac{r}{p}\right)^{p \times t}} \tag{8}$$

where

    FV Future Value;
    PV Present Value;
    r Nominal or compound interest rate;
    p Number of interest payments per annum;
    t Time in years.

If you invest US$100 for 2-years, assuming that the 2-year semi-annual interest rate is 4.00%, what is the investment worth at maturity?

$$FV = 100 \times \left(1 + \frac{4.00\%}{2}\right)^{2 \times 2}$$

$$FV = \text{US\$108.2432}$$

How much would you need to invest today so that you would have US$100, in 2-years' time, assuming that the 2-year semi-annual interest rate is 4.00%?

$$PV = 100 \times \frac{1}{\left(1 + \frac{4.00\%}{2}\right)^{2 \times 2}}$$

$$PV = \text{US\$92.3845}$$

Continuous compound interest rates

A continuously compounded interest rate assumes that interest is paid continuously rather than at discrete monthly, quarterly or annual intervals. A zero coupon bond for example is assumed to calculate continuous interest rather than periodic interest. We can derive the formulas for continuous interest compounding if we use FV (Equation (7)) and PV (Equation (8)) and assume that p is a very big number, in fact as p approaches infinity the equations break down to:

Formula:

$$FV = PV \times e^{(r_c \times t)} \tag{9}$$

Where

    PV Present Value;
    r_c Interest rate with continuous compounding;
    t Time in years.

What is the future value (FV) if you invest US$100 for 2-years at a continuous compound interest rate of 4.00%:

PV = US$100
r_c = 4.00%
t = 2

$$FV = 100 \times e^{(4.00\% \times 2)}$$
$$FV = 108.3287$$

Rearrange Equation (9) to obtain the continuously compounded interest rate for a given present value (PV) and future value (FV):

$$r_c = \frac{\ln(FV/PV)}{t} \tag{10}$$

What is the continuously compounded interest rate (r_c) if:

FV = US$100
PV = US$80
t = 5

$$r_c = \frac{\ln(100/80)}{5}$$
$$r_c = 4.4629\%$$

In general we can look at the relationship between annual effective rates (r_e) and continuously compounded interest rate (r_c) as:

$$r_c = \ln(1 + r_e) \tag{11}$$

What is the continuously compounded interest rate (r_c) if the effective annual rate (r_e) is 4.081%?

$$r_c = \ln(1 + 4.081\%)$$
$$r_c = 4.00\%$$

We can also easily convert the continuously compound rate (r_c) rate to an annual effective rate (r_e).

$$r_e = e^{r_c} - 1 \tag{12}$$

What is the effective annual rate (r_e) if the continuous compound interest rate (r_c) is 5.25%?

$$r_e = e^{6.00\%} - 1$$
$$r_e = 6.184\%$$

Once we convert the continuous compound rate to an effective annual rate we can then convert it further to a nominal compound rate as described on p 4.

MONEY MARKET YIELDS

Money market instruments are short-term securities with maturity less than 1-year or 365 days. Money market instruments cover a variety of underlying securities, including:

❑ Interbank deposits;
❑ Certificate of deposits (CDs);
❑ Commercial paper (CP);
❑ Bills of exchange;
❑ T-Bills; and
❑ Repurchase agreements (repos).

They can be issued by a variety of entities as a means to finance short-term obligations, and provide short-term (cash) liquidity:

❑ banks (interbank deposits);
❑ corporates (commercial paper); and
❑ governments (t-bills).

Some of the instruments are non-negotiable, such as deposits, which means the holder cannot transfer from one investor to another, thus they need to hold the investment until maturity. Some securities, such as CDs and T-bills are negotiable (transferable securities), therefore a secondary market exists which allows investors to sell (as well as buy) the securities at any time prior to maturity.

In the case of a short-term deposit or money market deposit, the principal amount invested and repaid are the same. All interest is accrued based on the nominal or face value of the deposit. In the case of a term deposit, interest is paid at the end of the deposit. The nominal rate of interest (r) on the deposit or loan is normally linked to a benchmark or interbank rate, such as the London Interbank Offer Rate or LIBOR for US dollar.

We can use Equation (2) to calculating the future value of a term deposit, replacing the present value (PV) with the principal or face amount of the deposit (P):

Formula:

$$FV = PV \times \left(1 + r \times \frac{d}{basis}\right)$$

Where

PV	Principal or face value of the instrument;
FV	Future value;
r	Nominal interest rate;
d	Number of days;
basis	Day count basis (360 or 365).

If you deposited US$100 for 181 days at a rate of 4.25% what would the maturity or future value (*FV*) be?

PV = US$100
r = 4.25%
d = 181
$basis$ = 360

$$FV = US\$100 \times \left(1 + 4.25\% \times \frac{181}{360}\right)$$

$$FV = US\$102.1368$$

If interest rates instantaneously fell 1% from 4.25% (as above) to 3.25% what would be the new present value (*PV*) or price of the deposit?

FV = US$102.1368
r = 3.25%
d = 181
$basis$ = 360

$$PV = \frac{FV}{1 + r \times (days/basis)}$$

$$PV = \frac{102.1368}{1 + 3.25\% \times \left(\frac{181}{360}\right)}$$

$$PV = 100.4947$$

If interest rates decreased 1.00% the value of the deposit would increase from its initial value of 100% to 100.4947%, everything else being equal.

Generally money market yields are quoted on an Act/360 day-count basis (some currencies such as GBP are quoted on an Act/365 basis) while bond yields are quoted on an Act/365 daycount basis.

We can simply convert one yield to the other by converting the basis which each is quoted.

Formula:

$$BY = MMY \times \frac{365}{360} \qquad (13)$$

$$MMY = BY \times \frac{360}{365} \qquad (14)$$

where

      BY Bond Yield;

      MMY Money Market Yield.

What is the BY (Act/365) for an investment that earns 5.00% on a MMY (Act/360) basis?

$$BY = 5.00\% \times \frac{365}{360} = 5.0694\%$$

What is the MMY (Act/360) for an investment that earns 5.00% on a BY (Act/365) basis?

$$MMY = 5.00 \times \frac{360}{365} = 4.9315\%$$

Discount yields

Some financial instruments, such as US Treasury bills, are quoted on a discount basis. This means that the securities are issued at a discount to it nominal value and mature at Par or 100%. The amount that the investor pays for the security (the amount of the discount) is determined by the discount yield, which is different, than its yield to maturity (effective or nominal yield).

Pricing securities with discount yields

We can calculate the price of a discount instrument from its discount rate.

Formula:

$$\text{Price} = FV \times \left(1 - r_d \times \frac{d}{basis} \right) \qquad (15)$$

What is the price of a 90-day US T-Bill with a PAR value of US$100, quoted at a discount rate of 6.00%? T-Bills are quoted on an Act/360 day count basis.

r_d = 4.00%　　Discount rate
FV = US\$100　Future Value (PAR)
d = 181　　　Number of (actual) days
$basis$ = 360　　Day count basis (360 or 365)

$$\text{Price} = 100 \times \left(1 - 4.00\% \times \frac{181}{360}\right)$$
$$\text{Price} = 97.9889$$

We can also use the built in excel function to calculate the price of a US T-Bill from a given maturity date and discount yield.

Excel example
PRICE(*settlement, maturity, rate, yld, redemption, frequency, basis*)

❑ *Settlement* is the Treasury bill's settlement date, which is the date after the issue date when the Treasury bill is traded to the buyer. Dates may be entered as text strings within.
❑ *Maturity* is the Treasury bill's maturity date, which is the date when the Treasury bill expires.
❑ *Discount* is the Treasury bill's discount rate.
　(yld)

A Treasury bill has the following terms:

Settlement date:　　　　9-Dec-05
Maturity date:　　　　　8-Jun-06
Discount rate:　　　　　4.00%

The Treasury bill price is:
= PRICE ("10-jan-05", "10-jan-10", 7.00%, 6.75%, 100, 2, 4)
= 101.0462

We can also use the more generalised discount price excel formula and assume that the future or PAR value is 100 and the daycount basis is Act/360.

= PRICE ("10-jan-05", "10-jan-10", 7.00%, 6.75%, 100, 2, 4)
= 101.0462

Discount yields

We can calculate the discount rate (r_d) given the securities price or present value (PV) and its maturity value or future value (FV), which is normally PAR, as well as the number of days to maturity and the daycount basis for the underlying security.

Formula:

$$r_d = \frac{(FV - PV)}{PV} \times \frac{basis}{days} \qquad \text{(16)}$$

where

r_d	Discount rate;
FV	Future value;
PV	Present value (current price);
d	Number of days to maturity;
$basis$	Day count basis (360 or 365).

What is the discount rate (r_d) of a US T-Bill if the current price is US$98.25 per US$100 nominal amount maturing in 181 days?

FV = US$100
PV = US$98.25
d = 181
$basis$ = 360

$$r_d = \frac{(100 - 98.25)}{98.25} \times \frac{360}{181}$$
$$r_d = 3.5427\%$$

You can also use the built in excel function to calculate the discount yield or T-bill yield.

Excel example
=YIELDDISC(settlement, maturity, pr, redemption, basis)

❏ *Settlement* is the security's settlement date, which is the date after the issue date when the security is traded to the buyer.
❏ *Maturity* is the security's maturity date, which is the date when the security expires.
❏ *Pr* is the security's price per US$100 face value.
❏ *Redemption* is the security's redemption value per US$100 face value.
❏ *Basis* is the type of day count basis to use.

Basis	Daycount basis
0 or omitted	US (NASD) 30/360
1	Actual/actual
2	Actual/360
3	Actual/365
4	European 30/360

A security has the following terms:

Settlement date:	23-Apr-06
Maturity date:	21-Oct-06
Price:	96.25
Redemption value:	US$100
Basis:	Actual/360

The discount yield is:

   = YIELDDISC("23-Apr-06","21-Oct-06", 98.25,100,2)

   = 0.035427 or 3.5427%

We can also use the more specific excel formula to get the discount yield for a T-Bill. This formula assumes that the future value is 100 and the daycount basis is Act/360.

   The Treasury bill yield is:

   = TBILLYield("23-Apr-05","21-Oct-05",98.25)

   = 0.035427 or 3.5427%

Converting discount yields to money market rates

We can convert the discount yield (applicable to T-Bills) to a money market yield using the following formula:

Formula:

$$r_e = \frac{r_d}{1 - \left(r_d \times \dfrac{d}{basis} \right)}$$

(17)

What is the comparable effective annual interest rate (r_e) on a money market basis (Act/360) if:

$$r_d \quad = 4.00\% \text{ Discount rate}$$
$$d \quad = 181 \quad \text{Number of actual days of deposit}$$
$$basis = 360 \quad \text{Day count basis}$$

$$r = \frac{4.00\%}{1 - 4.00\% \times \dfrac{181}{360}} = 4.0821\%$$

Given how T-Bill and the discount rates are calculated the discount rate will always be lower than the money market equivalent yields.

Table 1 is an example of a Bloomberg pricing page showing the yield/price relationship for a discount security, a US T-Bill, and also provides the equivalent bond and money market rates. A discount rate is 4.00%, is equivalent to a 4.0821% money market yield, which can also be converted and compared to an equivalent bond yield (BY):

$$BY = MMY \times \frac{365}{360} = 4.0821\% \times \frac{365}{360} = 4.139\%$$

Table 1 Yield/price relationship

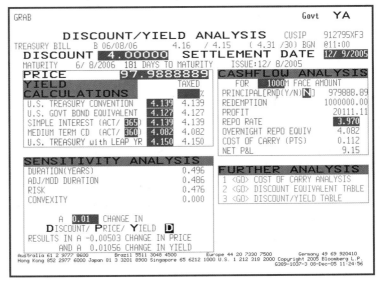

Source: Bloomberg

DAY COUNT BASIS CONVENTIONS

In order to determine the actual cash amount of interest to be paid we need to know the number days interest accrues and also the basis on which to calculate the amount of interest to be paid. The daycount basis or daycount fraction therefore refers to the following:

$$Daycount\ Fraction = \frac{d}{basis}$$

Where d is the number of days within an interest calculation period and the *basis* is the number of days during a year. Depending on the market conventions of the underlying interest-baring instrument there are different conventions for calculation daycount fractions. In most cases interest is calculated from (and including) the settlement date or start of the interest calculation period to (but excluding) the maturity or payment date.

Generally there are three ways to calculate the number of days (d) during an interest rate calculation period (as per ISDA: International Swaps Dealers Association, definitions):

Days calculations (d)

1. *Actual*

Count the actual number of days during the period:

From	To	Days (d)
1-Mar	31-Mar	30
1-Mar	29-Mar	28
1-Mar	1-Apr	31
1-Feb	1-Mar	28

2. *30*

Assume that each month has 30 days (remaining days are then subtracted from 30). Each month is assumed to have 30 days unless:

  (a) the last day of the interest or calculation period is the 31st day of the month and the first day of the month is a day less than the 30th (ie, not 30th or 31st) then the last month of the calculation period is considered to have 31 days; or

  (b) the last day of the calculation period is the last day of the month of February, in which case the month of February shall not be considered to be lengthened to a 30-day month.

We can calculate the number of days within the period using the following algorithm:

$$d = (Y_2 - Y_1) \times 360 + (M_2 - M_1) \times 30 + (d_2 - d_1)$$

where

D	Number of days within the period;
$d_2/M_2/Y_2$	End date of the period;
$d_1/M_1/Y_1$	Start date of the period.

We also make the following two conditions:
(i)   if $d_1 = 31$ then   set $d_1 = 30$
(ii) if $d_2 = 31$ and $d_1 < 30$ then   set $d_2 = 31$
      if $d_2 = 31$ and $d_1 \geq 30$ then   set $d_2 = 31$

From	To	Days (d)
1-Mar	31-Mar	30
1-Mar	29-Mar	28
1-Mar	1-Apr	30
1-Feb	1-Mar	30

3. *30E*

Assume that each month has 30, without regard to the date of the first day or last day of the calculation period, unless the last day of the calculation period is the last day of February, in which case the month of February shall not be considered to be lengthened to a 30 day month.

From	To	Days (d)
1-Mar	31-Mar	29
1-Mar	29-Mar	28
1-Mar	1-Apr	30
1-Feb	1-Mar	30

Excel example

Within Excel there is a function for determining the number of 30/360 days within a period:

=DAYS360(start_date, end_date, method)

Method = "False" or leave blank give you the number of days under the US (NASD) method (30):

=DAYS360("12/29/2000","1/31/2001") = 32 days

Method = "True" give you the number of days under the European 30 days a month method (30E):

=DAYS360("12/29/2000","1/31/2001") = 31 days

The following table provides examples of calculations of d for the three different conventions:

Day Count Conventions

| Date from | Date to | Number of Days | | |
		Act	30	30E
12-Feb-00	12-Aug-00	182	180	180
1-Jan-02	31-Jan-02	30	30	29
29-Dec-00	31-Jan-01	33	32	31
28-Feb-00	1-Mar-00	2	3	3
30-Dec-00	28-Feb-01	60	58	58
31-Dec-00	28-Feb-01	59	58	58
1-Mar-05	31-Mar-05	30	30	29
1-Mar-05	1-Apr-05	31	30	30
1-Feb-00	1-Feb-01	366	360	360
1-Feb-05	1-Mar-05	28	30	30

Basis calculations

There are also three different conventions for determining the basis.

1. *360:* Assume that each year has 360 days

Period	Days (d)
1-Mar-01 to 1-Mar-02	360
1-Mar-03 to 1-Mar-04	360

2. *365:* Assume that each year has 365 days

Period	Days (d)
1-Mar-01 to 1-Mar-02	365
1-Mar-03 to 1-Mar-04	365

3. *Actual:* Use the actual number of days within a full year coupon.

Period	Days (*d*)
1-Mar-01 to 1-Mar-02	365
1-Mar-03 to 1-Mar-04	366

If the interest period runs over two years, with one year a leap year and one not, the interest is calculated by dividing the payment/calculation into two parts.

Period	Days (*d*)
1-Feb-00 to 1-Feb-01	366 days
1-Feb-00 to 31-Dec-00	334 (leap year)
31-Dec-00 to 1-Feb-01	32 (non-leap year)

Day count basis and day count fraction

From the above outline there are nine different combinations of days and basis, however only five are used in common practice:

1. *Actual/Actual (ISDA[1])*

   The actual number of days in the calculation period divided by 365. If any portion of that interest calculation period falls within a leap year, the sum of (a) the actual number of days in that portion of the interest calculation period falling within a leap year divided by 366 and (b) the actual number of days in that portion of the interest calculation period falling within a non-leap year divided by 365.

   Example:
   Assume a semi-annual bond last paid a coupon on 2-June-2006 and pays the next coupon on 2-Dec-2006, which represents 183 actual days within the coupon period. What is the accrued interest to 5-Sept-2006, where there has been 95 actual days since the last coupon payment?

$$\mathrm{Act}/\mathrm{Act}_{(ISDA)} = \frac{95}{365} = 0.2603$$

(1b) Actual/Actual (ISMA²)

This method is used to calculate the accrued interest on US treasuries. When the interest calculation period is equal to or shorter than a regular interest period during which the coupon falls, then the actual number of days in the calculation period is divided by the product of the number of days in the regular period and the number of regular periods in a year.

$$\text{Actual/Actual}_{(ISMA)} = \frac{\text{Actual days}}{\text{Days in coupon period} \times \text{coupon frequency}}$$

Example:

Assume a semi-annual bond last paid a coupon on 2-June-2006 and pays the next coupon on 2-Dec-2006, which represents 183 actual days within the coupon period. What is the accrued interest to 5-Sept-2006, where there has been 95 actual days since the last coupon payment?

$$\text{Act/Act}_{(ISMA)} = \frac{95}{183 \times 2} = 0.25956$$

Under this calculation method there are equal coupon payments during the year regardless of how many actual days are in each period. For a semi annual coupon bond even though the first half of the year has 183 days and the second half of the year has 182 actual days there is an equal coupon paid for each semi-annual period.

2. *Actual/365 (Fixed)*

The actual number of days in the interest calculation period divided by 365, regardless of the fact that it may or may not be a leap year.

3. *Actual/360*

The actual number of days in the interest calculation period divided by 360, regardless of the fact that it may or may not be a leap year.

4. *30/360*

The number of days in the interest calculation period divided by 360 (see the above definition (30) to determine the number of days in the calculation period), regardless of the fact that it may or may not be a leap year.

5. *30E/360 or Eurobond basis*

The number of days in the interest calculation period divided by 360 (see above definition (30E) to determine the number of days in the calculation period), regardless of the fact that it may or may not be a leap year.

The table below shows an example of the daycount fractions for the five different conventions mentioned above.

Day Count Fractions						
		Day Count Fraction				
Date from	Date to	Act/360	Act/365	Act/Act	30/360	30E/360
12-Feb-00	12-Aug-00	0.506	0.499	0.4970	0.500	0.500
1-Jan-02	31-Jan-02	0.083	0.082	0.0820	0.083	0.081
31-Dec-00	28-Feb-01	0.164	0.162	0.1620	0.161	0.161
1-Mar-05	31-Mar-05	0.083	0.082	0.0820	0.083	0.081
1-Mar-05	1-Apr-05	0.086	0.085	0.0850	0.083	0.083
1-Feb-00	1-Feb-01	1.017	1.003	1.0000	1.000	1.000
1-Feb-05	1-Mar-05	0.078	0.077	0.0770	0.083	0.083
1-Feb-00	1-May-00	0.250	0.247	0.2459	0.250	0.250

The following table is a brief summary of the daycount basis conventions for the major currencies.

	Money market basis	Government bond basis
Australia	Act/366	Act/Act
Canada	Act/365	Act/365
Euro	Act/360	Act/Act
Japan	Act/360	Act/365
UK	Act/365	Act/Act
USA	Act/360	Act/Act

ROLL CONVENTION

If the expected interest payment date falls on a Saturday or Sunday (or a non-business day) we cannot make the payment so we must "roll" the payment to a good business day. We therefore need rules on how to roll the payment. For example, let's assume that interest is to be calculated up to and paid on 31-July-2005. However, since

31-July-2005 is a Sunday, we obviously cannot pay it. The rules or guidelines on when we pay the interest are refered to as the roll conventions. Not only do we roll or adjust for weekends we also adjust for non-business days within a particular business centre. For example for US$ we normally use New York as a business centre, so not only do we adjust for Sat and Sun we also adjust for New York holidays. There are generally three methods to roll interest payments for non-business days.

1. *Following business day convention*, if payment day is a non-business day then such a date shall be postponed to the next day that is a business day.
2. *Modified following business day convention*, if payment day is a non-business day then such a date shall be postponed to the next day that is a good business day unless it would thereby fall into the next calendar month, in which event such date shall be brought to the preceding business day.
3. *Preceding business day convention*, if payment day is a non-business day then such a date shall be brought forward to the immediately preceding business day.

Business day roll conventions					
		No adj.	Following	Mod following	Preceding
Roll date	DoW	1	2	3	4
25-Sep-05	Sun	25-Sep-05	26-Sep-05	26-Sep-05	23-Sep-05
25-Dec-05	Sun	25-Dec-05	28-Dec-05	28-Dec-05	23-Dec-05
25-Dec-06	Mon	25-Dec-06	27-Dec-06	27-Dec-06	22-Dec-06
31-Dec-06	Sun	31-Dec-06	1-Jan-07	29-Dec-06	29-Dec-06

The amount of interest paid can be adjusted (adjusted for non-business days), where the amount of interest reflects the roll or payments dates, or unadjusted, where the amount of interest is calculated based on the roll dates, regardless of when paid. If interest is unadjusted, interest roll dates and payment dates can be different.

1   ISDA: International Swaps Dealers Association
2   ISMA: International Securities Market Association (renamed the ICMA: International Capital Markets Association)

Short-Term Interest Rates and Futures

FORWARD-FORWARD

A forward-forward is a cash borrowing or deposit which begins on a forward date (a date beyond spot start) and matures on another forward date. All contract specifications, term, amount, and interest rate are all set out in advance. For someone who needs to borrow or lend cash at some time in the future a forward-forward contract removes any uncertainty with respect to what interest rate will apply. For a forward-forward there is principal exchange at the starting forward date and at maturity of the agreement. A forward-forward locks in an interest rate as well as commit both parties to borrow and lend cash on a specific future date. It is more common for counterparties to arrange borrowing and lending and then hedge the funding or lending rates using a separate agreement known as a forward rate agreement (FRA).

FORWARD RATE AGREEMENTS

Forward rate agreements (FRAs) are over the counter (OTC) contracts on short-term interest rates. They represent an agreement between two counterparties that wish to "fix" a future interest rate. There is no physical delivery of principal cash with FRAs, instead any profits and losses are realised by way of a cash settlement at the end of the contract period. There is also no premium or cash payment made at the time of entering into the contract, the only payment made is on settlement date at the end of the contract. If on the settlement date the FRA contract rate differs from a reference rate, (the reference rate is normally an interbank rate, for example LIBOR is used for US$) then a settlement payment is made from one counterparty to another. There is no principal exchange and there is no obligation by either party to borrow or lend cash. A FRA results in the same economics as a forward-forward. However, with a FRA the user enters into a deposit or borrowing at the current market rate and then a net cash payment is made by the FRA buyer or seller in order to make the net cash payment equal to a fixed interest rate (FRA contract rate). For a counterparty that wants to *pay* at the FRA rate they *buy* the FRA contract and lock in the rate payable. For example, a corporate may have a floating interest payment (linked to LIBOR) where the interest fixing is in 6 months time, the corporate can effectively hedge the interest rate risk and lock in a known forward rate by buying the FRA contract today for settlement in 6 months time. For a counterparty that wants to *receive* at the FRA rate they *sell* the FRA contract and lock in the rate to be received.

FRA applications
Example of FRA applications:

Current Market Rates:
6-Month LIBOR: 4.30%
6-Month FRA 6-Months Forward: 4.50/4.55%

1. *Hedge* against future interest rate risk by fixing the future interest rate today:
   A company borrows funds for 12 months, paying 6-Month US$ LIBOR + 100 bps. For these floating rate payments the normal market convention is to have the interest fixed at the beginning of the interest period and paid at the end or in arrears. The first interest payment in 6 months is fixed today at the current 6M US$ LIBOR rate, and paid at the end of the 6 months. The second interest rate is then fixed at the beginning of the next interest period and paid at maturity or in 12 months from the start of the loan. The company is exposed to increasing interest rates until the next interest rate is fixed 6 months from today. If rates increase over the next 6 months they will need to pay more interest, therefore they have interest rate exposure. In order to

eliminate this expose the company can buy (pay) a FRA from a bank which will fix the interest rate payable in 6 months' time regardless of where the actual rate ends up.

The company buys the 6-Month FRA at a contract rate of 4.55%. If in 6 months' time 6M LIBOR fixes at 4.75%, the company pays an interest payment of 5.75% (LIBOR + 100 bps) on the loan. They also settle the FRA contract, with the same notional amount, which they bought or agreed to pay at 4.55%, if the fixing is 4.75% then the FRA contract is settled which results in a 20 bps cash profit to the hedger. The NET cash flow to the corporate is equivalent to 5.55% (the fixed FRA rate + 100 bps).

Payment on Loan	−5.75%	(LIBOR + 100 bps)
FRA settlement	+0.20%	(4.75 − 4.55%)
Net Payment	−5.55%	(fixed at FRA rate + 100 bps)

2. *Speculate* on changes of future interest rates:
   One can profit from anticipated increases or decreases in interest rates by buying or selling a FRA respectively. If the trader has a view that LIBOR will be lower than 4.50% in 6 months' time, they will sell or enter into a short FRA position (effectively agree to receive at the FRA rate). If in 6 months' time LIBOR fixes at 4.25%, the FRA contract is cashed settled for a 25 bps profit (4.50% less 4.25%).

3. *Arbitrage,* take advantage of different prices of FRAs and other financial instruments such as exchange traded futures.
   Consider the following market prices for a financial future (Eurodollar future) which has a settlement date 6 months forward: if the FRA rate starting in 6 months and maturing in 12 months is 4.50/4.55% (bid/offer) and the 3-Month exchange traded future is priced at 95.41/95.43, which means an implied interest rate of 4.59/4.57% (100 less price):

3 × 6 FRA	4.50/4.55%
3-Month futures	95.41/95.43
Implied interest rates	(4.59/4.57%)

Arbitrage exists between the two prices, you can pay on the FRA at 4.55%, and buy or receiving on the futures contract at 4.57% (futures price of 95.43).

If (for example) in 1-month 3M LIBOR fixes at 4.40%:

FRA:

If the contract rate is 4.55% (you pay) and the settlement rate is 4.40%.
The settlement payment (or loss on the contract) is 15 bps (4.40%–4.55%)

Future:

Future settles at 95.60 (100 − 4.40)
Buy at 95.43 and settle or sell at 95.60 = profit of 17 bps

You have successfully locked in an arbitrage profit of 2 basis points to be realised in 6-month time. Normally, in an efficient market, these sort of arbitrage opportunities are rare, however for less liquid or less mature markets there may still exist arbitrage opportunities where FRA rates and futures are not priced efficiently.

FRA terminology
Spot FRA, Buy 6 × 12, US$ 10M at 4.50%

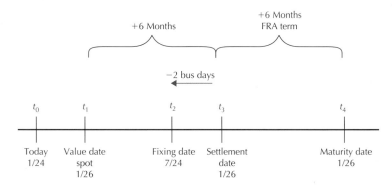

where

t_0 trade date;
t_1 value spot date: 2 business days after trade date;
t_2 reference rate fixing date: the difference between the contract rate and the reference rate is determined 2 business days before settlement date;
t_3 cash settlement date: the cash payment is exchanged;
t_4 Maturity date: Final maturity date of underlying FRA period, while there are no more payments to be made this is required

for the exact term of the FRA, final maturity less settlement date (t_3 less t_4) equals the number of days or period of FRA.

FRA interest rate: The agreed FRA contract rate, ie 4.50%.

FRA reference rate: The fixing rate, which you cash settle against the contract rate. The reference rate is usually based on 6M LIBOR for US$ or the specified interbank deposit rate for a particular underlying currency.

FRA purchase: A hedge for a forward short or borrowed cash position, which protects against rising interest rates. Purchase a FRA to lock in a rate you want to pay.

FRA sales: A hedge for a forward long or lent cash position, which protects against falling interest rates. Sell a FRA to lock in a rate you want to receive.

Settlement amount: The only cashflow that exists in a FRA, which is due on the settlement date. It is determined by the difference between FRA rate and reference rate multiplied by the Notional and daycount fraction and then the payment is discounted to the settlement date. Where the settlement amount (SA) equals:

$$SA = \frac{(Ref - FRA) \times (\pm Notional) \times (days/basis)}{1 + (Ref \times (days/basis))}$$

where

SA	Settlement Amount;
Ref	Reference Rate;
	LIBOR is the fixing rate for US$;
FRA	FRA or contract Rate;
Notional	Contract Amount ($+$ bought or $-$ sold);
basis	Day basis for interest calculations 360 (or 365);
days	Number of days contract or FRA Period.

The settlement amount equals the difference in the contract rate and the settlement rate at maturity in cash terms. It is then discounted back and paid on the settlement date, which is at the beginning of the FRA period, rather than wait until the end of the interest calculation period when the actual interest is paid.

FRA	6 $\times$ 12 purchase
Notional	US$ $+$ 10M

FRA rate	4.50%
LIBOR fixing	3.50%
Days of FRA	182

Settlement amount equals:

$$SA = \frac{(0.0450 - 0.0350) \times (+10M) \times (180/360)}{1 + (0.0350 \times (180/360))}$$

$$= US\$49,140.05$$

> We discount the actual settlement amount back to settlement date

A client initially purchases the FRA and thereby agrees to pay the FRA rate of 4.50%, and since rates have fallen the buyer must pay to the seller an amount equal to US$49,140. So even though the LIBOR rate has fallen the client must pay the difference between current LIBOR rates and the contract rate. In any interest rate scenario (higher or lower rates) the net interest payment is equal (on a net basis) to the contract rate of 4.50%.

Quotation

FRAs are usually quoted with reference to two numbers the first refers to the settlement date while the second refers to the final maturity date. The standard FRAs have underlying terms of 3, 6 or 12 months.

$$1 \times 4 \quad 3 \times 6 \quad 6 \times 9$$
$$1 \times 7 \quad 3 \times 9 \quad 6 \times 12$$

(where 6×12 referees to the FRA illustrated above). The settlement date is 6 months forward from spot date (2 business days forward) while the maturity date is 12 months forward from spot. Non-standard FRAs can also be quoted with terms of 1, 2, 4 months etc.). Given that FRA rates are money market instruments they are quoted based on an Act/360 (US$/EUR) or Act/365 (GBP/AUS/CAN/JPN) day count basis, the same as the underlying cash deposit rates which they are settled against.

Example:

Trade date:	14-April-06	(Friday)
Spot start:	18-April-06	(2 business days forward)
Start:	18-October-06	(6 months forward)

> Maturity: 18-April-07   (12 months forward)
> Number days: 183 days   (Actual days)

If one of the dates is not a good business day, generally following business days roll convention rules apply, which would be stated in the full FRA contract to which both parties agree.

Determination of a forward interest rate

Forward rates are interest rates set by market makers and reflect the market's expectations on future short-term interest rates. FRA rates are priced and traded on their own but they can also be derived from the prices of other market securities. We can derive the FRA from a combination of the zero coupon borrowing and lending interest rates.

For example,
If we could borrow cash for 1-year at 12-month LIBOR (5.00%), and
Lend cash for 6 months at 6-month LIBOR (4.00%),

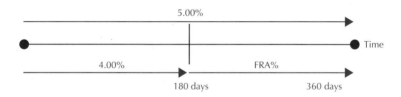

The forward rate (FRA rate) we can lend for 180 days forward can be derived from the no arbitrage relationship between the rates we can borrow and lend at. The interest you earn over the first 6 months at 4.00%, rolled over and compounded over the next 6 months at the implied FRA rate, the interest earned at maturity should be equal to what you would have earned if you had invested in just a 12-month deposit.

$$1 + 6MRate \times \frac{days6M}{basis} \times 1 + FRA \times \frac{daysFRA}{basis} = 1 + 12MRate \times \frac{days12M}{basis}$$

If we know the first 6-month rate and the 12-month rate then we can then solve for the implied 6-month rate FRA rate 6 months forward. If we re-arrange and generalise the above formula we can calculate FRA rates:

Formula:

$$FRA = \left[\frac{1+(r_L \times (days_L/basis))}{1+(r_S \times (days_S/basis))} - 1 \right] \times basis/days_{FRA}$$

(1)

where

r_L	5% Interest rate for longer period;
r_S	4% Interest rate for shorter period;
$days_L$	365 Number of days in longer period;
$days_S$	182 Number of days in shorter period;
$days_{FRA}$	183 Number of days in the FRA period;
$basis$	360 Day count basis.

Assuming that the interest rates are zero coupon rates.

In our example the implied 6 × 12 FRA rate is:

$$FRA = \left[\frac{1+(5.00\% \times (365/360))}{1+(4.00\% \times (182/360))} - 1 \right] \times \frac{360}{183}$$

$$FRA = 5.8757\%$$

If we have money market rates at which we can borrow and lend at, we can calculate the highest possible FRA rate and the lowest possible FRA rate, without arbitrage possibilities.

US$ Money Market (LIBOR) Rates (Act/360):

12 months (365 days):	5.00%	5.125%
6 months (182 days):	3.875%	4.00%

By doing a combination of a 12-month borrowing (or lending) with a 6-month lending (or borrowing) we can calculate the arbitrage free bid and offer FRA rates:

(a) Borrow 12 months at 5.125%   or   (b) Lend 12 months at 5.00%
     Lend 6 months at 3.875%   Borrow 6 months at 4.00%
     Sell FRA 6 × 12 at FRA_{offer}%   Buy FRA 6 × 12 at FRA_{bid}%

$$FRA_{offer} = \left[\frac{1+(5.125\% \times (365/360))}{1+(3.875\% \times (182/360))} - 1 \right] \times \frac{360}{183} = 6.2458\%$$

$$FRA_{bid} = \left[\frac{1+(5.00\% \times (365/360))}{1+(4.00\% \times (182/360))} - 1 \right] \times \frac{360}{183} = 5.8757\%$$

According to the current market rates, the FRA rate should be between 5.8757% and 6.2458%. If a trader quoted a FRA 6 × 12 rate

5.82/5.85% you could arbitrage the quote by entering into a combination of borrowing and lending to take advantage of the off market rate.

(a) Synthetically buy a FRA and:
Lend at 12-month LIBOR for 1-year spot start, at 5.00%
Borrow at 6-Month LIBOR for 6 months spot start, at 4.00%

(b) Sell the quoted 6 × 12 FRA at 5.85%
Which results in the following cashflows (based on a US$1M notional):

Rec +$50,694.44: 5.00% for 12 months, 5.00% × 365/360
Pay −$20,222.22: 4.00% for 6 months, 4.00% × 182/360,
Pay −$29,737.50: 5.85% for 6 months, 6 months forward,
   5.85% × 183/360
Net +$734.72   risk free profit.

SHORT-TERM INTEREST RATE FUTURES

Short-term interest rate futures represent standardised, exchange traded forward contracts on money market instruments. In general, most major currencies have a futures contract on a tradable short-term money market instrument such as a bank deposit or bank bill. The pricing and valuation of these instruments is very similar to FRAs and the two markets can often be viewed as direct substitutes.

For US$ the benchmark contract on short-term interest rates or 3-month LIBOR is the Eurodollar contracts traded primarily on the Chicago Mercantile Exchange (CME).

While a FRA can be tailor made to suit the users' needs, Futures have fixed parameters, such as underlying start dates, maturity dates and notional contract size. This standardisation makes futures more liquid and transparent but less flexible than FRAs.

Futures prices are quoted as discounts on the basis of 100. Thus, the formula to calculate the price of the future and the settlement amount is:

Formula:

$$Futures\ Price = 100 - Interest\ rate \tag{2}$$

$$SA = Notional \times \left(\frac{SP - PP}{100} \right) \times \frac{days}{basis} \tag{3}$$

where

SA	Settlement Amount;
SP	Settlement Price;
PP	Purchase Price;
Notiona	Contract size;
basis	Day basis for interest calculations 360 (or 365);
days	Number of days (underlying not to maturity).

For example, a forward interest rate of 5.50% equals a futures price of 94.50 (100 − 5.50). If the underlying forward rate increases from 5.50 to 6.00%, the future would decrease in price from 94.50 to 94.00; whereas if the forward rate decreased from 5.50 to 5.00%, the future price would increase from 94.50 to 95.00. If you purchase the futures contract on day 1 at a market price of 94.50 (albeit no cash is paid to purchase the contract) and at maturity the final settlement price is 96.00, then the settlement amount (SA) would be +US$2,500 (US$1million × (96.00 − 95.00)/100 × 90/360). If you are long in the contract, as rates fall the futures price increases and you earn a profit, if you had shorted the contract you would have lost − US$2,500. Futures, like FRAs, are settled against an inter-bank reference rate such as LIBOR.

A *tick* is the marginal movement of the futures price, where it is usually 0.01% (1 bp) in money market futures. The tick value is the standard value for all equivalent futures regardless of the maturity of the underlying future. The tick is equivalent to the concept of PV01, the present value of one basis point. The value of a tick can be calculated using the formula below:

Volume of the contract × Quantity of the tick × days/basis

For Eurodollar futures the contract size is standardised (US$1 Million) along with the underlying contract's term (90 days) and daycount basis (360). So for a US$ 90 day Eurodollar Futures contract a tick is worth:

US$1 million × 0.0001 × 90/360 = US$25

The following table summarises the contract specifications for most major currencies short term interest rate futures.

Currency	Futures exchange	Volume of contract	Underlying	Tick size	Tick value
EURO	EUREX	€1,000,000	3-Month EURIBOR	0.005	€12.5
GBP	LIFFE	£500,000	3-Month £ LIBOR	0.010	£12.5
US$	CME	US$1,000,000	3-Month US$ LIBOR	0.010	US$25
JPY	CME	¥100,000,000	3-Month ¥ LIBOR and 3-Month TIBOR	0.005	¥1250
CAD	Montreal	C$1,000,000	3-Month Bankers' Acceptance (BAs)	0.010	C$25
AUD	Sydney	A$1,000,000	90 Day Bank Accepted Bills	0.010	A$24*

*tick valuation on A$ bank bills varies depending on the level of interest rates, see www.sfe.com.au for details.

Eurodollar futures

Eurodollars are US$ deposits and savings outside of the United States (they have nothing to do with the Euro currency). They earn and pay a rate of interest, which is normally benchmarked against LIBOR.

Summary of Eurodollar contract specifications:

Feature	Description
Underlying	**90-day** Eurodollar time deposit
Face value	US$1 million
Delivery months	Mar, Jun, Sep, Dec, 40 months in the March quarterly cycle, and the four nearest serial contract months
Delivery method	Cash settled
Settlement rate	LIBOR rate for 3-month Eurodollar deposits on the last trading day
Last trading day	The second London business day immediately preceding the third Wednesday of the contract month
Quotation method	100 less the Interest rate
Tick	US$25
Margining	Initial margin and daily mark-to-market

Eurodollar futures are based on an underlying 90 days instrument, whereas 3-Month LIBOR is based on the actual number of days within a 3 month period, which may be more or less than 90 days. Eurodollar futures are based on a fixed 90-day term in order to have a tick amount of US$25 for each future contract regardless of the actual number of days in the underlying 3 month period.

You should note that the buying and selling terminology is opposite in futures and FRAs, and thus, a Eurodollar futures seller is equivalent to a FRA buyer as they both profit from a rise in interest rates.

Scroll	Last	⬛Change	Time	Bid ⬛	Ask	OpenInt	TotVol	Close
1)EDJ5 Apr05	96.8375s	+.0150	Close	96.8325	96.8400	61867	115	96.8225
2)EDK5 May05	96.685s	+.015	Close	96.680	96.690	51980	511	96.670
3)EDM5 Jun05	96.535s	+.025	Close	96.535		1474801	44113	96.510
4)EDN5 Jul05	96.365s	+.040	Close	96.365	96.385	635	100	96.325
5)EDQ5 Aug05	96.250s	+.050	Close	96.250	96.270	0	0	96.200
6)EDU5 Sep05	96.145s	+.065	Close	96.145	96.150	1366127	73289	96.080
7)EDZ5 Dec05	95.945s	+.070	Close	95.945	95.950	1144160	95354	95.875
8)EDH6 Mar06	95.825s	+.065	Close	95.825	95.830	910402	68715	95.760
9)EDM6 Jun06	95.720s	+.065	Close	95.720		674051	62006	95.655
10)EDU6 Sep06	95.625s	+.060	Close	95.625		478781	42003	95.565
11)EDZ6 Dec06	95.545s	+.050	Close	95.545		435954	31209	95.495
12)EDH7 Mar07	95.500s	+.040	Close	95.500		280038	32573	95.460
13)EDM7 Jun07	95.450s	+.035	Close			215448	13780	95.415
14)EDU7 Sep07	95.405s	+.030	Close	95.405		165459	13532	95.375
15)EDZ7 Dec07	95.345s	+.025	Close	95.340		147180	11357	95.320
16)EDH8 Mar08	95.310s	+.020	Close	95.305		128611	9357	95.290
17)EDM8 Jun08	95.265s	+.015	Close			125469	7279	95.250

Table header information:
- Session: PIT
- 90DAY EURO$ FUTR — Delayed monitoring enabled
- Exchange Web Page — Pricing Date: 4/13/05 — Price Display: 2
- Chicago Mercantile Exchange — Delayed prices — --LATEST AVAILABLE--- 2
- Grey date = options trading — 8223514 552047 Previous

Source: Bloomberg/CME

The Eurodollar futures market provides a good snapshot of where the market expects short-term interest rates to be on a given future date. As we can see from the current futures prices from 13-April-2005 the market's expectations were for interest rates to increase. Given that the futures contract settles against LIBOR we can say that the market expected 3-Month LIBOR in December 2005 to be 4.055% $(100 - 95.945)$. If current LIBOR was 3.155%, that indicates that the market is expecting rates to increase by 90 bps between April-05 and Dec-05. Given the fact that LIBOR closely tracks the US$ Fed funds rate the market's expectation for an increase in rates reflects the markets expectations that the US Federal Reserve (FEDs) will increase short-term interest rates by 90 bps over the next few meeting between April and Dec 2005. This implies that any rate increase is expected and already priced into the forward or future rates. If you ever want to know the market's expectations for an upcoming FED meeting, look into the futures.

Date	Cash market	Futures market
June	Corporate borrows US$10 million for 6 months at 3-Month LIBOR plus 1.00%	Sell 10 SEP Eurodollar future contracts at 95.50%
	Current 3-month LIBOR is 4.00%. First interest payment in September is 5.00% on notional	*Reflecting a 4.50% future yield.*
Sept	3-month LIBOR is now at 5.00%	The SEP futures contract expires and has a settlement price of 95.00, *which reflect the current 3-month LIBOR rate* (100 − 5.00%).
	Interest payment:	Settlement Amount:
	$= \text{US\$10M} \times 6.00\% \times 92/360$ $= -\$153,333.33$	$\text{US\$10M} \times \dfrac{(95.50 - 95.00)}{100} \times \dfrac{90}{360} + \$12,500$

Net payment −$140,833 (−$153,333.33 +12,500)
We can then solve for the implied rate (X) to be paid in 6 months time.

Using futures to hedge interest rate exposure

Corporate and financial institutions can use Futures to hedge interest rate exposure. Below is an example on how a corporate can hedge the floating rate of interest on cash borrowed:

The net payment made by the corporate is $140,833 ($153,333 − $12,500). Which equates to an interest rate of:

$$\$140,833 = \text{US\$10M} \times X\% \times 92/360$$
$$X = 5.511\%$$

If you hedged your forward interest payment with a future you would have been able to fix your interest rate at 5.511%. Why is the hedge rate not 5.50%, which was the implied rate from the future? The variance arises from the difference in underlying number of days, the interest period for the borrowing was 92 days while the underlying hedge was for 90 days. In order to have a better hedge you must adjust the number of futures contracts bought or sold to reflect this daycount difference:

$$\frac{\text{Notional amount of underlying}}{\text{Notional amount of futures contract}} \times \frac{\text{days}}{90}$$
$$= \frac{\$100M}{\$1M} \times \frac{92}{90} = 102 \text{ contracts}$$

A total of 102 contracts need to be sold. In the above example if 102 contracts were sold the implied forward or hedged rate would be 5.501%. In order to hedge a LIBOR FRA or any borrowing or lending obligation which is based on an Act/360 daycount basis, you need to hedge every US$1 million with a grossed up futures amount equivalent to 1.0222 times the underlying notional. Given that each contract may have a different number of underlying days this adjustment will need to be recalculated for each future contract (ie the 1.0222 adjustment is not a fixed number).

For further information on short-term futures specifications refer to the CME, LIFFE, Euronext online. Historical and delayed prices is also available

www.cme.com
www.liffe.com
www.euronext.com
www.sfe.com.au
www.m-x.com (montreal)

CONVEXITY WITH FUTURES

In the short term futures markets, the "tick value" is constant, regardless of the time to expiry of the contract. For example, each basis point change in the underlying interest rates is worth one cent on the Eurodollar future which in turn is worth $25 per contract. However for a FRA the value of one basis point (PV01) is not a constant US$25 (for the same notional size), actually the PV01 changes (decreases) the longer the underlying term of the FRA. While the future and FRA are priced and settle against the same underlying (3M LIBOR) the PV01s are not equal. If you were to hedge a FRA with a future contract (or vice-versa) you would have a realised gain or loss as a result of the convexity.

In order to convert the Eurodollar futures implied interest rate to equal the forward rate we must make a convexity adjustment (source from Hull, p 111).

$$F_{adjusted} = F_{unadjusted} - bias \tag{4}$$

where

$$bias = \frac{1}{2}\sigma^2 t_1 t_2$$

σ = Annual standard deviation of the change in short term rates (absolute change not a relative change);

t_1 = Time to maturity of the futures contract;

t_2 = Time to maturity of the underlying rate.

If we assume σ is 1.1%, which is based on historic data, the bias can be calculated for each given future contract. The following table shows the bias for each future, assuming the first future expires in 3 months, and then they roll every quarter thereafter. If the future expiring in 4-years had an implied interest rate of 5.00% the adjusted forward rate would be:

$$\text{Bias} = \frac{1}{2} \, 1.1^2 \times 4 \times 4.25 = 10.29\text{bps}$$

$$F_{adjusted} = (100 - 95.00) - 0.1029 = 4.8971\%$$

As you can see the bias is only significant for longer-term futures.

Time	Bias
0.25	0.08
0.50	0.23
0.75	0.45
1.00	0.76
1.25	1.13
1.50	1.59
1.75	2.12
2.00	2.72
2.25	3.40
2.50	4.16
2.75	4.99
3.00	5.90
3.25	6.88
3.50	7.94
3.75	9.08
4.00	10.29
4.25	11.57
4.50	12.93
4.75	14.37
5.00	15.88

CALCULATING STRIP YIELD

You can calculate longer term (zero coupon) interest rates implied by future rates by calculating the *strip yield*. A strip can be calculated by combining cash deposits (or borrowings) with a long (or short) position in the futures contracts. It involves a series of consecutive legs that are compounded together to provide a longer-term rate, the calculation is the reverse of how we calculated the implied FRA rate in the previous section. Purchase or sale of a series of such contracts with successive expiration dates can enable an investor to lock in a yield for the length of the strip.

The basic method for evaluating the strip Rate:

Formula:

$$[(1 + R_{cash} \times (n/360)) \times (1 + R_{futures1} \times (n/360))$$
$$\times \cdots \times (1 + R_{futuresN} \times (n/360)) - 1] \times 360/tn \qquad (5)$$

Where

n	Number of days within specific interest period,
R_{cash}	Cash interest rate;
$R_{futures1...N}$	Futures interest rate;
t	Number of days between trade date and final maturity date of last futures contract.

The first cash rate (R_{cash}) is called the "front fail" or "stub", which is the implied cash or zero rate from trade date up to the start of the first future.

Assuming:

Spot date:	16-March-2005
3-month LIBOR	3.00%
Jun-05 Future	96.535 (3.456%)
Sep-05 Future	96.145 (3.855%)
Dec-05 Future	95.945 (4.055%)

Using Equation (5) we can calculate the strip rate (zero coupon, Act/360) from 16-March 2005 to 21-Sept 2005, assuming that the stub or cash rate is equal to the 3M LIBOR rate: 3.00%.

$$[(1 + 3.00\% \times 91/360) \times (1 + 3.456\% \times 98/360) - 1]$$
$$\times (360/(91 + 98) = 3.25\%$$

Start date	Maturity date	Strip rate
16-Mar-05	15-Jun-05	3.00%
15-Jun-05	21-Sep-05	3.25%
21-Sep-05	21-Dec-05	3.47%
21-Dec-05	15-Mar-06	3.63%

The implied zero coupon rate from 16-Mar-05 to 21-Sept-05, which is implied from the current cash and futures market is 3.25%. We can also calculate longer-term strip rates from the available futures.

FUTURES VS. FRAS

A FRA is an OTC contract equivalent to an exchange trade short term interest rate future. FRA traders will price FRAs off future prices and normally use futures to hedge FRAs bought or sold.

Settlement

Both FRAs and futures are cash settled against interbank deposit rates (LIBOR) on settlement date (at the beginning of the underlying interest rate period). Futures are mark to market each day and gain or loss is settled on a daily basis, FRAs are settled in full at maturity. The cash settlement of a FRA is discounted from maturity date of the underlying interest period to the settlement date of the FRA, cash settlement of futures are not discounted.

Term

For most underlying FRAs a daycount basis of Act/360 (US) or Act/365 (GBP) is used. The actual number of days will normally be different than that used in future contracts, which normally will have a fixed 30- or 90-day term. This slight difference can effect the hedging.

Specifications

FRAs are tailor made to suit the users' needs, from specific dates to defined notional amounts. Futures are standard contracts, with fixed dates and notional amounts.

Liquidity

Given that futures trade on a regulated market they have more liquidity vs. a tailor made FRA contract. The futures market for Eurodollar futures is the largest futures market in the world and can be traded on a 24-hour basis. The liquidity for FRAs arises from another counterparty willingness to make a price, which may be difficult or inefficient especially for broken periods (odd dates).

Credit risk

When you enter into a contract with another counterparty for a FRA obligation you have potential credit exposure to that counterparty. If upon settlement day the counterparty owes you money given that interest rates have moved, you have credit risk on the other counterparty. Whereas when you buy futures you have no counterparty credit risk other than credit with the futures exchange which is assumed to be zero.

3

Bonds: Pricing, Risk and Hedging

BOND PRICE

The price of a bond, an interest-bearing security, is equal to the present value of all its future cash flows; coupon payments and the principal received at maturity. The net present value of all future cash flows is equal to the bond's price.

Consider a bond with price BP_0 at time $t = 0$, and maturing in T years' time. Let C denote the coupon of the bond and let the par value equal 100% (face value). We discount all cashflows using the present valuing method and formula we discussed in Chapter 1.

Formula: PV of bond's cashflows

$$BP_0 = \frac{C/p}{(1+r/p)^{t_1 \times p}} + \frac{C/p}{(1+r/p)^{t_2 \times p}} + \cdots + \frac{C/p}{(1+r/p)^{m \times p}} + \frac{PAR}{(1+r/p)^{m \times p}}$$

Which can be simplified to:

$$BP_0 = \sum_{t=1}^{m \times p} \frac{C/p}{(1+r/p)^{t \times p}} + \frac{PAR}{(1+r/p)^{T \times p}} \quad (1)$$

Where

BP_0 Bond price or present value at time 0;
r Yield to maturity;
t Time to payment, in years;
C Coupon or interest payment;
p number of coupons within the year;

PAR Face Amount/ Principal Redemption;

T Time to maturity, in years.

All bond cashflows (individual cash coupons $= C/p$ and the PAR amount at maturity) are effectively discounted to t_0 in Equation (1), where the applicable discount factor to time t_i, assumes the interest rate to the time of cash payment is equal to the bond's yield to maturity, r (YTM or the internal rate of return).

$$dcf = \frac{1}{\left(1+\dfrac{r}{p}\right)^{t_i \times p}}$$

Settlement date	10-Jan-05
Maturity date	10-Jan-10
Coupon	7.00%
Yield to Maturity	6.75%
Payment frequency	2 (semi-annually)
Basis	30E/360

What is the price (BP_0) or present value, per US$100 face value, of the following bond?

$$BP_0 = \frac{7.00\%/2}{(1+6.75\%/2)^{0.5\times2}} + \frac{7.00\%/2}{(1+6.75\%/2)^{1\times2}} + \cdots + \frac{7.00\%/2}{(1+6.75\%/2)^{5\times2}}$$
$$+ \frac{100}{(1+6.75\%/2)^{5\times2}}$$

The calculation returns the price (BP_0) per US$100 face value of a security that pays periodic interest. Table 1 provides the detailed calculations for the above equation.

Excel also has a built in function to calculate the price of a bond, which provides the same results.

Table 1

Settlement 10-Jan-05
Maturity 10-Jan-10   excel yield: 7.00%
Coupon 7.00%   excel price: 101.0462%
YTM 6.75%
frequency semi-annual basis 30/360 BP_0: 101.046%

	t	C/P (%)	dcf	PV CPN (%)	PV PAR	PV Total (%)
10-Jan-05	0.00	3.50	0.000	0.000	–	0.00
10-Jul-05	0.50	3.50	0.967	3.386	–	3.39
10-Jan-06	1.00	3.50	0.936	3.275	–	3.28
10-Jul-06	1.50	3.50	0.905	3.168	–	3.17
10-Jan-07	2.00	3.50	0.876	3.065	–	3.06
10-Jul-07	2.50	3.50	0.847	2.965	–	2.96
10-Jan-08	3.00	3.50	0.819	2.868	–	2.87
10-Jul-08	3.50	3.50	0.793	2.774	–	2.77
10-Jan-09	4.00	3.50	0.767	2.684	–	2.68
10-Jul-09	4.50	3.50	0.742	2.596	–	2.60
10-Jan-10	5.00	3.50	0.718	2.511	0.7175	74.27

Excel formula

PRICE(*settlement, maturity, rate, yld, redemption, frequency, basis*)

- *settlement* security's settlement date
- *maturity* security's maturity date
- *rate* security's annual coupon rate
- *yld* security's annual yield
- *redemption* security's redemption value per US$100 face value
- *frequency* number of coupon payments per year
(frequency options within excel:

Payments	Frequency
Annual	1
Semi-annual	2
Quarterly	4

Basis day count basis to use (basis options within excel:

Basis	Day count basis
0 or omitted	US (NASD) 30/360
1	Actual/actual
2	Actual/360
3	Actual/365
4	European 30/360

Using the excel function, what is the price of a bond with the following characteristics?

Settlement date	10-Jan-05
Maturity date	10-Jan-10
Coupon	7.00%
Yield to Maturity	6.75%
Payment frequency	2 (semi-annually)
Basis	4 (30E/360)

The bond's price is therefore:

= PRICE ("10-jan-05", "10-jan-10", 7.00%, 6.75%, 100, 2, 4)

= 101.0462

The YTM or IRR method of pricing bonds is based on two basic underlying assumptions:

All cashflows are discounted at the same rate (r) regardless of when they are received, which thus assumes a flat yield curve. Not only do we assume that we discount all cashflows at the same rate we also assume that we can reinvest all received cashflows at the same rate (r) as well. While we know that the yield curve is typically not flat (at least 90% of the time the yield curve is upward sloping) this method is the market standard for pricing bonds primarily given its relative simplistic mathematics. To find the true value of the bond we would need to discount each cashflows at the appropriate interest rate to the time that the individual cash flow is paid. The 1-year coupon is discounted at the 1-year interest rate, the 2-year coupon is discounted at the 2-year interest rate (and so on for all coupon payments), and the PAR amount paid at maturity in T years is discounted at the T year interest rate. While we know that Equation 1 is only an approximation, the difference in price from the true value is not significant. When we price cashflows associated with an interest rate swap we will use the more appropriate method of discounted each cashflows at the appropriate interest rate, and takes into account the term structure of interest rates (shape of the yield curve).

BOND YIELDS

In order to calculate the bond's yield to maturity (YTM) it requires a time consuming trial and error process, using Equation (1) and solving for r for a given bond price. We can easily calculate the bond's YTM using a calculator, which normally has a built-in function to calculate a bond's YTM or utilise the function built into excel.

Excel formula

YIELD(*settlement, maturity, rate, pr, redemption, frequency, basis*)

settlement	security's settlement date
maturity	security's maturity date
rate	security's annual coupon rate
pr	security's price per US$100 face value
redemption	security's redemption value per US$100 face value
frequency	number of coupon payments per year
basis	type of day count basis to use

Using the excel function, what is the yield to maturity of a bond with the following characteristics?

Settlement date	10-Jan-05
Maturity date	10-Jan-10
Coupon	7.00%
Current price	101.0462
Payment frequency	2 (semi-annually)
Basis	4 (30E/360)

The bond's yield is:

= YIELD ("10-jan-05","10-jan-10", 0.07, 101.0462, 100, 2, 4)

= 0.0675 or 6.750%

BOND PROCEEDS: CLEAN VS. DIRTY PRICE

The bond price quoted in the market (and the price that excel provides) is known as the clean price. However this price is only for newly issued bonds or bonds bought on coupon payment dates, bonds however can be purchased in the secondary market (after initial issue date) in between coupon payment dates. The amount we need to pay for the bond or the total proceeds paid must compensate the previous holder for any accrued interest they earned while they held the bond. When you buy a coupon-bearing instrument you therefore need to pay the clean price plus any accrued interest, which is known as the bond's *Dirty price.*

The amount of interest we need to pay to the previous owner is known as the accrued interest to the bond's settlement date. Interest is said to accrue each day, based on the respective calculation methods or the bond's basis, and paid on coupon payment dates. We use the following formula to determine how much accrued interest needs to be paid.

Formula:

$$AccInt = par \times rate \times \frac{AccruDays}{basis} \qquad (2)$$

where

AccInt	Amount of interest accrued;
par	Face value of the bond, usually 100%;
rate	Coupon rate;
AccruDays	Number of applicable days since lat coupon payment;
basis	basis of the bond.

A USD bond, with a 4.00% semi-annual coupon, maturing on 14-Feb-2010 is sold at a clean price of 101.0538%. The last coupon date was 14-Aug-2004, and the settlement date of the bond is 10-Jan-2005. Assuming that the bond pays semi-annual coupons on a 30E/360 basis, adjusted, following. What is the accrued interest and full proceeds which the purchaser must pay for USD1mil notional of bonds?

Last Coupon Date: 14-Aug-2004
Next Coupon Date: 14-Feb-2005
Settlement Date: 10-Jan-2005

Based on the 30E day count convention the number of applicable days (accrual interest days) between the previous coupon payment (14-Aug-04) and the bond's settlement date (10-Jan-05) is 146 days.

Hence, the accrued interest (AccInt) is:

$$AccInt = US\$1M \times 4.00\% \times 146/360$$
$$= US\$16,222.22$$

Therefore, the purchaser must pay the clean price plus accrued interest or total proceeds.

$$
\begin{aligned}
\text{Total Proceeds} &= (101.0538\% \times US\$1M) + (4.00\% \\
&\quad \times 146/360 \times US\$1M) \\
&= US\$1,010,538.00 + US\$16,222.22 \\
&= US\$1,026,760.22
\end{aligned}
$$

These total proceeds represent a dirty price of:

$$
\begin{aligned}
\text{Dirty Price} &= \text{Clean Price} + \text{Accrued Interest} \\
&= US\$102.676 \ (101.0538\% + 4.00\% \times 146/360)
\end{aligned}
$$

Below is the Excel function that calculates the accrued interest for a security that pays periodic interest.

Excel formula
ACCRINT(*issue, first_interest, settlement, rate, par, frequency, basis*)

Issue	security's issue date
first_interest	security's first interest date
settlement	security's settlement date
rate	security's annual coupon rate
par	security's par value.
frequency	number of coupon payments per year
basis	type of day count basis to use

Using the excel function, what is the accrued interest of a bond with the following characteristics?

Issue date	14-Aug-04
First interest date	14-Feb-05
Settlement date	10-Jan-05
Coupon	4.00%
Par value	100
Payment frequency	2 (semi-annually)
Basis	4 (30/360)

The accrued interest is:

= ACCRINT("14-aug-04", "14-feb-05", "10-jan-05", 4.00%, 100, 2, 4)
= 1.62222

Note that the accrued interest for the above bond is therefore US$1.62222 per US$100 of notional or face value of the bond, which is the same result we obtained through the manual calculation using Equation (2).

ODD COUPON BONDS

Each bond or interest bearing security will have interest payment or roll dates. Normally these roll dates are the same each year. For example if a bond has an issue date of 1-Mar-2005 and matures on the 1-Mar-2010, and has semi-annual coupons; the normal roll or payment dates would be 1st Mar, and 1st Sept each year. However, there are cases when the rolls are not as straightforward. For instance, if the bond is issued on 1-Feb-2005 and matures on 1-Mar-2010, what would the roll dates be?

When there are odd coupons you first need to determine when the stub or odd coupon occurs. Normally the stub is at the front, and then roll dates are determined from and including the maturity date, alternatively you can have a stub at the end where the roll dates are determined from and including the start or settlement date. You can also have a long or short stub. A short stub refers to an interest period less than a normal interest period (C_{short}). A long stub refers to the fact that the coupon period is longer than a normal interest period (C_{long}).

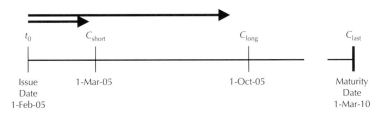

Interest details:

Settlement date	19-Apr-2000
Maturity date	12-Feb-2004
Coupon	5.00%
Payment frequency	2 (semi-annually)

While we could manually calculate the price of a bond with an odd coupon payment, excel provides a build in function to price this type of bond. Once the odd coupon rolls off it then becomes a normal bond with regular roll dates and can be priced using the standard pricing formulas.

Excel formula
ODDFPRICE (*settlement, maturity, issue, first_coupon, rate, yld, redemption, frequency, basis*)

settlement	security's settlement date
maturity	security's maturity date
issue	security's issue date
first_coupon	security's first coupon date
rate	security's interest rate
yld	security's annual yield
redemption	security's redemption value per US$100 face value

frequency   number of coupon payments per year
basis   the type of day count basis to use

Using the excel function, what is the price of a bond with the following characteristics?

Settlement date	10-Jan-05
Maturity date	10-Jan-10
Issue date	05-Jan-05
First coupon date	10-July-05
Coupon	7.00%
Yield	6.75%
Payment frequency	2 (semi-annually)
Basis	4 (30E/360)

The price per US$100 face value of a security having an odd (short or long) first period is:

= ODDFPRICE ("10-jan-05, "10-jan-10", "5-jan-05", "10-july-05",
    0.07, 0.0675, 100, 2, 4)

= 101.043

There is also a specific function in excel to calculate the yield of a bond that has an odd coupon.

Excel formula

ODDFYIELD(*settlement, maturity, issue, first_coupon, rate, pr, redemption, frequency, basis*)

Using the excel function, what is the yield of a bond with the following characteristics?

Settlement date	10-Jan-05
Maturity date	10-Jan-10
Issue date	05-Jan-05
First coupon date	10-July-05
Coupon	7.00%
Price:	101.50
Redemption value	100
Payment frequency	2 (semi-annually)
Basis	4 (30E/360)

The yield of a security that has an odd (short or long) first period is:

=ODDFYIELD("10-jan-05,"10-jan-10","5-jan-05", "10-july-05",
    7.0%, 101.50, 100, 2, 4)

= 6.642%

We can also calculate the price and yield for a bond where the stub (long and short) is the last coupon period, using the following excel formulas:

=ODDLYIELD (*settlement, maturity, last_interest, rate, pr, redemption, frequency, basis*)

=ODDLPRICE (*settlement, maturity, last_interest, rate, yld, redemption, frequency, basis*)

BOND PV01

The price of a bond changes as underlying interest rates change, there is an inverse relationship between the bond's price and yield, as yields increase (decrease) the bond price decreases (increases). We measure the price sensitivity to changes in interest rates by calculating the change in price for a one basis point (0.01%) change in the YTM. The change in price is the present value difference for a 1 basis point (PV01) change in yield. We can calculate the bond's PV01 by manually calculating the change in the bond's price for an increase in the bond's YTM (by 1 basis point).

Formula:

$$PV01 = BP_{up} - BP_0 \qquad (3)$$

BP_0 Initial Bond price with YTM equal to r
BP_{up} Bond price with YTM equal to $r + 0.01\%$

This calculation assumes a yield increases; you could also look at PV01 when yields decrease but you will find the answers very similar for very small (1 bp) change in yields. While market standard is to look at the PV01 for an increase in yield, we can also measurement PV01 by examining the effects yield increases and decreases and then take a simple average. The PV01 number will always be negative or at least assumed to be negative (it is common to quote PV01 in absolute terms), given the fact that the bond's price moves inversely with changes in interest rates.

What is the present value of a 1 bp (BP_0) in a bond's YTM, of the following bond?

Settlement date	10-Jan-05
Maturity date	10-Jan-10
Coupon	7.00%
Yield	6.75
Payment frequency	2 (semi-annually)
basis	30E/360

$$BP_0 = \text{US\$101.046}$$
$$\Delta y = 1\,\text{bp}$$
$$BP_{up} = \text{US\$101.0041}$$
$$\text{PV01}_{up} = (101.0041 - 101.046) = -0.0419 \text{ per 1 bp}$$

We can use PV01 to estimate the change in the underlying bond price for a given change in interest rates. If the YTM on the above bond increased by 50 bps we can approximate the new price.

$$BP_{new} = BP_0 + \text{PV01} \times \Delta y$$
$$= 101.046 - 0.0419 \times 50\,\text{bps}$$
$$= \text{US\$98.951}$$

Using the PV01 calculation we have estimated that the bond price should decrease from US\$101.468 to US\$98.951, for a given 50 bps increase in the bond's yield to maturity. The actual price is 98.967%, thus the PV01 price estimate is reasonably accurate for small changes in yields.

While the PV01 calculation is used to estimate the change in an individual bond's price we can also use it to estimate the change in market value of an investor's holdings. If an investor holds US\$10 million worth of the above bond at a current market price of 101.046, the market value of the position is US\$10,104,600 (US\$10 m × 101.046%). We can then estimate a loss as a result of an increase in interest rates. For a 50 bps increase in rates the price falls to US\$98.951, which means the market value of the position falls to US\$9,895,100 (US\$10 m × 98.951%), which means an estimated market value loss of US\$210,000 (for an assumed 50 bps increase in yields).

Note: Sometimes PV01 (present value of 1 basis point) is refered to as DV01 (dollar value of 1 basis point) both references have the same meaning.

BOND PORTFOLIO PV01

We have outlined how we calculate the PV01 for a single bond. If we examine not one bond but a portfolio of bonds we can calculate

Table 2 Bond portfolio: PVO1

Notional	Maturity	Coupon (%)	Yield (%)	Price (US$)	Market value	PV01
10,000,000	10-Jul-07	3.00	5.70	93.79	9,379,083	0.022
20,000,000	10-Jul-07	5.00	5.70	98.39	19,678,043	0.023
30,000,000	14-Feb-09	7.00	6.30	102.48	30,745,115	0.036
10,000,000	14-Feb-09	7.00	6.75	100.87	10,087,256	0.035
30,000,000	14-Feb-10	7.00	6.75	101.05	30,316,151	0.043
100 Mil					100,205,648	0.034

the PV01 on the overall portfolio. If we assume that the YTM for each bond within our portfolio changes equally at the same time (a parallel shift in our portfolio's YTM) we can calculate the change in market value for a change in yields. This manual calculation method thus provides us with the PV01 on the entire portfolio, as provided in Table 2.

The PV01 result of US$.034 (for a 1bp change in interest rates) allows us to estimate the change in the portfolio's market value for a given 25 bps increase in interest rates.

$$\Delta \text{ Market value} = \text{Notional} \times \text{PV01} \times \Delta r$$
$$= \text{US\$100,000,000} \times \text{US\$0.0341} \times (+25\,\text{bps})$$
$$= \text{US\$852,500}$$

For a 25 bps increase in yields the market value of the entire portfolio would decrease by an estimated US$852,500. The actual decrease would be US$845,278.

BOND DURATION AND MODIFIED DURATION

Duration is used to describe the effective life of a bond, and is quoted in terms of years. It is used to assess and analyse the risk profile of different bonds regardless of differences in term, coupons or yields to maturity. It provides a measure of the risk level of the bond and can be used in portfolio immunisations – hedging an investor against small changes in interest rates. Duration is similar in concept to the PV01 in that both measure the sensitivity of a bond's price to changes in yield to maturity. While PV01 is an absolute change in price while duration measures the percentage change in price for a given change in yields.

Given the fact that longer term bonds are more price sensitive to changes in underlying interest rates, we can use duration to measure and manage the interest rate risk of a bond or portfolio of bonds. The shorter the duration of a bond the less sensitive the price will be to changes in interest rates, and the longer the duration the more sensitive the price will be to changes in interest rates. Traders and bond fund managers will utilise the duration of a bond (or portfolio of bonds) to manage their exposure to interest rates. If you think interest rates will fall, and thus bond prices to increase, you can extend duration so that the price increase will be relatively greater. If you think interest rates will increase, and thus bond prices will decrease, you can shorter duration so that the price decrease will be relatively lower.

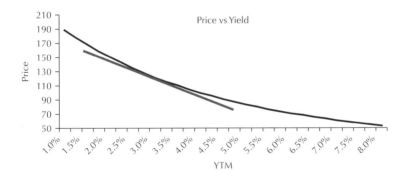

Duration is the slope of a line drawn tangent to the price yield curve. Duration is defined as the weighted average of a bond's cash flow payments, where the weights are the proportions of the cash flows in present value terms. It is defined as:

Formula:

$$\text{Macauly Duration} = \frac{\sum_{t=1}^{n}(PVCF \times t)}{BP_0} \qquad (4)$$

$PVCF$ = present value of bond's cashflows (coupons and notional), t = time (in years) when cashflow is received, BP_0 = Bond Price.

We can represent duration graphically, using a weighted balance (below). Duration is the point where the time weighted cashflows are balanced.

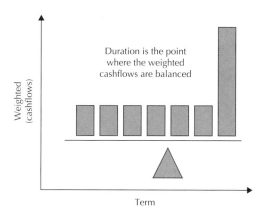

What is the duration if a bond has the following characteristics?

Settlement date	10-Jan-05
Maturity date	14-Feb-10
Coupon	7.00%
Yield	6.75%
Payment frequency	2
Basis	Actual/365

Table 3 provides the manual calculations for duration and modified duration.

Table 3 Duration and modified duration

t	Cashflows	DCF	PV cashflows	Weighted PV cash * time
0.50	3.500	0.9674	3.386	0.0168
1.00	3.500	0.9358	3.275	0.0324
1.50	3.500	0.9052	3.168	0.0470
2.00	3.500	0.8757	3.065	0.0607
2.50	3.500	0.8471	2.965	0.0734
3.00	3.500	0.8194	2.868	0.0851
3.50	3.500	0.7927	2.774	0.0961
4.00	3.500	0.7668	2.684	0.1062
4.50	3.500	0.7418	2.596	0.1156
5.00	103.500	0.7175	74.265	3.6748
	PV cashflows		101.046	
			Duration	4.3081
			Modified duration	4.1675

Another more useful measurement of duration is modified duration, which can be directly applied to estimate the change in price of a bond for a given change in YTM.

Formula:

$$\text{ModDuration} = \frac{\text{Duration}}{1+\left(\dfrac{\text{Yield}}{\text{Coupon Frequency}}\right)} \quad (5)$$

From the above example we can then calculate the *Modified duration* (ModDuration) of the bond.

$$\text{ModDuration} = \frac{4.3081}{1+\left(\dfrac{0.0675}{2}\right)} = 4.1675$$

Modified duration can also be estimated using the following formula, which is less computational than the above:

$$\text{ModDur} = \frac{(\text{Price if Yield decreases}) \text{ less } (\text{Price if Yield Increases})}{2 \times \text{Initial Price} \times \text{Change in Yield}}$$

where

Δy change in yield;
BP_0 initial bond price;
BP_{up} bond price if yields increase by Δy;
BP_{dn} bond price if yield decreases by Δy.

We can then express the above as:

$$\text{ModDur} = \frac{BP_{dn} - BP_{up}}{2 \times BP_0 \times \Delta y} \quad (6)$$

What is the modified duration of a bond with the following characteristics?

Settlement date	10-Jan-05
Maturity date	10-Jan-10
Coupon	7.00%
Yield	6.75%
Payment frequency	2 (semi-annual)
basis	Actual/actual

$BP_0 = US\$101.046$
$\Delta y = 1\,bp$
$BP_{up} = US\$101.0041$
$BP_{dn} = US\$101.0883$

$$\text{ModDur} = \frac{(101.0883 - 101.0041)}{2 \times 101.046 \times 0.0001} = 4.1675$$

We can also use the excel function to calculate duration and modified duration also.

$= \text{DURATION}(\textit{settlement, maturity, coupon, yld, frequency, basis})$
$= \text{MDURATION}(\textit{settlement, maturity, coupon, yld, frequency, basis})$

Calculating the Duration and ModDur in Excel,

$= \text{DURATION}(10\text{-jan-05}, 10\text{-jan-10}, 7.00\%, 6.75\%, 2, 4) = 4.3081$
$= \text{MDURATION}(10\text{-jan-05}, 10\text{-jan-10}, 7.00\%, 6.75\%, 2, 4) = 4.1675$

We can then use this modified duration to approximate the percentage change in bond prices as a result of changes in interest rates using the following formula, which we can then use to approximate the new bond price for a given change in interest rates:

Formula:

$$\% \; \Delta \; \text{in} \; BP = -\text{ModDur} \times \Delta y \times 100 \tag{7}$$

$$\text{Price} \; \Delta \; BP_0 = BP_{0 \times} (-\text{ModDur} \times \Delta y \times 100) \tag{8}$$

In the above example the modified duration was 4.1675, which we can use to estimate the new price of the bond if interest rates increased by 10 bps:

$BP_0 = US\$101.046$
$BP_{\Delta 10BP} = BP_{0\,+} (BP_{0 \times} \% \Delta \; \text{in} \; BP)$
$= (101.046 + (-4.1675 \times 0.001 \times US\$101.046).$
$= US\$100.6250$

The actual price change is US\$100.6261; for small changes in yields the duration approximation of price change is reasonably accurate.

If we now consider a 100 bps increase in interest rates, we would estimate the price change to be:

$$\% \, \Delta \, BP_0 \; = \; -4.1675 \times 0.010 \times 100$$
$$\% \, \Delta \, BP_0 \; = \; -4.1675\%$$
$$BP_0 \qquad = \; \text{US\$101.046}$$
$$BP_{\Delta 100BP} \; = \; BP_0 + (BP_0 \times \%\Delta \text{ in } BP)$$
$$= \; 101.046 + (-4.1675 \times 0.010 \times \text{US\$101.046})$$
$$= \; \text{US\$96.835}$$

The new price is estimated at US\$96.835 while the actual price change is US\$96.939. The greater the interest rate changes the less accurate the duration-based estimate becomes. Table 4 shows how the error from our ModDur estimation increases as the magnitude of the YTM change increase.

Table 4 Duration price estimate

Settlement	10-Jan-05			
Maturity	10-Jan-10			
Coupon	7.00%		ModDur	4.1675
Yield	6.75%			

	Yield (%)	Actual price	Estimated price	Error
+100 bps	7.75	96.939	96.835	10.43
+10 bps	6.85	100.626	100.625	0.11
BP_0	6.75	101.046		
−10 bps	6.65	101.468	101.467	0.11
−100 bps	5.75	105.366	105.257	10.83

The error is caused by the fact that the duration measurement changes as interest rates changes, the price/yield curve is not a linear and thus duration is not constant.

PV01 estimates the absolute or dollar change of an existing bond while ModDur is the approximate percentage changes in a bond price for a given change in yields. We can convert the ModDur figure to an equivalent PV01 measure (ie, absolute price change for a given YTM change)

Table 5 compares the estimated change in bond price using modified duration compared with the PV01 for the same bond, as you would expect the results are very similar to each other.

Table 5 PV01 and estimated PV01 using Modified Duration

Maturity	Coupon (%)	Yield (%)	Price (US$)	ModDur	Est PV01	PV01 (US$)
10-Jul-07	3.00	5.700	93.791	2.357	0.022	0.022
10-Jul-07	5.00	5.700	98.390	2.314	0.023	0.023
14-Feb-09	7.00	6.300	102.484	3.527	0.036	0.036
14-Feb-09	7.00	6.750	100.873	3.515	0.035	0.035
14-Feb-10	7.00	6.750	101.054	4.235	0.043	0.043

BOND CONVEXITY

Another measurement of interest rate sensitivity is convexity. While duration is the first derivative of the change in the bond's price for a given change in yields, convexity is the second derivative. Duration measures the rate of change or slope of the price/yield curve, convexity measures the curvature of the curve. When comparing two bonds, the price of the bond with a higher convexity will rise higher when interest rates fall and the price will decline less when interest rates rise.

Most non-callable or vanilla fixed rate bonds have a positive convexity; the price-yield curve will be steeper as yield decreases, and flatter as yields increase. While callable bonds have a negative convexity, which means that the bond's duration will decrease as yields decrease.

Formula:

$$Convexity = \frac{BP_{up} + BP_{dn} - 2 \times BP_0}{2 \times BP_0 \times \Delta y^2}$$

(9)

Where

Δy	change in yield;
BP_0	initial bond price;
BP_{up}	bond price if yields increase by Δy;
BP_{dn}	bond price if yield decrease by Δy.

What is the convexity of a bond with the following characteristics?

Settlement date	10-Jan-05
Maturity date	10-Jan-10
Coupon	7.00%
Yield	6.75%
Payment frequency	2
Basis	30E/360

BP_0 = US$101.0462
Δy = 10 bps
BP_{up} = US$100.6261
BP_{dn} = US$101.4683

$$\text{Convexity} = \frac{(100.6261 + 101.4683 - 2 \times 101.0462)}{2 \times 101.0462 \times 0.001^2}$$

$$= 10.518$$

We can then estimate what the price of a bond will be for a given change in interest rates, where the change in price is a result of the convexity.

$$\% \, \Delta \, BP_0 = \text{Convexity} \times \Delta\text{Yield}^2 \times 100 \qquad \textbf{(10)}$$

If we then assume a 100 bps change in yields we can estimate the percentage change in the bond price caused by convexity.

$$\% \, \Delta \, BP_0 = \text{Convexity} \times \Delta\text{Yield}^2 \times 100$$
$$\% \, \Delta \, BP_0 = 10.518 \times 1.00\%^2 \times 100$$
$$= 0.10518\%$$

We can then add both the modified duration and convexity adjustment to estimate the bond price for a give change in interest rates.

For example for a given 100 bps or 1.00% *increase* in interest rates what is the estimated new bond's price?

Estimated % ΔBP_0 using ModDur	−4.1675%
Convexity Adjustment	0.10518%
Total Estimated % ΔBP_0	−4.0623%

The actual percentage change in price is −4.0642%

If the original price were US$101.046 the estimated price, for a given 100 bps increase in interest rates, would be US$96.941 [101.046 × (1 − 4.0642%)].

For example for a given 100 bps or 1.00% *decrease* in interest rates:

Estimated % ΔBP_0 using ModDur	4.1675%
Convexity Adjustment	0.10518%
Total Estimated % ΔBP_0	+4.2727%

The actual percentage change in price is +4.275%

If the original price was US$101.046 the estimated price, for a given 100 bps decrease in interest rates, is US$105.364 [US$101.046 × (1 + 4.275%)].

Table 6 examines the price estimation using both the modified duration and convexity adjustments. The results are closer to the actual price when compared to the price estimate derived from the ModDuration calculation alone, and as the magnitude of the interest rate change increase this degree of accuracy increases.

Table 6 Duration and convexity price estimate

Settlement	10-Jan-05				
Maturity	10-Jan-10			Convexity	10.5186
Coupon	7.00%			ModDur	4.1675
Yield	6.75%				

	Yield (%)	Actual price	Estimated price	Error	ModDur est. price
+100 bps	7.75	96.939	96.941	−0.195	96.835
+10 bps	6.85	100.626	100.626	0.000	100.625
BP0	6.75	101.046			
−10 bps	6.65	101.468	101.468	0.000	101.467
−100 bps	5.75	105.366	105.364	0.201	105.257

There are four basic "rules" for duration and convexity of a (normal non-callable) bond:

(1) Everything else being equal the higher the bond's *Coupon* the higher the duration and convexity.
   ❏ Higher coupons result in more "time weighted cashflows" to occur earlier resulting in the point of equilibrium to be closer rather than further away.

(2) Everything else being equal the higher the bond's *YTM* the lower the duration and convexity.
   ❏ An increase in interest rates reduces duration. Higher interest rates decrease discount factors. This decrease in the time value of money will have a greater effect on the cash received further away.

(3) Everything else being equal the longer the *Maturity* the higher the duration and convexity.
   ❏ The longer the maturity the longer it will be before you receive your principal back, which normally makes up the majority of the cashflows.

(4) For a *Zero coupon bond* the duration is equal to its term to maturity, since all cashflows occur at maturity.

Table 7 gives a sample of different bonds and their ModDur and convexity estimations, illustrating the rules above.

Table 7 Duration and convexity for different bonds

Maturity	Coupon (%)	Yield (%)	Price	ModDur	Convexity
10-Jul-07	3.00	5.700	93.791	2.357	3.403
10-Jul-07	5.00	5.700	98.390	2.314	3.319
14-Feb-09	7.00	6.300	102.484	3.527	7.534
14-Feb-09	7.00	6.750	100.873	3.515	7.489
14-Feb-10	7.00	6.750	101.054	4.235	10.857

MODIFIED DURATION AND CONVEXITY: BOND PORTFOLIO

A bond portfolio's duration and convexity can be estimated by calculating the weighted average of the duration and convexity of each bond within the portfolio. Mathematically the portfolio's duration and convexity can be calculated as follows:

Formula:

$$\text{Duration portfolio} = w_1D_1 + w_2D_2 + w_3D_3 \cdots + w_iD_i \quad (11)$$
$$\text{Convexity portfolio} = w_1C_1 + w_2C_2 + w_3C_3 \cdots + w_iC_i \quad (12)$$

where

w_i weighted market value of bond within portfolio;
D_i duration of bond i;
C_i convexity of bond i;
i number of bonds in portfolio.

In Table 8 the ModDur of the portfolio is 3.392, while its convexity is 7.320.

Table 8 Modified duration and convexity of a portfolio

Notional	Maturity	Coupon (%)	Yield (%)	Price (US$)	Market value	Weight (%)	Mod-Dur	Convx
10 Mil	10-Jul-07	3.00	5.70	93.791	9,379,083	9	2.357	3.403
20 Mil	10-Jul-07	5.00	5.70	98.390	19,678,043	20	2.314	3.319
30 Mil	14-Feb-09	7.00	6.30	102.484	30,745,115	31	3.527	7.534
10 Mil	14-Feb-09	7.00	6.75	100.873	10,087,256	10	3.515	7.489
30 Mil	14-Feb-10	7.00	6.75	101.054	30,316,151	30	4.235	10.857
100 Mil	–	–	–	–	100,205,648	100	3.392	7.320

We can examine the portfolio in Table 8 further and can approximate the change in value of the portfolio for a given 100 bps increase in interest rates:

% Δ *in Portfolio Market Value* (% Δ PMV)

Estimated % Δ PMV using
$\quad$ ModDur $\qquad\qquad\quad$ = $-$ModDuration $\times$ Δy $\times$ 100
+ Convexity Adjustment $\quad$ = $+$ Convexity $\times$ ΔYield^2 $\times$ 100

Estimated % Δ PMV using
$\quad$ ModDur $\qquad\qquad$ $-$ 3.3920% ($-$3.392 $\times$ 1.00% $\times$ 100)
+ Convexity Adjustment $+$ 0.0732% (7.320 $\times$ 1.00%^{2} $\times$ 100)
Total Estimated % Δ PMV $-$ 3.3188%

From the estimated percentage change in the portfolio's value we can calculate the equivalent absolute change.
$\quad$ Δ PMV = Original Portfolio Market Value $\times$ % Δ PMV
$\qquad\qquad$ = US$100,205,648 $\times$ $-$3.3188%
$\qquad\qquad$ = US$ $-$3,325,625

For a 100 bps increase in yields we can therefore approximate the portfolio's new market value, US$96,880,023 (US$100,205,648 $-$ 3,325,625). The actual market value of the portfolio would decrease to US$96,878,411 (most of the difference is due to rounding).

HEDGING A BOND PORTFOLIO

We will examine three techniques to hedge our portfolio of long bonds; each employs a measurement of interest rate sensitivity to determine the appropriate number of hedge bonds we should short in order to hedge against changes in the portfolio's value as a result of changes in underlying interest rates.

Hedging method 1: PV01

In order to hedge our entire bond portfolio we would need to short a bond with a similar PV01 or interest rate sensitivity. If we short a hedge bond with an equal PV01 as our portfolio, any loss (or gain) of the portfolio's market value should be offset by a gain (or loss) in the market value of the hedge bond.

But since the relative PV01 of the hedge bond will likely be different than that of the portfolio, we need to adjust the notional of the hedge bond to reflect the difference. In order to determine the amount of hedge bond to short we need to calculate the relative hedge ratio:

Formula:

$$\text{Hedge ratio} = \frac{\text{PV01 Portfolio}}{\text{PV01 of hedge bond}} \quad (13)$$

$$\text{Hedge ratio} = 0.341/0.312$$

$$= 109.3\%$$

For every US$100,000,000 (notional) in our portfolio we need to be short US$109,300,000 (notional) of our assumed hedging bond.

How well does our hedge work for a given 10 bps increase in interest rates?

Bond Portfolio

Initial Market Value (MV) of portfolio	$100,205,648
MV of portfolio, with 10 bps increase in YTM	$ 99,866,443
Change in market value:	$ −339,205 (loss)

Hedge Bond

Initial Market Value (MV) of portfolio	US$107,559,243
MV of portfolio, with 10 bps increase in YTM	US$107,218,496
Change in market value:	US$340,747 (gain)
Net gain or Loss (portfolio plus hedge)	US$1,542 (gain)

For a given 10 bps increase in interest rates, the overall increase in market value of the hedge bond plus the loss on the portfolio of bonds would have resulted in a net gain of US$1,542. For a given 10 bps decrease in interest rates, the hedging error would have been a net loss of US$1,375.

While it is not a perfect hedge, in relative terms to the overall market value of the portfolio, it is not a significant error. Table 12 provides the analysis on the gains and losses for different changes in interest rates using the PV01 hedging technique. The greater the changes in interest rate the greater the hedging error.

Table 9 Hedging a portfolio using PV01

Notional	Maturity	Coupon (%)	Yield (%)	Price (US$)	Market value	PV01
10,000,000	10-Jul-07	3.00	5.70	93.79	9,379,083	0.022
20,000,000	10-Jul-07	5.00	5.70	98.39	19,678,043	0.023
30,000,000	14-Feb-09	7.00	6.30	102.48	30,745,115	0.036
10,000,000	14-Feb-09	7.00	6.75	100.87	10,087,256	0.035
30,000,000	14-Feb-10	7.00	6.75	101.05	30,316,151	0.043
100,000,000					100,205,648	0.0341
Hedge bond						
109,308,922	14-Jul-08	5.00	5.50	98.42	107,584,439	0.031
109.3%	Hedge ratio					

Hedging method 2: modified duration

The second method we will consider employs our modified duration calculation in order to determine an appropriate amount of hedge bonds to short. The method is very similar to the PV01 method, however. The only difference in the hedge ratio is the weighting is relative to the market value rather than the notional amount as in the PV01 method. This is because the ModDur measure the percentage change in the portfolio value rather than the absolute change in value for a given notional, which the PV01 calculates.

If our portfolio has an initial market value of US$100,205,648, and a modified duration of 3.392, we will need to short an amount of hedge bond (in market value terms), which would result in the same offsetting modified duration. We calculate a hedge ratio based on the relative modified duration for the portfolio and the hedge bond.

$$\text{Hedge ratio} = \frac{\text{Mod duration portfolio}}{\text{Mod duration hedge bond}} = \frac{3.392}{3.174}$$

Hedge ratio $= 1.0687$

For our portfolio with a market value of US$100,205,648 we need to be short US$107,099,655 of the hedge bond. This is the market value which we need to be short, not the notional amount. We can then convert the market value to a notional amount, in order to determine how many bonds we need to short in order to hedge the portfolio. If the current market price of the bond is US$98.422 we then need to short a notional amount equal to:

$$\text{Notional hedge (short)} = \frac{\text{Required market value}}{\text{Price of hedge bond}} = \frac{\text{US\$107,099,655}}{98.422\%}$$

Notional hedge (short) = US$108,816,367

If you shorted the hedge bond with a notional amount equal to US$108, 816, 367, any loss or gain (as a result of a change in yields) on the underlying portfolio would be offset by the gain or loss on the hedge bond.

Table 10 Hedging a portfolio using modified duration

Notional	Maturity	Coupon (%)	Yield (%)	Price (US$)	Market value	ModDur
10,000,000	10-Jul-07	3.00	5.70	93.79	9,379,083	2.357
20,000,000	10-Jul-07	5.00	5.70	98.39	19,678,043	2.314
30,000,000	14-Feb-09	7.00	6.30	102.48	30,745,115	3.527
10,000,000	14-Feb-09	7.00	6.75	100.87	10,087,256	3.515
30,000,000	14-Feb-10	7.00	6.75	101.05	30,316,151	4.235
100,000,000					100,205,648	3.392
Hedge bond						
(108,816,367)	14-Jul-08	5.00	5.50	98.42	(107,099,655)	3.174
				Hedge ratio	106.9%	

How well does our hedge work for a given 10 bps increase in interest rates?

Bond portfolio

Initial Market Value (MV) of portfolio:	US$100,205,648
MV of portfolio, 10 bps increase in YTM	US$ 99,866,443
Change in value of portfolio:	US$−339,205 (loss)

Hedge portfolio

Initial Market Value (MV) of hedge bond	US$107,099,655
MV of hedge bond, 10 bps increase YTM	US$106,760,363
Change in market value of hedge bond:	US$339,292 (gain)
Net gain or loss (portfolio plus hedge)	US$87 (gain)

For a given 10 bps decrease in interest rates, the hedging error would also have been a net gain of US$87, insignificant given the value of the portfolio

Table 12 examines our hedging results for various changes in interest rates, we notice that the greater the change in interest rates the greater the hedging error. However, given that duration is a more accurate measurement of interest rate sensitivity, relative to PV01, the hedging error is less.

Hedging method 3: Using duration and convexity

The third method for hedging our portfolio will utilise both modified duration and convexity in order to determine an appropriate hedge. Using a more robust and accurate measurement of interest rate sensitivity should provide us with a more accurate hedge.

It would be impossible to find a hedge ratio, which we could apply to our single hedge bond that will allow us to have equal ModDur and convexity so we will need to utilise a second hedge bond. Since we now need to try and match both the ModDur and the convexity of the duration we will need to employ two different hedge bonds. A mix of two different hedge bonds plus cash (which has a duration and convexity of zero) will allow us to hedge both duration and convexity of our underlying long portfolio. From Equations (11) and (12) we can solve for a portfolio mix where the weighed average duration and convexity equals that of the bond portfolio and where the market values of both portfolios are also equal.

$$ModDur_{port} = w_1 MD_1 + w_2 MD_2 + w_3 MD_3$$
$$Convexity_{port} = w_1 C_1 + w_2 C_2 + w_3 C_3$$

Where

$ModDur_{port}$	modified duration of the portfolio;
$Convexity_{port}$	convexity of portfolio;
$w_{1,2}$	portfolio weight of hedge bond 1 and 2;
w_3	portfolio weight of cash;
$MD_{1,2}$	modified duration of hedge bond 1 and 2;
$C_{1,2}$	convexity of hedge bond 1 and 2.

We know what all the underlying variables are except w_1, w_2 and w_3, the weights of the hedging bonds and cash in our "hedging portfolio". If we assume that the entire portfolio is made up of the three instruments then:

$$100\% = w_1 + w_{2 +} w_3$$

	Portfolio	Hedge bond 1	Hedge bond 2
Duration	3.392	3.174	4.425
Convexity	7.320	6.040	11.447

We now have three equations and three unknowns (the weights) to solve for:

$$3.392 = w_1 3.174 + w_2 4.425 + w_3 0 \quad \text{(i)}$$
$$7.320 = w_1 6.04 + w_2 11.447 + w_3 0 \quad \text{(ii)}$$
$$100\% = w_1 + w_{2\,+} w_3 \quad \text{(iii)}$$

Solve for w_1, w_2 and w_3

$$w_1 = \frac{ModDur_{port} - w_2 \times D_2}{D_1}$$

$$w_2 = \frac{Convexity_{port} \times MD_1 - ModDur_{port} \times C_1}{C_2 \times D_1 - D_2 \times C_1}$$

$$w_3 = 100\% - (w_2 + w_1)$$

$$w_2 = \frac{7.320 \times 3.174 - 3.392 \times 6.04}{11.447 \times 3.174 - 4.425 \times 6.04} = 28.59\%$$

and therefore,

$$w_1 = 67.05\%$$
$$w_3 = 4.36\%$$

Table 11 uses these hedge weightings, which gives our hedging portfolio the same offsetting ModDur and convexity as the long bond portfolio.

Table 11 Hedging a portfolio using modified duration and convexity adjustment

Notional	Maturity	Coupon (%)	Yield (%)	Price ($)	Market value	Mod-Dur	Convx	Weight (%)
10,000,000	10-Jul-07	3.00	5.70	93.79	9,379,083	2.357	3.403	9
20,000,000	10-Jul-07	5.00	5.70	98.39	19,678,043	2.314	3.319	20
30,000,000	14-Feb-09	7.00	6.30	102.48	30,745,115	3.527	7.534	31
10,000,000	14-Feb-09	7.00	6.75	100.87	10,087,256	3.515	7.489	10
30,000,000	14-Feb-10	7.00	6.75	101.05	30,316,151	4.235	10.857	30
100,000,000					100,205,648	3.392	7.320	100
Hedge bond								
−68,264,542	14-Jul-08	5.00	5.50	98.42	−67,187,584	3.174	6.040	67.05
−31,299,305	10-Jan-10	4.00	6.00	91.47	−28,629,411	4.425	11.447	28.57
−4,388,654	Cash				−4,388,654	0.000	0.000	4.38
−103,952,500					−100,205,648	3.392	7.320	100

How well does our hedge work for a given 10 bps increase in interest rates?

Bond portfolio

Initial Market Value (MV) of portfolio:	US$100,205,648
MV of portfolio, 10 bps increase in YTM	US$99,866,443
Change in value of portfolio:	US$−339,205 (loss)

Hedge portfolio

Initial Market Value (MV) of hedge portfolio: US$100,205,648
MV of hedge Portfolio, 10 bps increase YTM US$99,866,443
Change in market value of hedge portfolio: US$339,205 (gain)
Net gain or loss (bond portfolio plus hedge) US$ 0 (perfect hedge)

For a given 10 bps increase in interest rates, the overall increase in market value of the hedge bond plus the loss on the portfolio of bonds would have resulted in a zero net gain or loss. For a given 10 bps decrease in interest rates, the hedging error would also have been zero (a perfect hedge!).

Examining Table 12 you see that employing method three, duration and convexity hedging provides the optimal hedging results. Even for large changes in interest rates the hedging error is very small. Regardless of which hedging method you use you should always re-evaluate your hedge position as interest rates move and of course when the underlying portfolio changes.

Table 12 Compare hedging strategies

	Notional	Market value
Portfolio	100,000,000	100,205,648
Hedge Bonds	−103,952,500	−100,205,648

		Hedge error (US$)		
	Portfolio market value	PV01 hedge	ModDur hedge	MD + Con hedge
+100 bps	96,878,411	22,686	8,373	−20
+10 bps	99,866,443	1,543	87	0
Mkt value$_{t0}$	100,205,648			
−10 bps	100,546,321	−1,375	87	0
−100 bps	103,679,630	−5,904	8,965	22

Change in market value (Hedge less Portfolio).

BASIS RISK

In the above hedging examples we have made one main assumption, the YTM of the hedge bond(s) will move in the same direction and with the same magnitude as that of the underlying bonds within the portfolio, we assume a parallel shift in yields for all bonds. If yields increase by 10 bps they increase by 10 bps for all bonds, within the portfolio and for our hedge bonds. If they do not then we have *basis risk*: the risk that the yields do not move together in the same direction by the same magnitude.

While we cannot eliminate the basis risk we can try to reduce it by selecting an appropriate hedge bond. Normally every corporate or Eurobond that is issued, is priced relative to a specific benchmark or government bond. Assuming we hedge our underlying bond with the appropriate benchmark bond our basis risk should be reduced.

Not only does basis risk arise when we do not hedge our bond with the most appropriate benchmark bond but also as a result of credit risk. Normally a bond will be priced at a fixed spread over a benchmark bond. If the benchmark bond is currently trading with a yield to maturity of 5.50% and the corporate bond is issued with a YTM 20 bps over the benchmark bond, then the yield to maturity of the corporate bond is 5.70%. The spread is relative to the credit worthiness of the underlying issuer, relative to the benchmark. While we can use the hedge bond to protect from changes in interest rates, we are still at risk as specific credit spreads changes. The spread can change as a result of many factors that affect the credit worthiness of the underlying issuer.

Table 13 Bond spreads

Description	Notional	Maturity	Coupon (%)	Spread (%)	Yield (%)	Price
B1 3% 07	10,000,000	10-Jul-07	3.00	20	5.700	93.791
B2 5% 07	20,000,000	10-Jul-07	5.00	20	5.700	98.390
B3 7% 09	30,000,000	14-Feb-09	7.00	30	6.300	102.484
B4 7% 09	10,000,000	14-Feb-09	7.00	75	6.750	100.873
B5 7% 10	30,000,000	14-Feb-10	7.00	75	6.750	101.054
Hedge bonds						
HB1 5% 8	−68,264,542	14-Jul-08	5.00	0	5.500	98.422
HB2 4% 10	−31,299,305	10-Jan-10	4.00	0	6.000	91.470

BOND FUTURES

A bond future is an exchange-traded contract that allows the seller of the future to deliver to the buyer an agreed amount of bonds, at an agreed time and price. Each future will have standard contract specifications. Normally bond futures are contracts on government bonds such as US treasuries.

While most note and bond futures are physically settled at maturity (delivery of a bond) it is normal market practice to close the contract out early and any gain or loss on the position will be realised through the margin account. Table 14 summarises some of the most liquid bond futures contracts and the eligible bonds, which can be delivered on physical settlement.

Conversion factor (CF)

In order to allow a wider range of underlying bonds to be delivered the Chicago Board of Trade (CBT) applies a delivery mechanism, which approximately equalises the cost of a wider set of eligible bonds, which can be delivered. This factoring algorithm is known as the conversion factor (CF).

Each CBOT futures contract is cash settled against an invoice price, which is dependent on the underlying bond's conversion

Table 14 Contract specifications

Currency	Exchange	Future	Contract size	Underlying (%)	Eligible bonds
US$	CBOT	2y UST Note	200,000	2y UST 6	1.75–2 yrs*
US$	CBOT	5y UST Note	100,000	5y UST 6	4.1667–5.25 yrs
US$	CBOT	10y UST Note	100,000	10y UST 6	6.5–10 yrs
US$	CBOT	30y UST Bond	100,000	30y UST 6	min 15 yrs
EUR	EUREX	Euro-Schatz	100,000	Euro-Schatz 6	1.75–2.25 yrs
EUR	EUREX	Euro-Bobl	100,000	Euro-Bobl 6	4.5–5.5 yrs
EUR	EUREX	Euro-Bund	100,000	Euro-Bund 6	8.5–10.5 yrs
GBP	LIFFE	Long Gilt	100,000	Long Gilt 7	8.75–13 yrs
JPY	TSE	5y JGB Future	100 mil	JGB 3	4–5.25 yrs
JPY	TSE	10y JGB Future	100 mil	JGB 6	7–11 yrs

*Original maturity less than 5 yrs.
Source:
   www.cbot.com
   www.liffe.com
   www.eurexchange.com
   www.tse.or.jp

factor, applicable accrued interest, and a price based on a standard-ised yield to maturity of 6.00%.

Each underlying cash bond eligible for delivery against a future contract has a conversion factor. The CF is determined through a simple process. The conversion factor for each eligible bond is equal to the bond's price given the following assumptions:

1. Adjust the settlement and maturity date of the underlying bond. The settlement date for all futures is the first day of the futures delivery month. The maturity date is "rolled down" to the near-est month for the 2 and 5 year future and to the nearest quarter for the 10-year and long bond future (1 March, 1 June, 1 September and 1 December).
2. Calculate the price of a deliverable bond assuming a 6.00% YTM. (A few European bond futures use a 7.00% YTM.)
3. The CF is the calculated bond's price rounded to four decimal points. Table 15, which is published by the CBOT the calculated conversion factors for all the bonds eligible for delivery against the 5-Year US Treasury Note future contract.

What is the conversion factor for Bond No. 7 from Table 15 if we assume the following characteristics?

Settlement Date	1-Sept-2005	(futures delivery date)
Maturity date	1-July-2010	(rolled down to nearest 1st month)

Table 15

CBOT® 5-YEAR U.S. TREASURY NOTE FUTURES CONTRACT

This table contains conversion factors for all medium-term U.S. Treasury notes eligible for delivery as of July 13, 2005. (The next auction is c

			Issue	Maturity	Cusip	Issuance	6% Conversion Factors
		Coupon	Date	Date	Number	(Billions)	Sep. 2005
1.)		3 1/2	11/15/04	11/15/09	912828DB3	$15.0	0.9090
2.)		3 1/2	12/15/04	12/15/09	912828DE7	$15.0	0.9074
3.)		3 1/2	02/15/05	02/15/10	912828DL1	$15.0	0.9042
4.)		3 5/8	01/18/05	01/15/10	912828DG2	$15.0	0.9105
5.)		3 5/8	06/15/05	06/15/10	912828DX5	$14.0	0.9030
6.)		3 7/8	05/16/05	05/15/10	912828DU1	$15.0	0.9145
7.)	@	3 7/8	07/15/05	07/15/10	312828DZ0	$13.0	0.9119
8.)		4	03/15/05	03/15/10	912828DP2	$15.0	0.9221
9.)		4	04/15/05	04/15/10	912828DR8	$15.0	0.9208
				Number of Eligible Issues		9	9
				Dollar Amount Eligible for Delivery		$132.0	$132.0

Source: CBOT www.cbot.com

Coupon	3 7/8	
Yield to maturity	6.00%	(as always)
Price	91.1912%	
CF	0.9119	

CBOT calculates and makes available on a regular basis the list of eligible bonds and their calculated CF, which is available on their website at www.cbot.com

You can also use the built in function within CurveBuilder to calculate the appropriate conversion factor. If the underlying bond is not eligible for delivery the result will be "NE" rather than a conversion factor.

= CF (IssueDate, Future, FutureDeliveryDate, Coupon, Maturity)
= CF (15-Jul-05, 5, 1-Sept-05, .03875, 15-Jul-10)
= 0.9119

Invoice price

The above future represents US$100,000 par amount of an eligible note per contract. Upon physical delivery of the note the following invoice price will be paid per contract:

$$\text{Invoice Price} = \text{Contract size} \times (\text{Futures Settlement Price} \times \text{CF}) + \text{Accrued Interest}$$

In our above example, what is the invoice price if we deliver Bond No. 7 from Table 15?

CF	0.9119

Futures settlement price	98.90% (given at settlement)
Settlement date	30-Sept-05
Accrued interest per contract	US$817.45 (77days/365 × Coupon × US$100,000)
Invoice price	100,000 × (98.90% × 0.9119) + 817.45 US$91,004

Cheapest to deliver: CTD

The cheapest to deliver (CTD) bond is the one bond from the available eligible bonds that has the lowest cost to the seller. An approximate rule of thumb to determine the CTD bond is the one that has the smallest conversion ratio, as calculated by dividing the bond's price by its conversion factor. This is only an approximation, since it does not take into account accrued interest and carry costs but given that these effects are minimal this rule of thumb will normally hold true.

$$CTD = min\left(\frac{Bond\ Price}{Conversion\ Factor}\right) \qquad (14)$$

	3.50% 11/15/09	3.50% 12/15/09	3 7/8 07/15/10
Price	100.7113	97.7344	99.1787
Conversion factor	0.9090	0.9074	0.9119
Conversion ratio	110.7935	107.7082	108.7616
Cheapest to deliver	No	Yes	No

Implied repo rate

In order to determine the true CTD bond we must take into account the relative cost of delivering, therefore we must consider the accrued interest and carry costs. The implied repo rate, which is calculated from the current bond's price, futures price and accrued interest determines the true CTD bond. The CTD Bond is the one with the highest implied repo rate. The higher the implied repo rate, the cheaper the bond is to deliver.

$$Implied\ Repo\ Rate = \frac{CashIn - CashOut}{CashOut} \times \frac{360}{n} \qquad (15)$$

n is the number of days until futures settlement

Implied Repo Rate

$$= \frac{(FutP \times CF) + AccInt_{end} + IntermCPN - (BondP + AccInt_{beg})}{(BondP + AccInt_{beg}) - (IntCPN \times d_2)} \times \frac{360}{d_1}$$

where

FutP	Futures Price;
BondP	Bond Price;
CF	Conversion factor;
AccInt$_{beg}$	Accrued Interest at beginning or on trade date;
AccInt$_{end}$	Accrued Interest at the end or on delivery (futures settlement) date;

IntermCPN	Interim Coupon paid;
if any, d_1	number of days between settlement and delivery dates;
d_2	number of days between interim coupon and delivery date.

What is the implied repo rate for Bond No. 2 from Table 15 if we assume the following characteristics?

Bond No. 2 = 3.5% of 12/15/04
Settlement = 27-July-05
Delivery = 30-Sept-05
FutP = 107.50
BondP = 97.7344
CF = 0.90740
$AccInt_{beg}$ = US$0.4027 (42/365 × 3.50%)
$AccInt_{end}$ = US$1.0260 (107/365 × 3.50%)
IntermCPN = none paid
d_1 = 65 days (27-July-05–30-Sept-05)
d_2 = 0 (since no interim coupon paid)

$$\frac{(107.50 \times 0.90740) + 1.0260 + 0 - (97.7344 + 0.4027)}{(97.7344 + 0.4027)} \times \frac{360}{65}$$

Implied Repo Rate = 0.02452 or 2.452%

The implied repo rate is annual rate of interest you earn from the date you buy the bond to the date of delivery or settlement of the future. Therefore the higher the implied repo rate the higher the interest you receive on the initial cash outlay, therefore the CTD bond. As you can see from Table 16 the bond with the highest implied repo rate is bond No. 2, with an implied rate of 2.45%, and therefore is the CTD. Note that this is the same result as we achieved with the conversion ratio analysis.

Table 16

CBOT® 5-YEAR U.S. TREASURY NOTE FUTURES CONTRACT

This table contains conversion factors for all medium-term U.S. Treasury notes eligible for delivery as of July 13, 2005.

September 2005 Futures Analysis
6% Conversion Factors

Futures Price **107.7082**

	Coupon	Issue Date	Maturity Date	Price	Issuance (Billions)	Conversion Factor	Price / ConvFactor	Implied Repo
1.)	3 1/2	11/15/04	11/15/09	100.7113	$15.0	0.909000	110.7935	-12.95%
2.)	3 1/2	12/15/04	12/15/09	97.7344	$15.0	0.907400	107.7082	2.45%
3.)	3 1/2	02/15/05	02/15/10	97.5938	$15.0	0.904200	107.9339	1.31%
4.)	3 5/8	01/18/05	01/15/10	99.4212	$15.0	0.910500	109.1941	-5.01%
5.)	3 5/8	06/15/05	06/15/10	98.0781	$14.0	0.903000	108.6136	-2.02%
6.)	3 7/8	05/16/05	05/15/10	99.0781	$15.0	0.914500	108.3413	-0.44%
7.)	3 7/8	07/15/05	07/15/10	99.1797	$13.0	0.911900	108.7616	-2.57%
8.)	4	03/15/05	03/15/10	99.6250	$15.0	0.922100	108.0414	1.17%
9.)	4	04/15/05	04/15/10	99.625	$15.0	0.920800	108.1940	0.40%

Number of Eligible Issues: 9

Dollar Amount Eligible for Delivery: $132.0

Source: www.cbot.com

HEDGING WITH BOND FUTURES

We can also hedge an individual bond or a bond portfolio using bond futures. The method and mechanics are very similar to that explained in the previous sections where we used plain vanilla fixed rate treasuries as a hedge against our long bond portfolio.

Just as was calculated before, we need to know the hedge ratio, but instead of calculating the number of bonds we need to short to hedge our position. We calculate the number of futures required to hedge our position:

$$Hedge\ Ratio = \frac{Portfolio\ PV01}{Futures\ PV01}$$

We have already discussed how to calculate the PV01 on our portfolio, the only remaining calculation is the PV01 on the underlying bond future. Unlike short term interest rate futures which have a fixed tick or PV01 value ($25 for Eurodollar futures) a bond future has a variable PV01 depending on which eligible bond is the cheapest to deliver.

It is assumed that the future seller will deliver the CTD bond, since it makes the most economic sense. Therefore the future's price itself will reflect changes in the CTD bond's price. Given the following relationship we can calculate the future's PV01:

$$Future\ price = \frac{CTD\ price}{Conversion\ factor} \qquad (16)$$

Therefore, a change in the CTD bond's price will be reflected in the future's price through the following relationship:

$$\Delta\ Future\ price = \frac{\Delta\ CTD\ price}{CTD\ Conversion\ factor}$$

And a specific 1 bp change in the yield of the CTD bond the future price will move by:

$$PV01\ future = \frac{CTD\ PV01}{CTD\ Conversion\ factor}$$

The first step is to calculate the PV01 for the CTD bond assuming the following characteristics?

CTD bond = 3.5% 12/15/09
Bond price = 97.7344
Settlement date = 30-June-2005
Conversion factor = 0.9074
Futures price = 107.7082.
Notional size = US$100,000
CTD PV01 = US$39.77 per US$100,000 notional (per futures contract)

$$PV01\ Future = \frac{US\$39.77}{0.9074} = US\$43.83$$

For a 1 basis point change in yields the underlying future contract's value will change by US$43.83.

Given the bond portfolio presented in Table 2, we see that the PV01 of the portfolio is US$0.0341, and portfolio's notional amount of US$100,000,000. Therefore, for a 1 bp change in yields the portfolio's market value will change by US$34,100 ($100,000,000 × US$0.0341). We can now calculate the appropriate number of futures to short in order to hedge this portfolio:

$$Hedge \; ratio = \frac{34,100}{43.83} = 778.006 \; Futures$$

However, since we can only buy and sell full future contracts we round down to 778 futures. Therefore, we need to short 778 September 2005 (5-year) bond futures to hedge our portfolio of US$100 m bonds. How well this hedge works depends on well the underlying cheapest to deliver bond represents the portfolio of bonds. While the futures contract will reduce the interest rate exposure there will probably be more basis risk when compared to hedging with specific benchmark bonds.

REPURCHASE AND SALE AND BUY BACKS

A sale and buy back and repurchase agreements (Repos) are bilateral contracts where one counterparty sells a security to another counterparty and also agrees to repurchase the security on a fixed forward date. The market makes a distinct difference between the two products, while the economics of each are very similar.

The primary purposes of these transactions are:

❏ finance a long securities position;
❏ short term cash investment; and
❏ cover short positions.

Repurchase agreements

A repurchase agreement is commonly referred to as a repo. A repo is a short-term money market instrument where one counterparty agrees to sell a security to another counterparty and at the same time agrees to buy it back on a forward date at an agreed forward price. Given the nature of the transaction is very similar in nature to a "secured loan". One counterparty lends the other funds and holds the underlying securities as collateral.

The terminology repo, reverse repo and repurchase agreement all refer to the same transaction. One counterparty's Repo is another's reverse repo. Generally the repo is viewed from the dealer or market maker's perspective.

A repo transaction (from the dealer's perspective) is where a client has excess cash to invest for a short period of time. The dealer sells securities (such as a US Treasury bond) to a customer in exchange for cash, and agrees to buy back the securities on an agreed forward date. The securities are valued and sold at the current market price plus accrued interest (total proceeds) and are repurchased at the original total proceeds plus repo interest. Repo terms range from overnight to several months. The rate, which is quoted by the dealer, is a function of the credit quality of the underlying collateral, the term of the repo and the level of interest rates in the market. The Fed fund rate for US$ is the benchmark rate against which most US$ repo rates are quoted.

During the life of the repo any coupons earned are passed from the counterparty holding the collateral to the original holder of the securities. The original holder also retains all credit risk on the

underlying securities. In the case of a default it would be the original holder that suffers the loss and not the actual holder of the collateral, since they have an agreed sell back price regardless of
whether the underlying has defaulted or not.

The cashflows under a typical repo
Initial cash proceeds:
Nominal bond amount × (clean price + accrued interest)

Final cash proceeds at maturity:
Initial cash proceeds × (1 + repo rate × repo Days/repo Basis)

A repo transaction: example
A client has US$10,000,000 to invest for 39 days, from 13-April-06 to
22-May-06 (39 actual days). A bank provides a US Treasury bond
(UST 5.00% May/2015) as collateral at a quoted repo rate of 2.50%
(Act/360)

Initial cash proceeds

Current market price	101.5496%	(clean price)
Accrued interest to 13-Apr-06	1.8630	(5.00% × 136/365)
All in price	103.3441%	(dirty price)

Nominal amount of bonds provided by the bank as collateral:

$$\frac{Cash\ investment}{Dirty\ price\ of\ collateral} = \frac{10,000,000}{103.4126\%} = US\$9,670,000$$

Repo interest earned by the customer, paid by the bank:

$$Repo\ interest = Cash\ investment \times r \times \frac{days}{basis}$$

$$US\$10,000,000 \times 2.50\% \times \frac{39}{360} = US\$27,083$$

Final cash proceeds to be returned to customer at maturity

Initial cash proceeds	10,000,000
Plus repo interest	27,083
Final cash proceeds	US$ 10,027,083

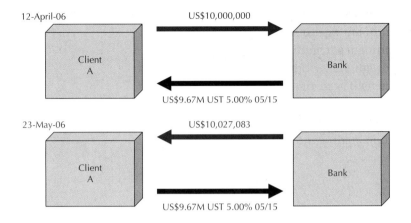

A reverse repo transaction

A client can fund a long securities position using a reverse repo transaction. A client receives cash and in return lends the securities to a dealer. The client retains all the economic value of the security they provide it as collateral for the cash received.

Example

A client has US$10,000,000 of US Treasury bonds (UST 5.00% May/2015), which they need to fund. They want to retain all the economics of holding the security but need cash to fund the long position. They want to carry the position from 12-April-06 to 2-June-06 (51 actual days). The repo dealer has quoted a repo rate of 3.00% (Act/360).

Initial cash proceeds

Current UST market price:	101.4811%	(clean price)
Accrued interest to 12-Apr-06	1.9315	(5.00% × 141/365)
All in price	103.4126%	(dirty price)

Cash provided by bank to client on start of reverse repo:
  Nominal amount of bonds × All in price
$$= US\$10,000,000 \times 103.4126\%$$
$$= US\$10,341,260$$

Coupon received by the bank during the life of the repo:
  US$10,000,000 × 5.00% × (181/365) = US$247,945

On coupon payment date the bank passes this payment to the client.

Final cash proceeds to be returned to bank at maturity
Repo interest to be earned by the bank, paid by the customer at maturity:

$$Investment \times Repo\ Rate \times \frac{days}{basis} = 10{,}341{,}260 \times 3.00\% \times \frac{51}{360} = US\$43{,}950$$

Total Proceeds to be returned to customer at maturity:
  Initial bond proceeds plus repo interest = 10,341,260 + 43,950
  US$10,385,210

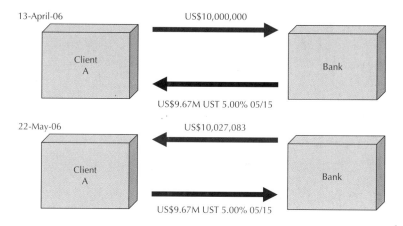

In a repo/reverse repo transaction the original owner of the bond keeps all the economic value of the bond, the market risk, underlying credit risk and any income that is received. While the legal title of the collateral passes for the term of the repo to ultimate holder of the security. In the USA the repo agreement is generally documented under the PSA agreement whereas in Europe the ISMA General Master Repo Agreement (GMRA) is generally used.

The lender of cash in a repo transaction has the underlying security as collateral against the loan. In the above example the amount of loan was dependent on the market value of the bond at the start of the transaction. In order to ensure that the lender has sufficient collateral they may require additional *margin*, to ensure that as the bond's price falls there is sufficient collateral to cover the loan. This initial margin is also refereed to as the *haircut*. In the previous example the dealer may require to hold 105% of collateral against any cash loan.

Original cash proceeds, assuming a 5.00% haircut:

$$US\$10,341,260/105\% = US\$9,848,819$$

Then at maturity the original cash proceeds plus the repo interest (paid on the haircut cash amount) is returned.

Amount to be repaid given a 105% haircut, at maturity:

$$US\$ 9,848,819 + US\$41,857 = US\$9,890,676$$

Implied repo rate

If the repo rate is not explicitly stated but we know the proceeds of the repo transaction we can calculate the *implied repo rate*.

$$Implied\ Repo\ Rate = \frac{CashIn - CashOut}{CashOut} \times \frac{360}{days}$$

Example

If a repo involved an underlying UST as collateral, where the initial total proceeds were US$101,020,668 and the final proceeds which were paid back after 23 days was US$101,202,382 then the implied repo rate would be:

$$Implied\ Repo\ Rate = \left[\frac{101,202,382 - 101,020,668}{101,020,668} \right] \times \frac{360}{23} = 2.82\%$$

Buy and sell back transaction

A buy and sell back is an agreement to exchange securities for cash today and then to transfer the securities back at a specified future date. Unlike a typical repo, both deals are treated as separate transactions, even though they are executed simultaneously. A buy/sell-back transaction closely mirrors that of two cash transactions. The lender of cash receives full legal ownership of the securities and is entitled to the accrued interest and coupon payment (if any) although the forward price would reflect any payments of interest made on the bond. In the US buy/sell-back and sell/buy-backs are also referred to as *Dollar rolls*.

A dealer purchases a security for a specific period of time with a simultaneous transaction to sell back the security on a future date, at a price, which is adjusted to reflect the implied repo-financing rate. The underlying security is valued at the current market value plus accrued interest (dirty price) and the initial transaction done in a similar way as a normal bond would settle in the cash market. At the end of the term the securities are sold back at a pre-determined price, which is calculated using the initial price and the financing rate.

Example
A client has US$10M UST bond (UST 3.50% 12/Dec/14) to finance from 5-Oct-06 to 2-Dec-06 (58 actual days). A dealer quotes a financing rate of 4.25%.

Purchase price initially

Current market price:	99.3973%	(clean price)
Accrued interest to 5-Oct-06	1.1027	(3.50% × 115/365)
All in price	100.5000%	(dirty price)

Cash paid by the bank for the securities, initially
 Nominal Amount of Bonds × bond all-in price
 US$10,000,000 × 100.5000% = US$10,050,000

Financing interest to maturity:

$$Investment \times Financing\ rate \times \frac{days}{360} = 10,050,000 \times 4.25\% \times \frac{58}{360}$$
$$= US\$68,815$$

Sell back price at maturity
All-in proceeds at maturity = Initial proceeds + financing interest
 = US$10,050,000 + US$68,815
 = US$10,118,815

This equates to an all-in price
All-in price at maturity = US$10,118,815/10,000,000
 = 101.1882%

Less accrued interest = 1.6589% (3.50% × 173/365)
(As of 2/Dec/06)

Sell back price (clean price) = 99.5293%

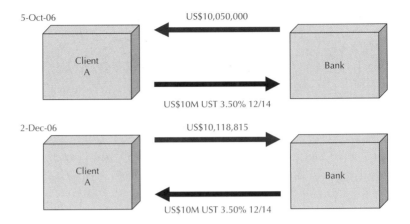

A security sell/buy-back works in the opposite direction, where the client has cash to invest and the bank wants to lend out or finance an underlying security.

Securities lending

In order for a dealer to short a bond or security they must make a physical delivery of the underlying bond. They can borrow it from another counterparty, which then results in the desired short position for the dealer.

If a dealer thinks that interest rates will increase over the next week, they can short the UST in order to profit from such a view (assuming they are correct). The dealer wants to short the UST 6.25% July-08 bond for 1 week from 2-June-06 to 9-Jun-06, to do so they must borrow the bond from another counterparty. The dealer buys the bond on 2-Jun at the current market price and then on sells it in the open market, on the same day they agree to return the security back on 9-Jun-06, at the same original price. On 9-Jun they buy the security back in the open market at the current market price and give it back to the lending counterparty. The dealer retains all the economic value of the bond that it has shorted.

Example
A dealer wants to short the UST 6.25% 08 bond, for 7 days. In order to short the bond they need to borrow the security from a client, who is willing to lend them the bond and quotes a rebate rate of 2.75% (Act/360).

Purchase price initially

Current market price	97.7500%	(clean price)
Accrued interest	2.4144	(6.25% × 141/365)
All-in price	100.1644%	(dirty price)

Cash paid by dealer to client
All-in price × notional
US$10,000,000 × 100.1644% = US$10,016,440

The dealer then sells the bonds they have just borrowed at the same all in proceeds. On the initial trade date the dealer has a flat cash position, but is short the UST, which they have promised to return in 7 days. During the life of the transaction the client has the use of the cash proceeds which they then must pay a financing charge or rebate back to the dealer.

Financing fee to be paid by the client to the dealer

$$Cash\ proceeds \times Rebate\ rate \times \frac{days}{360} = 10,016,440 \times 2.75\% \times \frac{7}{360}$$
$$= US\$5,356$$

Cash paid back at maturity
Initial all in proceeds plus rebate
US$10,016,440 + 5,356 = US$10,021,796

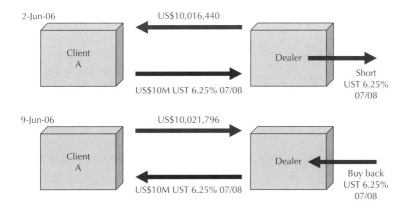

In this example the dealer has borrowed the UST 6.25% 07/08 at the current market price and agrees to sell them back to the client at the same price plus a financing rebate.

Initially the dealer borrows the securities from the client and then sells them in the cash market. At maturity the dealer must buy back the securities at the current market price. If the price has fallen they would have made a profit. If the price has increased they will have to buy the bonds back at a higher price and therefore incur a trading loss.

Example continued
Initially on 2-Jun-06, the total proceeds of the bond purchased and sold match. There is no profit or loss on day one; it is considered a back-to-back trade. On 9-Jun-06, if interest rates have increased and the price of the bond has fallen, the dealer buys the bonds back at the current market price.

New market price	97.0000%	(clean price)
Accrued interest	2.5343	(6.25% × 148/365)
All-in price	99.5343%	(dirty price)

Therefore the dealer must re-purchase the bonds back in the open market at the new all in price of 99.5343% which means they must pay an all in proceeds of US$9,953,430 (US$10M × 99.5342%).

The dealer delivers the bonds back to the original client and receives the pre-agreed total proceeds of US$10,021,796. Given that the new total proceeds to purchase the bonds back is only US$9,953,430 they would have earned a profit of US$68,366. The client earns the difference in the market price less the amount of accrued interest on the bond during the lending period plus they earn the financing rebate:

Clean price:	Notional × (97.75% less 97.00)	+ 75,000
Bond AI:	Notional × 6.25% × 7/365	− 11,986
Rebate	Cash proceeds × 2.75% × 7/360	+ 5,347
Total profit/loss		US$ + 68,370 (profit)

*difference due to rounding

Or another way to look at it, from a total proceeds and from the dealer's point of view.

Initial all-in proceeds	+US$10,016,440
Final all-in proceeds	−US$ 9,953,430
Rebate	+US$ 5,347
Net Profit/loss	+US$ 68,366 (profit)

4

Interest Rate Swaps

WHAT IS AN INTEREST RATE SWAP

An interest rate swap (IRS) is an agreement between two counter-parties to exchange coupon flows. There is only an exchange of coupons or interest flows and no exchange of the principal, and all payments are made in the same underlying currency. IRSs have two legs: a fixed interest leg and a floating interest leg. One counter-party is the fixed rate payer (and floating rate receiver) thus known as the payer, while the other is the floating rate payer (and fixed rate receiver) and thus known as the receiver. IRSs are used to man-age interest rate exposure on underlying assets and liabilities, as well as allowing counterparties to speculate on directional moves of interest rates.

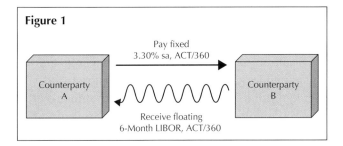

Figure 1

Pay fixed
3.30% sa, ACT/360

Counterparty A

Counterparty B

Receive floating
6-Month LIBOR, ACT/360

PAR swap rates

A current or at the money swap rate is called a PAR swap rate. A PAR swap rate is the fixed rate which the market maker is willing to pay (received) in return for receiving (paying) the Floating Coupons. A PAR swap rate is the fixed rate which the value of the IRS, Pay (Rec) Fixed PAR swap rate *vs.* Rec (Pay) Floating Interest, is zero[1] on trade date. There is no economic value to the transaction, as such there is no premium paid on settlement date by either counterparty.

We can value the fixed leg of an IRS just as we value any fixed rate bond. We calculate the present value of the discounted cash-flows. For a PAR swap rate we know that the NPV of the fixed leg is PAR. We also discount the cashflows (coupons and principal) at the applicable interest rate when the cashflow is received. This reflects the true value of the cashflows given the shape of the underlying yield curve, rather than assuming a flat interest rate which we use in valuing vanilla fixed rate bonds.

The value of the fixed leg of an IRS:

$$PAR = \sum_1^i \frac{CPN}{1+r_i} + \frac{100}{1+r_n}$$

And if the discount factor to a specific date can be calculated, applying the interest rate (r_i) to the actual date:

$$dcf_i = \frac{1}{1 + r_i \times \dfrac{days}{basis}}$$

the we can rewrite the value of the fixed leg as:

$$100 = \sum_1^i PAR \; Swap \times dcf_{1toi} + 100 \times dcf_i \qquad \text{(1)}$$

While this may not seem very important characteristic, we will revisit this equation when we look at deriving discount factors from PAR swap rates in Chapter 5.

HOW INTEREST RATE SWAPS ARE QUOTED

IR swaps can be quoted either as an absolute rate or as a spread over the yield of a benchmark government bond, such as on-the run US Treasuries in case of US$, UK Gilts for GBP, or JGBs (Japanese government bonds) in JPY. A market maker will nor-mally provide a "rate sheet" of their current PAR swap rates. An example is Table 1.

Table 1

Term	UST yield sa	Swap spread		Swap rate	
2 yr	3.50	37	42	3.87	3.92
3 yr	3.65	40	45	4.05	4.10
4 yr	3.75	42	47	4.17	4.22
5 yr	3.82	45	50	4.27	4.32
3M LIBOR		3.15%			
6M LIBOR		3.35%			

The rate at which the dealer will pay fixed is known as the swap OFFER rate (lower rate), while the rate they are willing to receive fixed is the BID rate (higher rate). For example, the market maker quotes a five-year IRS at a fixed offer rate of 3.80% and a bid rate of 3.85%. The swap dealer will Pay 3.80% *vs.* receiving Floating,[2] and Receive 3.85% *vs.* Paying Floating.

While at inception the value of an IRS is normally zero, immediately after trade date as time and interest rates change the swap will have a positive or negative value. The value depends on changes in interest rates and which side of the swap you are on (ie payer or receiver of the fixed rate). We will consider in more detail in the next chapter how to value and mark to market (MTM) IRS but for now let us consider the applications.

Figure 2 is a historical graph of the 5 and 10-year US$ absolute swap rates since 1990.

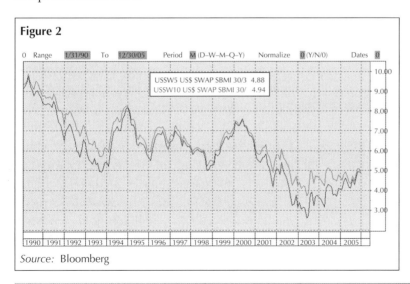

Figure 2

Source: Bloomberg

WHAT IS A SWAP SPREAD?

The fixed swap rate can also be considered the fixed rate at which banks can borrow cash from the interbank market, longer term. Swap spreads represent the difference between the fixed swap rate and the risk free government rate. The difference (or swap spread) represents the credit spread banks, in general, would have to pay relative to that of the risk free government rate. Even if swap rates are quoted on an absolute basis there is still an implicit spread or credit differential implied by the swap rate relative to an underlying risk free rate. Figure 3 plots the US Treasury and PAR swap rate yield curves.

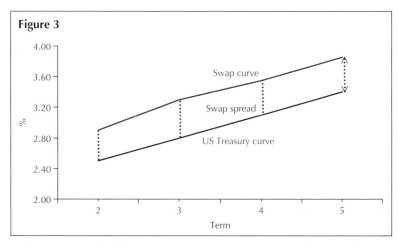

Figure 3

Swap spreads change over time as market conditions change. Supply and demand of fixed rate payers and receivers will ulti-matly drive the absolute swap rates and thus the implicite swap spreads. However given the fact that swap spreads represent the "average cost of credit" in the market any factor that effects the probability of default will cause swap spreads to change. During an economic slowdown, the probability of default (on average) increases thus swap spreads widen. During an economic boom the probability decreases causing a decrease in spreads. Swap spreads thus reflect changes in the underlying credit markes. Any factor that is seen as positive for the credit market, which reduces the default probability, will cause spreads to tighten, and anything bad for the credit market, which increases the default probability, will cause spreads to widen. Figure 4 is a hsitorical graph of 5 and 10-year US$ swap spreads since 1990.

Figure 4

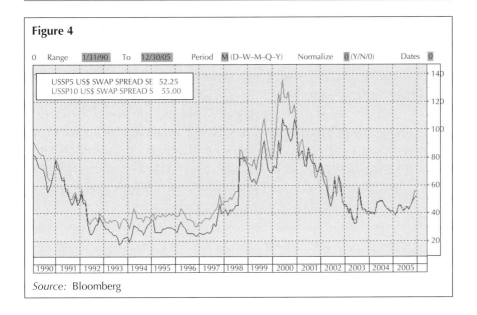

| 0 | Range | 1/31/90 | To | 12/30/05 | Period | M (D–W–M–Q–Y) | Normalize | 0 (Y/N/0) | Dates | 0 |

USSP5 US$ SWAP SPREAD SE 52.25
USSP10 US$ SWAP SPREAD S 55.00

Source: Bloomberg

While there are no strict rules which drive the level of spreads, if we observe historic spreads we notice there are four variables which affect the level of swap spreads.

Absolute level of yields

As overall interest rates (UST rates) decrease, initially there tends to be a widening of swap spreap. Swap rates seem to lag the fall in the underlying government rates. Also, with lower rates, corporates tend to want to take advantage of the lower cost of funding and pay fixed on their liabilties, thus more will want to enter into pay fixed rec floating swaps, which given the effects of supply and demand will cause spreads to widen. However, lower interest rates implies a lower cost of financing for banks and corporates which is seen as a positive for the credit markets and thus will eventually cause spreads to tighten. This effect can be seen in Figure 4, as interest rates were falling starting in 1990, spreads were tightening.

Bond supply

The relative supply and demand of bonds within the market will also have an effect on spreads. During times of very low interest rates more corporates will want to issue bonds, this over supply and lower demand (as a result of lower yields) will cause an imbalance. In order to establish equilibrium the yields of new issues will have to increase which results in a gradual widening of credit spreads.

Shape of the yield curve

Swap spreads tend to widen as the yield curve flattens. A flatter or even an inverted yield curve generally implies an expectation of a economic slow down. This expectation of a poor economic situation is bad for the credit market and thus will cause spreads to widen. The curve was relatively steep in 1992/1993, which caused spreads to tighten, and in 2005 as the curve became flat and spreads started to widen.

Credit spreads

The most obvious and generic of all the underlying factors affecting swap spreads is the overall market's perception on credit spreads. Any macro event that may effect the general markets perception on credit (positive or negative) will have a direct impact on the level of swap spreads. Macro events may include the economic outlook for the world (or US) economy, or a credit specific event such as Russia defaulting on its external debt, which may have a rippling effect on "other" credits/markets. Just like interest rates, credit spreads go thru "cycles", there are periods when the absolute number and frequency of defaults are low and credit spreads tighten, followed by period when default frequencies increase as a result of higher interest rates or poor macro economics and spreads tend to widen.

QUOTATION BASIS

In order to calculate the actual coupon payments we need to know how interest is calculated. In order to determine the cash amount we need to know the interest calculation basis, day count basis as well as the payment frequency for the fixed and floating coupons.

Table 2

Currency	Basis for floating interest			Basis for fixed interest	
	Quotation basis	Payment freq	Index	Quotation basis	Payment freq
US$	Act/360	3M	LIBOR	Act/360	Ann
GBP	Act/365	3M	LIBOR	Act/365	Semi-Ann or Ann
EUR	Act/360	6M	EURIBOR	30/360	Ann
JPY	Act/360	3M	LIBOR or TIBOR	Act/365	Semi-Ann
CAD	Act/360	6M	BAs	Act/365	Semi-Ann
AUD	Act/365	90D	Bank bills	Act/365	Semi-Ann

While there is a standard market convention, as outlined in the tables above, different market makers may quote rates with different underlying basis. When comparing rates quoted by different dealers always make sure they are quoting on the same basis.

Table 3 outlines a typical quote for a fixed floating IRS (notice that the quotation basis is different than above) as well as its applicable cashflows.

Table 3 IRS cashflows

Notional	US$100 Million
Trade date	15-Apr-05
Settlement date	19-Apr-05 (spot)
Maturity	19-Apr-07 (2 years)
Pay	4.050%, semi-annual,
Fixed rate	30/360
Receive	6 M US$ LIBOR (6 ML)
Floating rate	Act/360
Floating rate spread	0 bps

Date	Days	Floating rate payment	Fixed rate payment
19-Apr-05	–	–	–
19-Oct-05	183	$6ML_0 \times 183/360 \times US\$100M$	$-4.05\% \times 180/360 \times 100M$
19-Apr-06	182	$6ML_1 \times 182/360 \times US\$100M$	$-4.05\% \times 180/360 \times 100M$
19-Oct-06	183	$6ML_2 \times 183/360 \times US\$100M$	$-4.05\% \times 180/360 \times 100M$
19-Apr-07	182	$6ML_3 \times 182/360 \times US\$100M$	$-4.05\% \times 180/360 \times 100M$
19-Oct-07	183	$6ML_4 \times 183/360 \times US\$100M$	$-4.05\% \times 180/360 \times 100M$
19-Apr-08	183	$6ML_5 \times 183/360 \times US\$100M$	$-4.05\% \times 180/360 \times 100M$

Example of cashflows

Payment 19-October-05

If 6M LIBOR for the first period ($6ML_0$) was set at 2.30%

    The floating rate receipt would be:

        2.30% × 183/360 × US\$100M   =   US\$+1,169,167

    The fixed interest payment would be:

        4.05% × 180/360 × US\$100M   =   <u>US\$−2,025,000</u>

Net payment made by (fixed rate) payer   US\$−855,833

Payment 19-April-06

If 6M LIBOR for the first period ($6ML_2$) were set at 2.50%

    The floating rate receipt would be:

        2.50% × 182/360 × US\$100M   =   US\$+1,263,888

    The fixed interest payment would be:

        4.05% × 180/360 × US\$100M   =   <u>US\$−2,025,000</u>

Net payment made by (fixed rate) payer   US\$−761,112

Table 3 outlines the cashflows but to value the IRS we need further information. In order to estimate the NPV of the IRS we need the present value of each of the swap's legs (floating and fixed). We therefore will need to estimate what the 6M LIBOR will be and also the discount factor applicable for each payment date outlined above. The 6ML rates are the forward rates or FRAs, which we can estimate from current market rates. We will look at how to estimate the FRAs and discount factors by constructing a "zero curve" from current market rates, which we will cover in detail in Chapter 5.

Floating rate fixing

While the amount of interest paid on the fixed leg is predetermined, the amount of interest on the floating leg changes from interest period to interest period. The floating interest payments are fixed against an underlying interest rate index. The interest rate for most currencies is the inter-bank deposit rate. This is the average rate at which banks will borrow and lend funds to each other. The rate itself is fixed every business day basis and then published on Telerate or Reuters, as shown in Figure 5.

LIBOR

LIBOR is the floating rate index used for US\$, GBP and JPY (among others). LIBOR is an acronym for the London Interbank Offer Rate.

The LIBOR fixing is set or determined each London business day at 11 am by taking the average interbank deposit rate from a pre-set panel of banks. The market convention is for the LIBOR fixing rate to be applicable for a period starting spot, which for most currencies is two business days forward from trade date (T + 2) and maturity X months from spot date. The six-month LIBOR fixing on Wednesday is the applicable interest rate for funds valued two days forward (Friday) and maturing six months from Friday. Most markets have a two-business day spot start with a notable exception of GBP, which has a spot start or value date of same day. Spot start refers to value date of the floating coupon and is normally the market convention for the value date of the IRS.

Figure 5

BRITISH BANKERS'
 ASSOCIATION   Pa

04/14	03:34 GMT	[BRITISH BANKERS ASSOCIATION LIBOR RATES]		
[13/04/05]	RATES AT 11:00 LONDON TIME 13/04/2005			14/
CCY	USD	GBP	CAD	EUR	JPY
O/N	2.80625	4.92875	2.56750	2.08563	SNO.03750
1WK	2.84500	4.84125	2.57833	2.09213	0.03875
2WK	2.85000	4.84813	2.58167	2.09375	0.04000
1MO	2.95375	4.85688	2.59417	2.10388	0.04000
2MO	3.07000	4.90000	2.61417	2.12422	0.04688
3MO	3.14063	4.94063	2.63417	2.13881	0.05188
4MO	3.22000	4.95875	2.67167	2.15234	0.05500
5MO	3.31000	4.97438	2.71167	2.16278	0.05563
6MO	3.41000	4.98563	2.75000	2.17669	0.06500
7MO	3.48000	4.99625	2.79667	2.19066	0.06500
8MO	3.55250	5.00625	2.84333	2.20138	0.06750
9MO	3.62000	5.01625	2.88917	2.21925	0.07625
10MO	3.68000	5.02625	2.93500	2.23925	0.08000
11MO	3.73500	5.03563	2.97750	2.25900	0.08375
12MO	3.78250	5.04563	3.02333	2.28113	0.09125

Source: Bloomberg/BBA

Normal market convention is to use the LIBOR fixing two business days (T + 2) prior to the start of the interest rate period and then pay it at maturity. This is referred to as set in advance and paid in arrears, which is illustrated in Figure 6. There are other Non-standard market conventions such as set and paid in arrears, where the interest fixing is taken two business days before the end or payment date of the interest period. LIBOR in arrears (LIA) will be discussed in more detail in a later chapter.

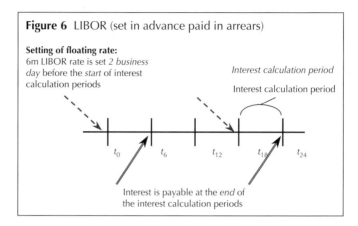

Figure 6 LIBOR (set in advance paid in arrears)

Setting of floating rate:
6m LIBOR rate is set *2 business day* before the *start* of interest calculation periods

Interest calculation period

Interest calculation period

t_0 t_6 t_{12} t_{18} t_{24}

Interest is payable at the *end* of the interest calculation periods

For further information on LIBOR, detailed definitions and historic rates see the British Bankers' Association web site at www.bba.org.uk/

EURIBOR

For EURO denominated IRS the floating coupon is fixed using the EURIBOR reference rate (Euro Interbank Offered Rate). EURIBOR has a similar fixing mechanism as LIBOR; the main differences are the business centre and the composition of the panel of banks, which decides the rate fixings.

Euribor is quoted for spot value (T + 2) and on an act/360 day-count convention, to three decimal places. While there is an Euro LIBOR fixing as well, market convention is to use EURIBOR as the fixing rate for most EUR swaps.

For further information on Euribor, detailed definitions and historic rates see the following link: www.euribor.org/

Figure 7

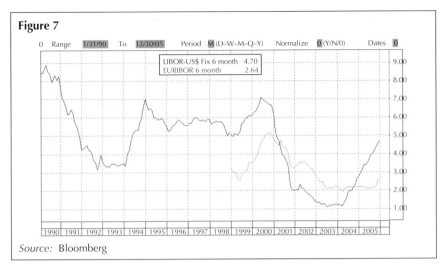

| 0 | Range | 1/31/90 | To | 12/30/05 | Period | M (D–W–M–Q–Y) | Normalize | 0 (Y/N/0) | Dates | 0 |

Source: Bloomberg

Business centres

When specifying the details of an IRS transaction we must designate the business centre for floating rate fixing. For example we can only obtain a US$ LIBOR fixing when it is a good business day in London (ie banks are open). There will also be a business centre for the cash payment. For example if we receive our US$ funds in a clearing bank in NY we will need to have a good business day in New York so that we can actually receive the funds. If it is not a good business day we then rely on the business day roll convention to determine the actual fixing or payment date. We therefore must specify in our swap contract, the business centre for the floating rate fixing as well as the centre for cash payment (for both the fixed and floating interest payments). In some cases they may not be the same centre and may include more than one centre for various reasons.

The business centre for LIBOR fixings is London, and for Euro the business centre is TARGET. Because the Euro has more than one major business centre, the Governing Council of the European Central Bank (ECB) decides the appropriate business days. The Euro business days are known as, "TARGET", which stands for the Trans-European Automated Real-time Gross settlement Express Transfer. The ECB has mandated that the system will be closed, in addition to Saturdays and Sundays, on the following days:

New Year's Day, Good Friday, Easter Monday,
1st May (Labour Day), Christmas Day, 26 December

INTEREST RATE SWAP APPLICATIONS
Liability management

Banks and corporates spend a lot of time looking for markets that can provide cheap sources of financing, on a relative basis. "On a relative basis" means the same common or domestic terms. Many borrows are attracted simply to "lower interest payments" but on a relative basis the funding may actually be more expensive. So while a bond denominated in JPY lower may have lower coupon payments compared with a US$ bond, the foreign exchange exposure may actually result in significantly higher payments over the long run. Similarly, when short-term interest rates are very low many corporates may choose to pay a floating rate of interest on their liabilities, since the rate is significantly lower than the longer term fixed rate, which they can lock in. However as short term rates increase these liability payments will increase which again may result in higher overall payments in the long run. So regardless of how you fund you should always compare the funding on a relative or after hedged basis, which is normally denominated in the currency of domicile of the head office and on a similar fixed or floating spread basis. Your choice to hedge or not is a separate matter, the choice of funding alternatives is a matter of relative costs. To illustrate how we manage our liability exposure let us consider a simplified example.

A corporate (BBB Co.) issues a floating rate note (FRN) with a floating rate coupon of LIBOR + 75 basis points. As LIBOR increases their interest payments increase, they therefore have interest rate exposure. In order to eliminate this exposure they want to swap from paying FLOATING to FIXED payments. In general corporates prefer to have fixed rate liabilities, as they generally want to have known or fixed expenses.

At the same time, a bank (AAA) issues a fixed rate bond. In general bank's prefer to manage all their assets and liabilities on a floating rate basis, therefore they want to swap their fixed rate obligation into a floating liability. Banks will borrow funds at LIBOR (regardless of the underlying tenor) and then lend it out at LIBOR plus a spread, resulting in a fixed profit margin, regardless of changes in interest rates. Hence, each party is actually asking for an opposite hedge.

A swap dealer acts as an intermediary between the two counter-parties. It manages to match the two trades together, however, nei-ther counterparty is aware of the other, nor do they have any credit or econimic exposure to the other party.

Figure 8 illustrates how the hedge works for all parties involved. The swap dealer receives from Corp BBB fixed at 3.85% against paying 6M LIBOR; the dealer then pays 3.80% fixed *vs.* receiving 6M LIBOR from Bank AAA.

In this example the dealer's margin is 5 bps. This margin is the profit the swap dealer requires in order to enter into the trades. The size of the margin is a function of two factors: liquidity – the ability of the dealer to offset the position with another trade, and credit risk. In the event of default by one of the counterparties the swap dealer is responsible for ensuring the hedge remains. Therefore they will have to replace the defaulted swap in the open market at current market rates, which therefore results in credit risk to the dealer. While initially there is generally no credit risk (zero NPV), over time as interest rates change, one side of the trade will have a positive NPV and thus credit risk, so it is this potential credit risk

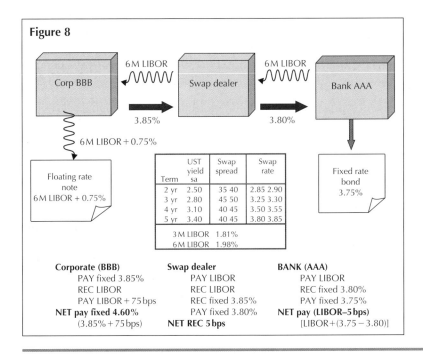

Figure 8

Term	UST yield sa	Swap spread	Swap rate
2 yr	2.50	35 40	2.85 2.90
3 yr	2.80	45 50	3.25 3.30
4 yr	3.10	40 45	3.50 3.55
5 yr	3.40	40 45	3.80 3.85

| 3 M LIBOR | 1.81% |
| 6 M LIBOR | 1.98% |

Floating rate note
6M LIBOR + 0.75%

Fixed rate bond
3.75%

Corporate (BBB)
PAY fixed 3.85%
REC LIBOR
PAY LIBOR + 75 bps
NET pay fixed 4.60%
(3.85% + 75 bps)

Swap dealer
PAY LIBOR
REC LIBOR
REC fixed 3.85%
PAY fixed 3.80%
NET REC 5 bps

BANK (AAA)
PAY LIBOR
REC fixed 3.80%
PAY fixed 3.75%
NET pay (LIBOR–5 bps)
[LIBOR + (3.75 – 3.80)]

that the dealer must be compensated for. The amount of credit risk is dependent not only on the potential MTM of the trade but also the credit rating of the underlying counterparty. In the case where one of the counterparties has a lower credit rating the dealer may require additional spread to be paid. In the above example the dealer may require the corporate (whom is rated BBB) to pay a fixed rate which is an additional 5 bps higher to compensate them for contingent credit risk. While swap dealers will provide a general quote for fixed swap rates they may also appply differential pricing depending on the underlying trade and counterparty's credit rating.

Asset/liability management

Financial institutions manage the interest rate exposure of their assets and liabilities using interest swaps. Banks manage a huge portfolio of assets and liabilities; all have different tenors and interest rates. Banks can borrow and lend on any basis required, as a function of cost or client preferences, and then use IRS to manage any mismatch.

As an example, assume bank ABC offers only 1 asset and 1 liability product. Cash comes in from deposits, which they agree to pay a floating rate of interest linked to LIBOR, and lends cash out as five-year fixed rate loans. While the short-term cash deposit can be called at any time and pays LIBOR the consumer loan will have a fixed rate of interest for five years. While there is a difference in tenor, which will need to be managed (cash management), the biggest risk to the bank is the interest rate exposure.

If interest rates go up the interest paid on the deposits will increase, while the interest received from the loans remains fixed. Hence the bank is at risk if rates go up, and this risk is known as "GAP Risk". The GAP risk is defined as the duration of the Assets less the duration of the bank's Liabilities. In the above example the duration of the deposit is short term, less than three months, while the duration on the Loan is longer term, probably around three years. Banks manage the GAP risk using IRSs, by effectively changing the duration of the underlying liabilities and/or assets.

In the above example the bank eliminates the exposure by entering into an IRS. They enter into a pay fixed receive floating IRS, effectively converting the fixed rate liability into a floating rate

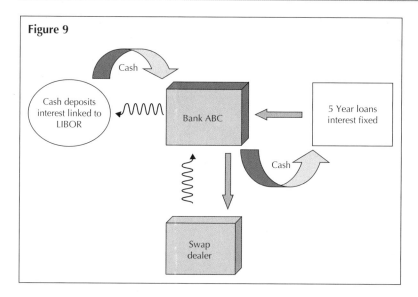

Figure 9

liability. Since both asset and liability are on a floating rate basis the durations should match, thus a zero gap risk. The bank now makes a fixed profit regardless of the absolute level or change in underlying LIBOR.

In the real world a bank's portfolio of assets and liabilities can be huge and thus need to be monitored and managed at a macro level, using IRS to manage the overall portfolio rather than individual assets and liabilities. This is referred to as asset liability management (ALM) within a financial institution.

Asset swaps

Institutional investors (banks or fund managers) can also use IRSs to alter the interest profile of an investment. As an example, assume Bank ABC wants to buy a fixed rate bond (FRB). However, the bank needs to have the coupons match its funding, which is 6M US$ LIBOR. The Bank can purchase the five-year fixed rate note paying a 5.00% semi-annual coupon, at a price of PAR (100%), and then overlay an IRS to manage the interest rate exposure.

Bank ABC receives a 5.00% coupon from the bond and then pays that to the swap dealer in exchange for a floating rate of income (in order to match its funding). Given the current PAR swap rates quoted by the dealer we can figure out what spread the dealer should be paying over LIBOR. The dealer is quoting a five-year PAR

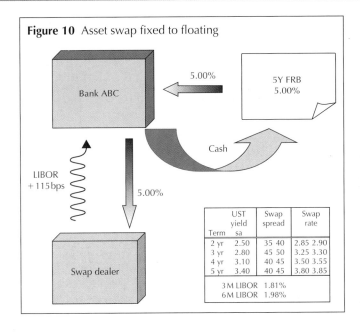

Figure 10 Asset swap fixed to floating

Bank ABC

5.00%

5Y FRB
5.00%

Cash

LIBOR
+ 115 bps

5.00%

Swap dealer

Term	UST yield sa	Swap spread	Swap rate
2 yr	2.50	35 40	2.85 2.90
3 yr	2.80	45 50	3.25 3.30
4 yr	3.10	40 45	3.50 3.55
5 yr	3.40	40 45	3.80 3.85

3 M LIBOR 1.81%
6 M LIBOR 1.98%

Bid swap rate of 3.85%. This is the rate at which they will receive in return for paying floating. Since the counterparty is paying the full bond's coupon of 5.00%, and not the PAR rate of 3.85%, the dealer is willing to pay LIBOR + 115 bps. This 115 bps spread comes from the difference between the PAR rate and the actual rate received. Since we are receiving 115 bps more than the PAR rate we are willing to pay 115 bps more on the floating leg. As back of the envelope pricing we can add or subtract equivalent basis points from one side to the other in order to keep the Net NPV of both legs at zero. Variance between this pricing and actual pricing can be explained by the differences in coupon basis. This approximate pricing only works if the fixed and floating legs are quoted on the same basis, in other works if the PV01s for the fixed and floating legs are equal.

Interest rate speculation

Hedge funds make money by correctly predicting future movements in interest rates. If we assume that a hedge fund believes that interest rates will fall, they can make money by entering into one of two different trades (assuming their view is correct):

Alt 1:   Purchase US$10 Million 5-Year US Treasuries

Alt 2:   Enter into a 5-Year IRS, receiving fixed and paying floating

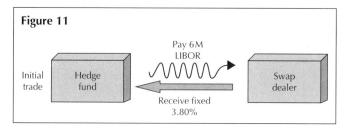

Figure 11

Initial trade — Hedge fund — Pay 6M LIBOR → Swap dealer — Receive fixed 3.80%

The hedge fund will make a profit in either case if interest rate fall. If interest rates fall a profit is realised by selling the UST at the higher price (as a result of lower rates). For the hedge fund to realise a profit under Alt 2 they must enter into an offsetting IRS, pay fixed *vs.* receive floating, effectively cancelling out the initial trade. For the Hedge fund to earn a profit they want long-term swap rates to fall. Alt 2 involves some additional risk (basis risk), the risk that swap rates and US treasury rates do not move in the same direction. Swaps allow the hedge fund to enter into a directional market trade without the need of any upfront cash. The hedge fund does not require any upfront capital, only credit lines with a swap dealer. This allows the hedge fund to have a similar speculative position but the ability to leverage the position using interest rate derivatives.

If long-term swap rates fall the hedge fund makes a profit, just as they would if they had purchased US Treasuries. If immediately after the initial trade the five-year fixed swap rate fell to 3.50% the hedge fund could enter into a offsetting IRS and lock in a guaranteed profit of 30 bps per annum (3.80% less 3.50%). They could enter into an offsetting trade, and if the IRS was entered into with the same counterparty they could cancel both swaps and cash settle the NPV differences. Given that the underlying swap is five years the total upfront profit would be approximately 1.50% (30 bps received for each year for five years) albeit on a discounted basis.

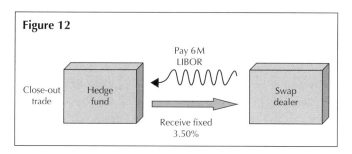

Figure 12

Close-out trade — Hedge fund — Pay 6M LIBOR → Swap dealer — Receive fixed 3.50%

NON-STANDARD INTEREST RATE SWAPS

There is also some non-standard IRS.

❑ **Amortising swaps** are similar to plain IRS except that the notional amount decreases over time. Normally they are linked to a loan where the underlying principal decreases or amortises over time.

❑ **Zero coupon swaps** have a zero fixed rate. The receiver of fixed will pay a floating rate of interest and receive a lump sum at end of the swap.

❑ **Constant maturity swaps (CMS)** A vanilla IRS normally has one floating leg which is linked to a floating index, such as LIBOR, a CMS swap is where one floating leg is linked not to a short term LIBOR rate but to a variable long term swap rate. The CMS rate is the fixed swap rate, which is fixed each day and fluctuates as the long-term interest rate changes over time.

❑ **Basis Swap** is a swap where both legs of the swap are floating. You can have an IRS where you Rec 3-Month US$ LIBOR *vs.* paying 6-Month US$ LIBOR. In the case where both legs are floating but are denominated in different currencies you have a cross-currency basis swap (see cross-currency swaps in Chapter 8).

❑ **LIBOR-in-arrears swaps** Normal market convention is to have the floating interest rate to be set in advance (prior to the start of the interest period) and then paid in arrears (at the end of the interest rate period). An alternative is to have the floating interest fixed in arrears or at the end of the interest period and then paid immediately thereafter.

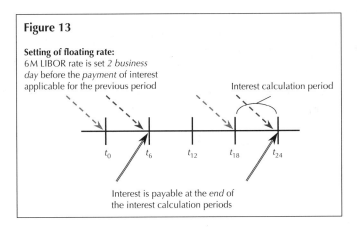

Figure 13

Setting of floating rate:
6 M LIBOR rate is set *2 business day* before the *payment* of interest applicable for the previous period

Interest calculation period

t_0 t_6 t_{12} t_{18} t_{24}

Interest is payable at the *end* of the interest calculation periods

In general these swaps can be priced just like a conventional IRS. The value is simply the NPV of the underlying cashflows. The only complication exists in mapping out the underlying cashflows, or modifying when and how interest is paid. The key to valuing any non-generic swap is to have a principal schedule fixed upfront. If we have a known principal schedule we can estimate the amount of interest to be paid and thus value the stream of cashflows. Where the notional changes, unexpectedly over time it is impossible to price using this conventional NPV method.

We will look at how to value these non-standard IRSs in later chapters.

CASE STUDIES

In this section we will consider several case studies on how to apply interest rate swaps. We will only consider the application of the interest rate derivatives and use approximate pricing to examine what the hedging results should be. We will look at the actual detailed pricing in Chapter 6.

Asset swaps

You are running a bond fund. You are not allowed to run any interest rate risk, which means you cannot hold floating rate notes (FRNs). You need all your assets to earn a fixed rate of interest. You can however buy an FRN and enter into a Pay Floating *vs.* Receive Fixed IRS in order to eliminate any interest rate exposure. You have been offered the following bond:

❏ 5-Year FORD FRN, offered with a coupon of 6M US$ LIBOR + 100 basis points at a price of PAR.
❏ There is an equivalent fixed rate bond which you can purchase, it is being offered with a current YTM of 135 bps over the similar term US Treasury.

Should you buy the FORD FRN and asset swap it into a fixed rate security, or buy the vanilla fixed rate bond? To answer this question we need to determine the fixed rate we could receive after hedging the FRN's coupons with an IRS.

Table 4 Current market rates

Term	UST yield sa	Swap spread		Swap rate	
2 yr	2.50	35	45	2.85	2.95
3 yr	2.80	40	45	3.20	3.30
4 yr	3.10	45	55	3.55	3.65
5 yr	3.40	50	60	3.90	4.00
3M LIBOR		1.81%			
6M LIBOR		1.98%			

If our swap counterparty is willing to pay 3.90% *vs.* receiving 6M US$ LIBOR, then they should be willing to pay 4.90% (3.90% + 100 bps) *vs.* receiving 6M US$ LIBOR + 100 bps. We effectivly add 100 basis points to each leg, in oreder to keep the fair value NPV of the IRS at zero.

We now need to determine what this fixed rate or equivalent yield to maturity is relative to the US Treasury. From the current market rates we see that the 5Y UST is currently trading with a YTM of 3.40%. If the fixed coupon we receive is 4.90% this implies that our asset swap package can provide a fixed rate asset at a spread of 150 basis points over the UST's yield (4.90% less 3.40%). Therefore, buying the floating rate FORD bond and then entering into a Fixed-Floating IRS the bond fund can achieve a fixed rate which is better than an equivalent plain vanilla fixed rate FORD bond, which is only being offered at a fixed spread of 135 bps over UST.

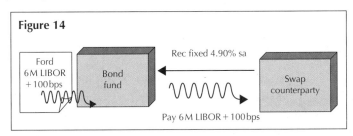

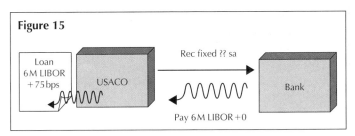

Treasurer's tips

One year ago, USACO entered into a swap transaction to hedge a five-year floating rate loan. The loan was priced at 6M LIBOR + 50 basis points. At the time of the initial hedge USACO obtained three quotes for a 5Y US$ IRS (all quoted on a semi-annual 30/360 basis *vs.* 6-month LIBOR).

Bank A: 5.77 − 5.74%
Bank B: 5.75 − 5.72%
Bank C: 5.76 − 5.71%

Which was the best quote offered to USACO?
In order to hedge the initial interest rate exposure USACO needs to enter into a Pay Fixed received floating IRS. USACO wants to pay the lowest rate possible. The bank (market maker) receives on the BID side (high side) and pays on the OFFER (low side) we therefore must consider each bank's BID, and given that USACO wants to pay fixed, they want the lowest BID possible. Therefore, given the three quotes above USACO should enter into an IRS with bank B at a fixed rate of 5.75%.

What is the effective (after hedge) funding cost for USACO?
The effective funding cost for the corporate is therefore:

Pay 6M US$ LIBOR + 50 bps	Loan
Rec 6M US$ LIBOR + 0	IRS floating leg
Pay Fixed Rate of 5.75%	IRS fixed leg
Net or effective Funding Cost	
Fixed Rate + floating Spread:	6.25% (5.75 + 0.5%)

Today (1-year later), the treasurer is convinced that interest rates are likely to fall further, as they have over the last 12 months. Therefore he decides to enter into another IRS to swap the fixed funding costs into a floating cost in order to take advantage of possible lower rates. The new swap they enter into will offset the original hedge, swapping their liability back to the original floating rate obligation. The treasurer calls the same three banks for quotes in order to re-swap the proceeds.

Bank A: 4.93 − 4.88%
Bank B: 4.93 − 4.90%
Bank C: 4.95 − 4.90%

Which is the best quote now?

To offset the initial hedge USACO wants to enter into a receive fixed *vs.* pay floating IRS. This will effectively cancel the initial swap and leave them to benefit from lower rates. The quoting bank receives on the BID side (high side) and pays on the OFFER (low side), therefore we need to consider the bank's OFFER rates. Given that USACO wants to receive the fixed rate they want the highest OFFER possible. Given the above quotes, the best quote is banks B and C at 4.90%. Given that our initial swap is with bank B and since we are doing the reverse transaction of our initial trade, it would make sense to do the trade with bank B from a credit perspective. The two trades cancel each other out in terms of exposure, they could in fact cancel the first trade and enter into just one at the new effective rate, reducing the overall credit exposure the counterparties have to each other.

What is the new effective funding cost?

The *new* effective funding cost for the corporate is therefore:

(a) Pay 6M US$ LIBOR + 50 bps   Loan
(b) Rec 6M US$ LIBOR + 0   IRS floating leg
(c) Pay Fixed Rate 5.75%   IRS fixed leg
(d) Pay 6M US$ LIBOR + 0   *new* IRS floating leg
(e) Rec Fixed rate 4.90%   *new* IRS fixed leg

Effective *new* funding cost:
Since (b) and (d) cancel each other out, we are left with:

Pay 6M US$ LIBOR + 50 bps   ((a) as above)
Pay Net Fixed rate 0.85%   (5.75% less 4.90% Net basis of (c) and (e))

Net *new* effective funding:

6M US$ LIBOR + 135 bps (50 + 85 bps)

Does the initial swap have a positive or negative MTM from USACO's point of view?

The initial trade USACO is paying fixed, and given the fact that interest rates have fallen the first hedge is out of the money (negative MTM) from USACO's perspective. The fixed rate they paid on the initial trade was 5.75% and if they wanted to offset the initial hedge they would need to receive fixed and since the new rate they could receive is lower they are worse off and thus a the initial hedge has a negative MTM. The initial hedge is out of the money by 85 bps (Pay 5.75% Rec 4.90%) which they will need to continue to pay for the remaining four years of the hedge or close out both trades and pay an upfront premium to settle the difference in NPVs. The amount USCO would need to pay today to close out both hedges is approximately 3.40% times the notional amount (85 bps $\times$ 4 years) albeit on a discounted NPV basis.

Hedge fund trading

You work as a derivative salesperson at an investment bank and have a client, which is a hedge fund. Your client believes interest rates are going to fall and rather than buy US treasuries outright you have convinced them to use IRSs as a means to speculate and profit from a correct view on changes in long term interest rates.

The hedge fund had a view that interest rates were going to fall. So they entered into a Rec Fixed Pay Floating IRS, which would allow them to benefit from a drop in long term swap rates. As the long-term rates fall they could close out the original swap pay fixed (at a lower fixed rate) and rec floating. Given that the floating legs would cancel out the profit would be the spread difference between the fixed rate received and the fixed rate paid. This profit (or loss) would be in basis points and would be for the remain life of the underlying swaps which they could realise on a periodic basis or (more common) they could PV all the cash flows, cancel both offsetting swaps and cash settle the NPV differences.

One year later, General Electric, which was rated (AAA/Aaa), has defaulted on a bond, which has caused all credit spreads to widen (including swap spreads). At the same time the US Federal Reserve has unexpectedly cut interest rates by 25 bps, which has caused a parallel shift down in the US treasury yield curve by 25 bps.

Your client at the hedge fund calls you up to close out the initial trade and is not very happy. "You convinced me to enter into an IRS *but* swap rates have not moved while the Treasury bond I wanted to buy has increased in price, thanks for nothing!"

What do you tell your client?

Rates: 1-Year ago

Term	UST yield (%)	Swap spread		Swap rate	
2 yr	2.50	35	40	2.85	2.90
3 yr	2.80	45	50	3.25	3.30
4 yr	3.10	40	45	3.50	3.55
5 yr	3.40	40	45	3.80	3.85
6M LIBOR		1.98%			

Rates: Today

Term	UST yield (%)	Swap spread		Swap rate	
2 yr	2.25	60	65	2.85	2.90
3 yr	2.55	70	75	3.25	3.30
4 yr	3.85	65	70	3.50	3.55
5 yr	3.15	65	70	3.80	3.85
6M LIBOR		1.73%			

Initially, the hedge fund would have entered into a Rec Fixed *vs.* Pay Floating IRS, since the bank pays the fixed OFFER (lower) rate and Recs the Fixed Bid (higher) rate the hedge fund would receive 3.80% *vs.* paying 6M US$ LIBOR. In order for the hedge fund to realise a profit they would need to reverse the initial swap, thus they would need to pay fixed to offset the initial trade. However, since the trade is to be unwound one year from start, they no longer need to reverse a five-year swap, since it is now only a four-year trade. While the five-year rate has not changed, given the fact that they need to enter into a four-year swap to reverse the trade and given the fact that the four-year swap rates are lower than the initial five-year rate the hedge fund would have actually made a profit.

The hedge fund, in order to cancel the first trade would need to pay the bank's four-year swap BID (higher) rate of 3.55%. This would result in a net benefit or positive trading profit of 25 bps per annum.

Initial Trade:

      Rec   Fixed 3.80%, 5-Years

      Pay   6M US$ LIBOR

1-Year later (4Y remaining on initial trade)

      Pay   Fixed 3.55%, 4-Years

      Rec   6M US$ LIBOR

Net benefit: 25 basis points per annum (3.80% less 3.55%) for 4-Years

Normally you would NPV the 25 bps per annum profit and make a full cash payment upfront and close out the trade (cancel or tear up the two undelying swaps). Therefore the approximate profit would be a total of approximately 91 bps * Notional. That does not include the positive carry the Hedge fund benefited from during the last 12 months, where they were paying LIBOR and receiving the higher 3.80% fixed rate.

---

1   A swap, PAR swap rate *vs.* floating rate interest has an initial NPV of zero. However, given the bid and offer between rates, there will be a positive profit to the market maker on trade date.

2   For US$ the floating leg is normally 6M US$ LIBOR.

5

Deriving a Zero Coupon Curve

BUILDING A ZERO COUPON CURVE

An interest rate swap comprises a series of cashflows or coupon payments, normally exchanging fixed interest coupons for floating interest coupons. We value a swap similar to how we value a fixed income bond; the price or value is equal to the net present value of the cashflows (coupons and principal).

Table 1 is an example of an interest rate swap valuation. We have valued both legs (fixed and floating) independently, where the Fixed (receiving) leg is worth an NPV of US$+7,716,519, and the NPV of the Floating (paying) leg is US$−7,716,519, which results in an NPV or mark to market of US$0 (NPV fixed leg + NPV floating leg).

In order to value this swap we need to perform the following tasks:

(1) Generate the relevant coupon dates, based on the appropriate day roll conventions and payment frequency for both the fixed and floating legs.
(2) Calculate the relevant coupon flows for the known fixed rate, based on the appropriate daycount basis.
(3) Calculate the expected floating rates for the required floating interest periods.
(4) Calculate the discount factors to the relevant payment dates.

Given the parameters for the swap provided in Table 1 we can calculate steps 1 and 2, but for steps 3 and 4 we need the appropriate discount factors (DCFs) and FRA rates. In order to calculate the

Table 1

Trade date	15-Apr-05
Swap term	2 years
Spot start	19-Apr-05
Maturity	19-Apr-07
Notional	100,000,000
Fixed coupon	4.050 %
Fixed accrual basis	30/360
Fixed coupon frequency	semi-annual
Floating accrual basis	Act/360
Floating coupon frequency	semi-annual
Floating coupon spread	0.00 bps

NPV fixed leg	7,716,519
NPV floating leg	−7,716,519
Total NPV	0

Receiving Fixed

Dates	t	DCF	Coupon	CPN value	NPV coupons
19-Apr-05		0.99969			
19-Oct-05	0.5000	0.98261	4.05	2,025,000	1,989,795
19-Apr-06	0.5000	0.96300	4.05	2,025,000	1,950,078
19-Oct-06	0.5000	0.94249	4.05	2,025,000	1,908,537
19-Apr-07	0.5000	0.92252	4.05	2,025,000	1,868,109

Paying Floating

Dates	t	DCF	LIBOR (%)	CPN Value	NPV coupons
19-Apr-05		0.99969			
19-Oct-05	0.5083	0.98261	3.418	−1,737,554	−1,707,346
19-Apr-06	0.5056	0.96300	4.029	−2,036,690	−1,961,336
19-Oct-06	0.5083	0.94249	4.282	−2,176,581	−2,051,400
19-Apr-07	0.5056	0.92252	4.281	−2,164,106	−1,996,437

DCF and FRAs we need to generate a zero coupon curve using the price or interest rates from tradable market securities. These underlying financial instruments are available for the dealer to buy and sell which effectively represent the rates at which they can borrow or lend cash. These rates allow us to determine the NPV of US$1 received or paid at some time in the future (as we discussed in Chapter 1, the time value of money).

The objective of generating a zero coupon or discount factor curve is to allow us to present value any cashflow paid or received on any given date using current market rates. The instruments we use to generate our zero curve are a combination of deposits, futures (if available and liquid) and Par Swaps Rates. We also need

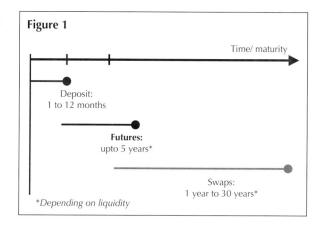

Figure 1

Time/ maturity

Deposit:
1 to 12 months

Futures:
upto 5 years*

Swaps:
1 year to 30 years*

*Depending on liquidity

to make sure these rates blend together in terms of time, overlapping one another in order to avoid GAPS within the curve. Figure 1 shows how these instruments should fit and overlap each other.

Deposit rates range from overnight (O/N) to 12-Months, these financial instruments generate discount factors for the short-term part of the yield curve. The minimum number of deposit rates depends on the maturity date of our first future, if included or the maturity of our first PAR swap rate if no futures are used. The maturity date of the last deposit included should overlap the next instrument we use in our curve in order to avoid gaps within our curve.

Futures rates are then used to calculate the discount factors for the medium term part of the curve. The number of futures *used* depends on the liquidity of the underlying futures. For US$, futures are liquid out to at least five years, while for other currencies futures may only be liquid for up to 12 months or not available at all. The number of futures *required* depends on the shortest tenor swap instrument we have included. If futures are not used and only deposit and swap rates are inputted, we may need to imply an interest rate or discount factor to a specific date in order to complete our curve generating calculations.

Par swap rates are then used to calculate the discount factors for the medium to long part of the curve. Deposits and futures represent zero coupon instruments and therefore are relatively easy to transform into discount factors. Par swap rates are slightly more difficult to convert to discount factors given their coupon payments; we will need to strip the coupons so that we have a zero coupon rate.

Table 2

Basis Cash	Act/360
Basis Swaps	30/360 semi-annual
Spot	2 business days
Spot Date	19-Apr-05
Curve Date	15-Apr-95

Input	Name	Price	Yield	Grid point
Cash	O/N		2.806	18-Apr-05
Cash	T/N		2.806	19-Apr-05
Cash	1 Month		2.950	19-May-05
Cash	3 Month		3.140	19-July-05
Cash	6 Month		3.410	19-Oct-05
Futures	Jun-05	96.535	3.465	21-Sep-05
Futures	Sep-05	96.145	3.855	21-Dec-05
Futures	Dec-05	95.945	4.055	15-Mar-06
Futures	Mar-06	95.825	4.175	21-Jun-06
Futures	Jun-06	95.720	4.280	20-Sep-06
Futures	Sep-06	95.625	4.375	20-Dec-06
Swap	2 Year		4.050	19-Apr-08
Swap	3 Year		4.250	19-Apr-09
Swap	4 Year		4.350	19-Apr-09
Swap	5 Year		4.450	19-Apr-10

The combination and mix of underlying instruments used to generate a zero curve is a matter of choice and not a fixed rule. Traders that price and hedge short term instruments may use more futures, while traders that price and hedge longer dated interest rate swaps will use less futures and more swaps. In a liquid market the choice should not result in an economic difference, since the instruments should be perfectly interchangeable.

Our discussion and the Curveßuilder model which is included on the CD relies on some simple curve generating rules in order to avoid gaps in our zero curve:

(1) The maturity date of our last deposit must be at least equal to the settlement date of our first future, or equal to the second last coupon payment date associate with our first swap input if no futures are included.

(2) If futures are included, the last future used must have a grid-point date at least equal to the second last coupon payment date.

(3) We use the shortest tenor swap available out to the longest tenor swap available.

We use the following market rates, deposits, futures and par swap rates to generate a zero curve.

THE BOOTSTRAPPING ALGORITHM

We generate a discount factor curve using tradable instruments with interest or market rates that represent the rate at which banks can borrow or lend cash in order to synthetically replicate (and thus value) paying or receiving cash at some future date.

Short-term discount factors are generated using cash or deposit rates, in the medium term futures are used, while the long end of the curve uses par swap rates. This process, building up the discount factors from deposit, futures and then swap rates is known as bootstrapping. We begin the process by generating a discount factor from the instrument with the earliest maturity date then successively building up until we have a discount factor for our longest tenor instrument. For each maturity date, for the underlying instruments we will calculate a discount factor, for each of these dates we call "grid points" on our curve.

Deposit rates

We start the bootstrapping algorithm by generate discount factors from deposit and future rates from the following formula:

$$dcf = \frac{dcf_{start}}{1 + r \times \dfrac{days}{basis}} \tag{1}$$

For US$ deposit rates (LIBOR) the daycount basis (*days/basis*) is Actual/360.

For an *overnight (O/N) deposit rate*, the deposit starts on trade date and matures one business day forward. O/N deposit rates always start on trade date therefore dcf_{start} will always equals 1 and the maturity date is one business day forward, which is three actual days (since the term runs over a weekend) for the purposes of our calculations. The discount factor to the maturity of an overnight deposit rate is:

$$dcf_{O/N} = \frac{1}{1 + 0.02806 \times \dfrac{3}{360}} = 0.999766$$

For a *tomorrow next* (T/N) *deposit rate*, the deposit starts one business day forward, and matures one business day later. In our example, the deposit starts one business day or three actual days forward, and matures one business and one actual day thereafter. The dcf_{start} for the T/N deposit is equal to $dcf_{O/N}$. The discount factor to the maturity of T/N deposit rate is:

$$dcf_{T/N} = \frac{0.999766}{1+0.02806 \times \dfrac{1}{360}} = 0.999688$$

For all other deposit rates (1–12 months) the are spot start and matures X months from the spot. For US$ spot is two business days forward from trade date and therefor the discount factor to the start of our remaining deposits is equal to the DCF of our T/N deposit:

$$dcf_{spot} = dcf_{T/N} = dcf_{start} = 0.999688$$

(for spot start equal to two business days).

The remaining discount factors are calculated as follows, using Equation (1):

$$dcf_{1M} = \frac{0.999688}{1+0.0295 \times \dfrac{30}{360}} = 0.997237$$

$$dcf_{3M} = \frac{0.999688}{1+0.0314 \times \dfrac{91}{360}} = 0.991816$$

$$dcf_{6M} = \frac{0.999688}{1+0.0341 \times \dfrac{183}{360}} = 0.982655$$

Note: If no O/N and/or T/N rate is included, in order to avoid gaps in the curve we assume that the first deposit rate (regardless of the underlying tenor) is the missing O/N and/or T/N rate. While this may not be technically correct, given the insignificance in the rate itself it will have little effect on our generated curve and subsequent pricing.

We now have the discount factors for each of the grid points (maturity dates) associated with the deposit rates.

Table 3

Instrument	Period begin date	Period end date	Rate	DCF
O/N	15-Apr-05	18-Apr-05	2.806	0.999766
T/N	18-Apr-05	19-Apr-05	2.806	0.999688
1 Month	19-Apr-05	19-May-05	2.950	0.997237
3 Month	19-Apr-05	19-July-05	3.140	0.991816
6 Month	19-Apr-05	19-Oct-05	3.410	0.982655

Future rates

We now calculate the appropriate discount factors derived from futures. The first futures instrument in our example is the Jun-05 future, and the Jun-05 future gives us the implied zero coupon interest rate for the FRA starting approximately two months from the trade date, and maturing three months thereafter. In order to derive the discount factor we again use Equation (1). We therefore need to know dcf_{start} which is the discount rate to the settlement of the Jun 05 future, 15-Jun-05. This discount rate is known as the "stub rate". This stub rate is interpolated from the discount factors already calculated from the deposit rates (hence the reason why the maturity of our last deposit rate needs to be at least equal to the maturity of our first future). Figure 2 shows the appropriate timing and dates for our first future and the underlying FRA associated with the first future.

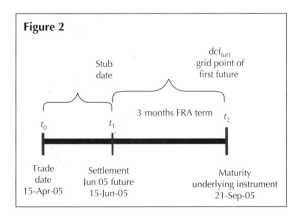

Figure 2

If the stub date (settlement date of the first future, Jun 05) is 15-Jun-05, and

$$dcf_{19\text{-May-05}} = 0.997237$$
$$dcf_{19\text{-Jul-05}} = 0.991816$$

Then the interpolated discount factor to the stub date is:

$$dcf_{stub} = 0.994837$$

We now calculate the discount rates to the maturity of the underlying interest rate associated with the first future:

$$dcf_{fut1} = \frac{dcf_{stub}}{1 + futrate \times \dfrac{days}{basis}} \qquad (2)$$

Futures are quoted as a price, rather than as an interest rate, therefore we need to convert the price into an implied interest rate. The price is 100 less the implied interest rate, therefore to convert from a futures price to an interest rate we simply subtract the future's price from 100 (eg $100 - 97.25$ implies an interest rate of 2.75%). Table 2 already has the future prices converted into interest rates or the required *futrate* for our calculations.

$$dcf_{fut1} = \frac{0.994837}{1 + 0.03465 \times \dfrac{98}{360}} = 0.98554$$

Dcf_{fut1} is then the discount factor to the maturity of the underlying interest rate associated with the first futures contract and is also the discount factor to the settlement of the second futures. $dcf_{fut1} = dcf_{start}$ of the second future. The DCF derived from the second and third futures are calculated as follows:

$$dcf_{fut2} = \frac{0.98554}{1 + 0.03855 \times \dfrac{91}{360}} = 0.97603$$

$$dcf_{fut3} = \frac{0.97603}{1 + 0.04055 \times \dfrac{84}{360}} = 0.96688$$

We continue the calculations for all the available futures.[1] We now have the applicable discount factors derived from all available futures included in our curve.

Table 4

Futures

Instrument	Period begin date	Period end date	Rate	DCF
Jun-05	15-Jun-05	21-Sep-05	3.465	0.985541
Sep-05	21-Sep-05	21-Dec-05	3.855	0.976030
Dec-05	21-Dec-05	15-Mar-06	4.055	0.966882
Mar-06	15-Mar-06	21-Jun-06	4.175	0.956017
Jun-06	21-Jun-06	20-Sep-06	4.280	0.945784
Sep-06	20-Sep-06	20-Dec-06	4.375	0.935439

If no futures are used (or not enough futures are available or liquid) it is likely that there will be a gap in our curve and therefore we will have to interpolate an interest rate and then derive an implied DCF in order to continue the bootstrapping process.

Swap rates

We now derive the discount factors from the par swap rates. While deposit rates and futures are zero coupon instruments and as such are easily convertible into discount factors, par swaps rates have coupons which require a more complex calculation in order to derive the discount factors.

The swap rates we are using are PAR rates, which mean that the net present value of all the cash flows from the fixed leg discounted back at the appropriate discount factors equals PAR (100%), as at spot date.

$$NPV_{spot} = PAR\ (100\%)$$

$$100 = \sum_{1}^{i}\left(swaprate \times dcf_{1toi} \times \frac{days}{basis} \right) + (100 \times dcf_i)$$

where i is the number of coupon payment dates.

If we know that the swap has an NPV of PAR on Spot date then we will need to discount the NPV to reflect the fact that spot maybe a date a few days into the future. For US$ spot is two business days forward and from our example we know that our $dcf_{spot} = 0.999680$. Therefore, if the swap's NPV_{spot} is PAR (100%) value spot, then the NPV on trade date (t_0) NPV_{t0} must be, $PAR \times dcf_{spot}$.

$$NPV_{t0} = 100 \times dcf_{spot}$$

We can then derive a generalized formula to price PAR swaps, which we can then use to derive discount factors to the swap's maturity date.

$$100 \times dcf_{spot} = \sum_{1}^{i} \left(swaprate \times dcf_{1toi} \times \frac{days}{basis} \right) + (100 \times dcf_{maturity}) \quad \text{(3)}$$

In our example the first swap instrument has the following details:

Par swap rate	4.05%
Coupon frequency	semi-annually
Daycount basis	30/360
Number of coupons	4 ($i = 4$)

If we rewrite Equation (3) to stripe out the DCF and cashflows at the swap's maturity date we have the following equation:

$$100 \times dcf_{spot} = \sum_{1}^{3} \left(swaprate_{2Y} \times dcf_{1to3} \times \frac{days}{360} \right) + \left(swaprate_{2Y} \times \frac{days}{basis} + 100 \right) \times dcf_{2yr}$$

If we know the discount factors[2] associated with the first three coupon payment dates, which we have obtained from our deposit and futures DCFs, then the only unknown is the discount factor at the maturity date of our 2-year swap (dcf_{2yr}), which we solve for.

$$dcf_{2yr} = \frac{100 \times dcf_{spot} - \sum_{1}^{3} \left(swaprate_{2Y} \times dcf_{1to3} \times \frac{days}{360} \right)}{100 + swaprate_{2Y} \times \frac{180}{360}}$$

$$dcf_{2yr} = \frac{100 \times 0.999688 - \sum_{1}^{3} \left(4.05 \times dcf_{1to3} \times \frac{days}{360} \right)}{100 + 4.05 \times \frac{180}{360}}$$

$$dcf_{2yr} = \frac{100 \times 0.999688 - 5.8484}{100 + 4.05 \times \frac{180}{360}}$$

$$dcf_{2yr} = 0.92252$$

Table 5

Term	2		
Coupon	4.05		
	Time (yrs)	DCF	Period × DCF × CPN
19-Apr-05			
19-Oct-05	0.5000	0.982615	1.989795
19-Apr-06	0.5000	0.963001	1.950078
19-Oct-06	0.5000	0.942487	1.908537
19-Apr-07	0.5000	?	
		Sum Coupons	5.8484
		DCF	**0.92252**

Given the DCFs associated with the first three coupon payment date the DCF at maturity must be 0.92252 in order for the fixed rate to be a PAR swap rate, where the sum of the discounted cashflows equals 100%.

Our next swap rate is a 3-year rate but in order to calculate the discount factor to the maturity of the 3-year swap we need to know the discount factors for all but the last payment date (maturity date). We have all the DCFs required except the discount factor for the coupon received at 2.5-years. We need to estimate the swap rate at 2.5-years by interpolating between the 2 and 3-year rates, and then follow the same logic as we did for the 2-year swap rate. (We use straight-line interpolation method for this exercise).

$$\text{Interpolated 2.5 year swap rate} = \frac{4.05 + 4.25}{2} = 4.15\%$$

We can now solve for the DCF to the maturity of our implied 2.5-year swap rate.

$$100 \times dcf_{spot} = \sum_{1}^{4}\left(swaprate_{2.5Y} \times dcf_{1to4} \times \frac{days}{360}\right)$$
$$+ \left(swaprate_{2.5Y} \times \frac{days}{basis} + 100\right) \times dcf_{2.5yr}$$

Solving for the $dcf_{2.5yr}$:

$$dcf_{2.5yr} = \frac{100 \times dcf_{spot} - \sum_{1}^{4}\left(swaprate_{2.5Y} \times dcf_{1to4} \times \frac{days}{360}\right)}{100 + swaprate_{2.5Y} \times \frac{180}{360}}$$

$$dcf_{2.5yr} = \frac{100 \times 0.999688 - \sum_{1}^{4}\left(4.15 \times dcf_{1to4} \times \frac{days}{360}\right)}{100 + 4.15 \times \frac{180}{360}}$$

$$dcf_{2.5yr} = 0.90190$$

Table 6

Term	2.5		
Coupon	4.15		

	Time (yrs)	DCF	Period × DCF × CPN
19-Apr-05			
19-Oct-05	0.50	0.982615	2.038926
19-Apr-06	0.50	0.963001	1.998228
19-Oct-06	0.50	0.942487	1.955662
19-Apr-07	0.50	0.922523	1.914235
19-Oct-07	0.50	?	
		Sum Coupons	7.90705
		DCF	**0.90190**

Now that we have the discount rate to 2.5-years we can now continue the calculation process, calculating the dcf to the maturity date of the 3-year swap rate.

$$dcf_{3yr} = \frac{100 \times 0.999688 - \sum_{1}^{5}\left(4.25 \times dcf_{1to5} \times \frac{days}{360}\right)}{100 + 4.25 \times \frac{180}{360}} = 0.8808294$$

Table 7

| Term | 3 | | |
| Coupon | 4.25 | | |

	Time (yrs)	DCF	Period × DCF × CPN
19-Apr-05			
19-Oct-05	0.50	0.982615	2.088057
19-Apr-06	0.50	0.963001	2.046378
19-Oct-06	0.50	0.942487	2.002786
19-Apr-07	0.50	0.922523	1.960362
19-Oct-07	0.50	0.901903	1.916545
19-Apr-08	0.50	?	
		Sum Coupons	10.01413
		DCF	**0.880829**

We continue the bootstrapping algorithm until we have a grid point equal to the maturity date of the last input.

$$dcf_{3.5yr} = \frac{100 \times 0.99969 - 12.025723}{100 + 4.30 \times \frac{180}{360}} = 0.860921$$

$$dcf_{4yr} = \frac{100 \times 0.99969 - 14.038060}{100 + 4.35 \times \frac{180}{360}} = 0.841016$$

$$dcf_{4.5yr} = \frac{100 \times 0.99969 - 16.049652}{100 + 4.40 \times \frac{180}{360}} = 0.821127$$

$$dcf_{5yr} = \frac{100 \times 0.99969 - 18.059042}{100 + 4.45 \times \frac{180}{360}} = 0.801270$$

The combined end results in the following (Table 8) zero discount curve, which provides the underlying grid points and discount factors. We now have a generic discount factor curve, with specific grid points and DCFs. This discount or zero curve now becomes the engine behind most of our pricing and hedging going forward.

Table 8

Basis Cash	Act/360	
Basis Swaps	30/360 semi-annual	
Spot	2 business days	
Spot Date	19-Apr-05	
Curve Date	15-Apr-05	

Input	Name	Price	Yield	Grid point	Discount factor
Cash	O/N		2.806	18-Apr-05	0.999766
Cash	T/N		2.806	19-Apr-05	0.999688
Cash	1 Month		2.950	19-May-05	0.997237
Cash	3 Month		3.140	19-July-05	0.991816
Cash	6 Month		3.410	19-Oct-05	0.982655
Futures	Jun-05	96.535	3.465	21-Sep-05	0.985541
Futures	Sep-05	96.145	3.855	21-Dec-05	0.976030
Futures	Dec-05	95.945	4.055	15-Mar-06	0.966882
Futures	Mar-06	95.825	4.175	21-Jun-06	0.956017
Futures	Jun-06	95.720	4.280	20-Sep-06	0.945784
Futures	Sep-06	95.625	4.375	20-Dec-06	0.935439
Swap	2 Year		4.050	19-Apr-07	0.922523
	2.5 Year	interp	4.150	19-Oct-07	0.901903
Swap	3 Year		4.250	19-Apr-08	0.880829
	3.5 Year	interp	4.300	19-Oct-08	0.860921
Swap	4 Year		4.350	19-Apr-09	0.841016
	4.5 Year	interp	4.400	19-Oct-09	0.821127
Swap	5 Year		4.450	19-Apr-10	0.801270

GENERATING GENERIC DISCOUNT FACTORS AND FRAS

Now that we have calculated a discount factor or zero coupon curve, we can interpolate a discount factor to any date; we can also calculate the implied FRA between any two dates.

Discount factors

In order to determine the discount factor to "any date" we simply interpolate the rate from the generated discount factors. We can then estimate the net present value (NPV) of any cashflow by multiplying the cashflow by the appropriate discount factor.

Given the zero curve derived in the previous section we can determine the applicable discount factor to any date, for example let us assume we have a cash payment on 15-Oct-05 and we need to determine the DCF to that specific date.

If we know the following DCFs:

> 21-Sept-05: 0.985541
> 21-Dec-05: 0.976030

Using straight-line[3] interpolations we then calculate the DCF to 15-Oct-05:

$$dcf_{15\text{-}oct\text{-}05} = neardcf + (keydate - neardate) \times \frac{neardcf - fardcf}{neardate - fardate}$$

$$dcf_{15\text{-}oct\text{-}05} = 0.985541 + (19\text{-}Oct\text{-}05 - 21\text{-}Sep\text{-}05)$$

$$\times \frac{0.985541 - 0.97603}{21\text{-}Sep\text{-}05 - 21\text{-}Dec\text{-}05}$$

$$dcf_{15\text{-}oct\text{-}05} = 0.985541 + 28 \times -0.0001045$$

$$dcf_{15\text{-}oct\text{-}05} = 0.982615$$

We can now calculate a DCF to any date to and including the maturity of our last inputted instrument.

Generic FRAs

Now that we have DCFs to any given date we can now calculate the implied FRA rate for any given interest rate period. In our initial interest rate swap pricing example (Table 1) we see that we have an implied FRA rate on 19-Oct-06 of 4.2818%. This is the expected LIBOR fixing, or the forward rate on 19-April-06 and thus the applicable floating rate for the interest period which matures and is payable on 19-Oct-06. The rate is set in advance (19-April-06) and paid in arrears (19-Oct-06).

Since we know that the FRA rates are zero coupon rates we can utilise Equations (4) and (2) to calculate our FRA rates.

Using Equation (4)

$$dcf = \frac{1}{1 + r \times \dfrac{days}{basis}}$$

and Equation (2)

$$FRA = \left[\frac{1 + r_L \times \dfrac{days_L}{basis}}{1 + r_S \times \dfrac{days_S}{basis}} - 1 \right] \times \frac{basis}{days_{FRA}}$$

By combining and rearranging the above equations we have a generic calculation for a FRA between any two dates calculated from discount factors at the start and maturity of the FRA instrument.

$$FRA = \frac{DCF_{(s)} - DCF_{(m)}}{DCF_{(m)}} \times \frac{basis}{days} \qquad \textbf{(4)}$$

where

$DCF_{(s)}$ discount factor to the FRA start date;

$DCF_{(m)}$ discount factor to the FRA maturity or payment date;

$days$ number of days between the start and maturity of the FRA;

$basis$ daycount basis of FRA (for US$ the basis is 360).

Example 1
Calculate the FRA rate on 19-April-2006 (Act/360 daycount basis)

FRA start date   19-April-06
Start date $DCF_{(s)}$ 0.963001 *(interpolated from our zero curve)*
Payment date   9-Oct-06 *(FRA maturity date, 183 actual days)*
Payment   0.942487 *(interpolated from our zero curve)*
date $DCF_{(m)}$

$$FRA = \left[\frac{0.963001 - 0.942487}{0.942487} \right] \times \frac{360}{183}$$
$$FRA = 4.2818\%$$

Example 2
Calculate the FRA rate between 21-Jun-06 and 20-Sep-2006 (Act/360 Basis):

Start date   21-Jun-06
Start date $dcf_{(s)}$ 0.956017   *(from Table 8)*
Payment date   20-Sep-2006   *(91 actual days)*
Payment date $dcf_{(m)}$ 0.945784   *(from Table 8)*

$$FRA = \left[\frac{0.96017 - 0.942487}{0.945784} \right] \times \frac{360}{91}$$
$$FRA = 4.280\%$$

If you examine the futures we used in generating our zero curve you will notice that this FRA rate equals the inputted rate for the Jun 06 future, which is what you would expect. Using Equation (5.4) we can now use the generated zero curve to calculate a zero coupon FRA rate between any two dates.

BUILDING A ZEROCURVE USING CURVEßUILDER

Curveßuilder is the excel workbook which does all the calculations explained in this chapter and then generates the zero curve. The user can modify and change the specific inputs to suit their specific choices as well as tailor it for specific currencies.

Figure 3

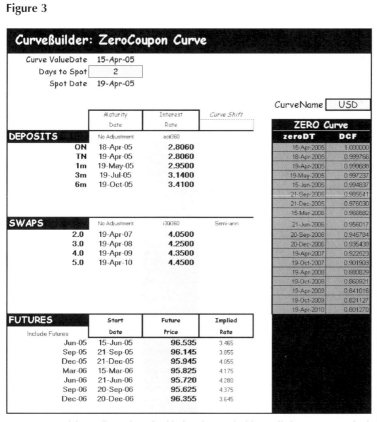

Note: Some of the sections described below have a hidden pull-down menu, which you can access by simply selecting or activating the appropriate cell. For example, daycount convention

(1) The first inputs tell us the trade date or valuation date. From a pricing perspective all calculations assume that the *Curve ValueDate* is today, regardless of the actual day it is. This allows you to look at pricing using historic curves. If you had saved all the market rates from the 15-April-05 we can generate the DCFs for that date at any time, this is useful if you need to look at historic pricing. Generally, you will have *ValueDate* set to today, using the excel formula = today().

The next input is the number of *Days to Spot*, for most currencies spot start is two business days forward, while some (such as GBP) spot date is same day start. Spot date is then automatically provided (*X* business days forward from *ValueDate*).

(2) The second section of our input screen is the Deposits; these are the current interbank deposit rats, such as LIBOR. We can include a maximum of eight different deposit rates, ranging from overnight (O/N), tomorrow next (T/N), and 1 through 12 pmonths. Once the instrument is included Curveßuilder automatically calculates the appropriate maturity date, as well as the correct start date for the instrument.

You can also select an appropriate roll convention for non-business days. For most currencies the roll convention is modified following. You also select the daycount basis for deposit or money market instruments, for US$ this is Act/360, while for some (such as GBP) the Daycount basis is Act/365. This Daycount basis will also be applicable for the futures if included.

(3) Section 3 is where the swaps are inputted, a maximum nine inputs can be included. These Par swap rates are inputted in terms of Years. For example, input 2 to include the 2-year PAR swap rate. Curveßuilder will again automatically calculate the appropriate maturity date. While there is no maximum tenor we can include for our calculations the size of the output table will constrain us on what we can include, make sure the maturity date of the last swap used is the final grid point in our Zero Curve table. In order to make sure all swap instruments are used make sure that the last *ZeroDT* in your table matches the maturity date for the long swap included.

You can also select the appropriate roll conventions, daycount conventions and coupon frequency of the underlying swap rates.

For the swap rate you can input either absolute swap rate or input swap and US Treasury yields and swap spreads as illustrated below:

Figure 4

SWAPS		No Adjustment	i30/360	Semi-ann	
	3.0	19-Apr-08	**4.1500**	**10**	**4.250**
	4.0	19-Apr-09	**4.2000**	**15**	**4.350**
	5.0	19-Apr-10	**4.2000**	**20**	**4.400**
	6.0	19-Apr-11	**4.5500**	**30**	**4.850**

(4) If you select to include futures, CurveßUilder will automatically input the required futures (includes only the quarterly futures) so that there are no gaps in our curve. It starts with the first available future and then includes all futures required to overlap our swap rates, as we described in earlier sections. CurveßUilder has a built in function which provides the next future from any given date, = nextfut(anygivendate).

If you select not to include futures ("*No Futures used*" on the spreadsheet), CurveßUilder will not provide any future dates, and will use only deposit and swap rate to calculate the zero curve.

(5) The Curve Shift Cell allows you to automatically shift the entire curve (parallel shift) up (X) or down ($-X$), the shift is in basis points. This basically adds the inputted value (in the curve shift cell) to every input rate, and recalculates the zero curve assuming the new rates. This will help us determine how changes in interest rates affect the value of any given structure.

(6) The name of the curve or currency of the curve you are generating. CurveßUilder allows you to construct more than one zero curve so we name each curve in order to call upon on the specific results for that particular currency.

BID AND OFFER CURVES

Given that the zero curve is the basic engine for all our further pricing models we need to make sure that the rates and data inputted is accurate and up to date for all instruments. Pricing errors can result if all data is not update simultaneously, which means if you update or change the swap rates make sure the deposits and future rate are updated as well. Given that the rates overlap if you change one set of rates without changing all rates, while the model will still provide valuations, the results may be spurious. Not only the accuracy of the inputs is important but also which side of the curve use is important as well. For all instruments there will be a bid and offer rate or price (as for futures). In order to have accurate rates you need to have the correct curve inputted.

Which curve you input will depend on the instrument we are pricing as well as which side of the market you are pricing from, a market maker or a market taker. The following Table 9 is from a market taker's (say a corporate treasury) point of view.

Table 9

Underlying	Curve	User example
Pay fixed	Bid (highside)	Swap a fixed rate bond into a floating rate asset
Receive fixed	Offer (lowside)	Swap a fixed rate bond issue into floating rate liability
Mark to market	Mid-market	MTM a portfolio

1 Futures have an underlying interest rate contract with a maturity of 90 days. However in order to avoid gaps in the curve we assume that each contract is back to back, from settlement of one future to the settlement of the subsequent future, our calculations are based on the actual number of days between the two futures rather than 90 days.

2 We require a dcf from either futures or deposits to cover at least the second last coupon date. In our example we need dcfs derive from deposits and futures to extend out to at least 19-Oct-06. If no dcf exists we will have to assume an interest rate and thus a dc in order to complete the swap's dcf calculation.

3 It is normal practice to use log linear interpolation on dcfs, and linear interpolation on zero interest rates, but for our calculations we will use linear interpolation for sake of simplicity and constancy.

6

Asset and Liability Swaps: Cashflows and Pricing

While a PAR or ATM interest rate swap has uniform cashflows, and is relatively simple to calculate and value, most swaps are designed to match an underlying transaction, which results in non-generic cashflows. Most non-generic swaps have either short or long first coupon (on the fixed or floating legs), involve a cash payment upfront or at maturity, or involve a changing notional over the life of the swap such as an amortising swap.

While these structures may seem more complicated to price, in fact they are not, as long as you can determine what the cashflows are. We will examine the cashflows of several asset swaps, where the coupon payments and cashflows of an existing bond are swapped, as well as various forms of liability swaps, where a borrower has a loan or bond outstanding and wants to hedge the interest rate exposure.

ASSET SWAPS

As we saw in Chapter 4 an asset swap package is the combination of a fixed income instrument overlaid with an interest rate or cross-currency swap which alters the coupon payments. Given that most financial institution (banks) fund on a floating rate basis, most want floating rate assets in order to eliminate any interest rate risk (matched assets and liabilities). The bank can however buy a fixed rate security and then enter into a pay fixed, receive floating interest rate swap. For investors who want fixed rate assets (bond funds) they can purchase an FRN (floating rate note) and then enter into an interest rate swap to transform a bond's floating rate coupons into fixed rate coupons, by entering into a receive fixed, pay floating IRS.

Given the fact that most fixed rate bonds trading in the secondary market are not priced at PAR or 100% and also given the need to consider accrued interest, an interest rate swap must be structured to fit the bond's specific cashflows. The total return of a fixed rate bond is made up of a combination of coupons and capital gains or losses, to get a net yield to maturity. For an asset swap we eliminate any capital gains or losses, and are left with only coupon payments (fixed or floating).

For a fixed rate bond, there are two methods which we can apply an underlying IRS, we can either swap the cashflows based on the bond's market value or based on the PAR value. Bonds are priced relative to their PAR value or 100%, bonds trading below 100% are considered discount bonds while bonds trading above PAR are considered to be trading at a premium. There will always be a cash payment adjustment for asset swaps since most bonds will trade at a premium or discount price.

Market value swap

An investor pays the total proceeds for a bond on the settlement date. Total proceeds include the market price of the bond plus any accrued interest (bond's dirty price). The investor then receives the floating coupon based on total proceeds amount. At *maturity*, when the bond matures and the notional or PAR is repaid, the difference between PAR and the initial total proceeds is either paid or received to the investor.

PAR value asset swap

Regardless of what the price and the total proceeds of the bond is initially, the investor pays the total proceeds for the bond plus they pay or receive a cash payment *upfront* based on the difference between PAR and the initial total proceeds. They then receive the floating coupon based on the PAR amount.

In either case the investor receives the floating coupon based on total amount paid out on the initial settlement day, they also will be returned (net of any payment) the same amount of money at maturity. The difference between a market value swap and a PAR value swap is that the "cash payment adjustment" is done upfront for a PAR value asset swap, and at maturity for a market value swap.

The interest rate swap will adjust the cashflows to take into account this premium or discount bond pricing. If we consider asset swapping the following fixed rate bond:

Fixed rate bond (FRB) details

Notional:	US$10,000,000
Settlement date:	19-April-05
Bond maturity date:	19-Jun-09
Coupon:	4.50%
Frequency:	Semi-annual
Basis:	30/360
Clean price:	96.66% *(price is at a discount to PAR)*
Days of accrued interest:	120 days *(based on 30/360)*
Amount of accrued interest:	$4.50\% \times (120/360) \times$ US$10,000,000 = US$150,000
Total proceeds to purchase:	Notional $\times$ Clean price + Accrued interest US$10,000,000 $\times$ 96.66% + 150,000 = US$9,816,000
Required Floating coupon details:	6-Month US$ LIBOR Semi-annual, Act/360

From the swap trader's perspective they will be looking to receive a fixed coupon from the bond's cashflows and pay floating to the investor. In this case the trader will need to generate the zero curve, using the offer side of the swap curve. The swap offer rates (lower rates) are the rates where the trader can pay away the fixed coupons they will be receiving from the fixed bond's cashflows.

Market value asset swap: (adjustment at maturity)
Principal and cash payments

❏ Investor pays the total proceeds of US$9,816,000 for US$10 M notional of the FRB on settlement date, 19-April-05.

❏ At maturity, the investor gets back US$10 M from the bond (assuming the bond has not defaulted).

❏ At maturity the investor pays (since it is a discount bond) the difference between the initial total proceeds (market value) and the PAR value (cash received at maturity). The investor pays the swap dealer US$184,000 (US$10 m − 9,816,000).

Coupon flows

❏ Investor receives a 4.50% fixed, semi-annual coupon.
❏ Investor pays to the swap dealer the same fixed coupon. The fixed coupon is received and paid based on the PAR amount of US$10 M. The initial fixed coupon received is a full coupon and the entire coupon is passed on to the swap dealer. The initial floating interest period starts on settlement date and matures on the first floating coupon roll, which may result in an initial coupon period, which is longer or shorter than the remaining periods.
❏ Swap dealer pays investor 6 M LIBOR plus a spread, where the floating rate coupon is calculated based on the bond's initial market value.
❏ The floating rate spread is calculated so that the floating leg's NPV equals that of the fixed leg's NPV, for a net NPV of zero. Solve for a zero NPV by changing the floating rate spread. From our cashflow calculator in Exhibit 1 we determine that the appropriate spread is LIBOR + 114.7 bps.

Figure 1 illustrates all the cashflows of the market value asset swap.

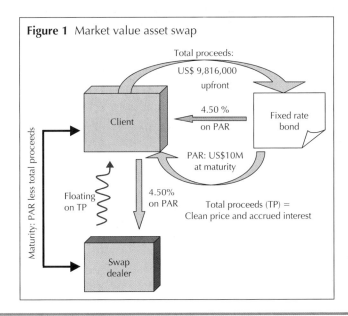

Figure 1 Market value asset swap

Exhibit 1 Market value asset swap

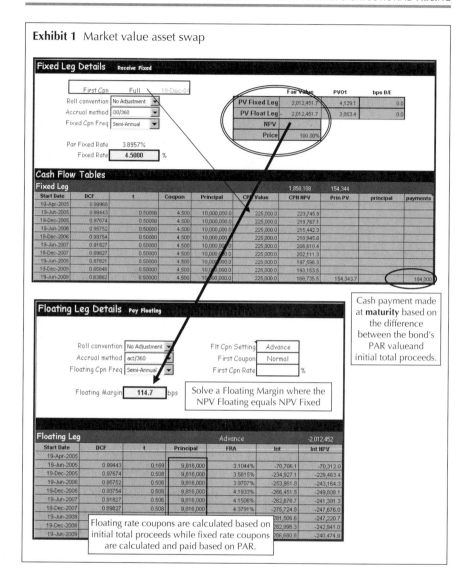

Exhibit 1 shows the actual pricing of the market value asset swap, given the principal and cash payments as well as the coupon flows. In this exhibit we solve for the appropriate floating rate coupon (LIBOR + spread) given the current bond's characteristics, as described above.

PAR value asset swap: (adjustment upfront)
Principal and cash payments

❑ Investor pays the total proceeds of US$9,816,000 for US$10 M notional of the FRB on settlement date, 19-April-05.

❑ On settlement date Investor pays (since it is a discount bond) the difference between the initial market value (total proceeds paid upfront) and PAR. The investor pays US$184,000 (US$10 M – US$9,816,000) to the swap dealer.

❑ Total initial investment is therefore US$10 M or PAR.

❑ At maturity, the investor gets back US$10 M from the bond (assuming the bond has not defaulted).

Coupon flows

❑ Investor receives a 4.50% fixed, semi-annual coupon.

❑ Investor pays to the swap dealer the same fixed rate coupon. The fixed coupon is received and paid based on the PAR amount of US$10 M. The initial fixed coupon received is a full coupon and the entire coupon is passed on to the swap dealer. The initial floating interest period starts on settlement date and matures on the first floating coupon roll, which may result in an initial coupon period, which is longer or shorter than the remaining periods.

❑ Swap dealer pays client 6 M LIBOR plus a spread, where the floating rate coupon is based on the bond's PAR value.

❑ The floating rate spread is calculated so that the floating leg's NPV equals that of the fixed leg's NPV, for a net NPV of zero. Solve for a zero NPV by changing the floating rate spread. From our cashflow calculator in Exhibit 1 we determine that the appropriate spread is LIBOR + 112.6

Figure 2 illustrates all the cashflows of the PAR value asset swap.

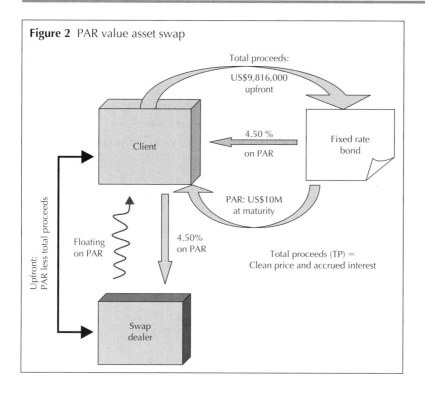

Figure 2 PAR value asset swap

Exhibit 2 shows the actual pricing of the PAR value asset swap, given the principal and cash payments as well as the coupon flows. In this exhibit we solve for the appropriate floating rate coupon (LIBOR + spread) given the current bond's characteristics, as described above.

Exhibit 2 Cashflows and pricing for a PAR value asset swap

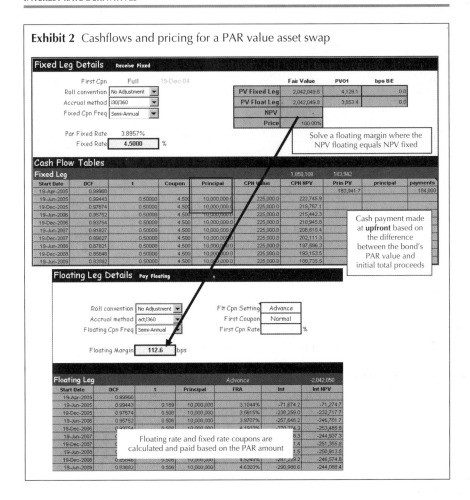

We can use the goal seek function within excel to solve for the required floating margin which results in a net NPV of zero (where the fixed NPV = floating NPV). In excel under tools/goal seek the following "goal seek" window will pop up. Enter the cell you want to set to zero, the cell that has the net NPV, solve for value 0 (zero), by changing the floating margin input. Once it solves for the correct margin, click okay to accept the calculation.

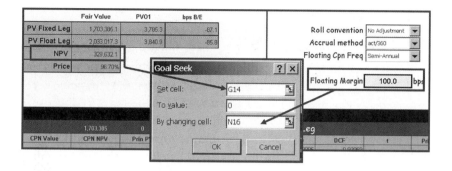

It is more common to apply and trade a PAR value structure. The only time that you may prefer to use the market value method is when the bond is priced at a deep discount, say below 90%.

Example
A fixed rate bond is currently trading a deep discount; total proceeds are equal to 80% (dirty price plus accrued interest per 100% PAR amount). An investor wants to buy the bond and then apply an IRS to convert the fixed coupons to floating rate coupons. They want to structure the swap as a PAR value asset swap. For a PAR value asset swap they would need to make a significant cash adjustment upfront. While the bond is only worth 80% the investor pays 100% (or PAR). What happens to the other 20% cash proceeds? The swap dealer assumes to invest the cash at the curve rate or LIBOR and then pay it back over the life of the swap. Therefore 80% of the investment is earning LIBOR + 100 bps while 20% of the cash is earning LIBOR. The net coupon (floating rate margin) would be the weighted average return (WAR).

WAR = [80% @ LIBOR + 100 bps] + [20% @ LIBOR]
WAR = 100% @ LIBOR + 80 bps

So instead of receiving a floating rate coupon of LIBOR plus 100 bps, as you would expect, the investor only receives LIBOR plus 80 bps. This can also have a leverage effect for bonds that are trading at a price over PAR.

Example

A fixed rate bond is currently trading at a premium, with total proceeds equal to 120% (dirty price plus accrued interest per 100% PAR amount). An investor wants to buy the bond and then overlay an IRS in order to swap the fixed coupons for floating coupons. They want to structure the swap as a PAR value asset swap. Given that the total proceeds are 120% of notional, the underlying IRS will require significant cash adjustment upfront. While the investor invests 100% (PAR) of their own funds in the bond they would need to borrow 20%, upfront, from the swap dealer to pay for the remaining total proceeds. We assume that the investor borrows the funds at LIBOR or the curve rate, and then repay the loan over the life of the swap, in the form of a higher coupon. So while 100% of their cash is earning LIBOR plus 100 bps the money they have borrowed (20%) at LIBOR is also earning the L+100 bps. The net coupon (floating rate margin) would be the weighted average return:

$$WAR = [100\% @ LIBOR + 100\,bps] + [20\% @ (LIBOR + 100 - LIBOR)]$$
$$WAR = 100\% @ LIBOR + 120\,bps$$

So instead of receiving a floating rate coupon of LIBOR plus 100 bps, as you would expect, the investor receives LIBOR plus 120 bps.

Some swap dealers recognise this borrowing and lending of cash and may require further adjustments to the price. Our method of valuing IRS transactions that involve cash payments or receipts assumes that we will borrow and lend cash at LIBOR (flat). This is sometimes not realistic especially in the above case when the dealer may in fact be making a significant cash loan to a counterparty with a weaker credit rating of BBB for example. In such a case the dealer should adjust the floating rate spread to reflect the fact that there is significant credit risk which the dealer is not getting compensated for.

BOND PRICING: GIVEN TARGET FLOATING SPREAD

You can also calculate the price at which you should buy the fixed rate bond if you have a target floating spread. Using the details from the previous example, assume you want to buy the fixed rate bond but you need to earn a floating rate margin of 150 bps over LIBOR. We need to calculate what clean price we should buy the

Exhibit 3 Solving for a bond's price for a given target floating margin

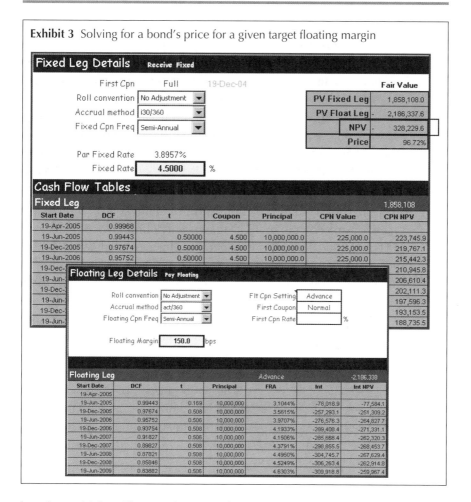

bond at which will provide us with an after hedge floating rate spread of 150 bps.

The first step is to use the swap-pricing model (Exhibit 3) to calculate the NPV of the swap, *without* any cash payment or receipt. The vanilla swap where the fixed leg mirrors that of the fixed rate bond and the floating leg reflects the desired coupons. The NPV of this IRS is −US$328,229. This means that if our trader entered into this IRS, with no cash payment, the trader would show a net loss. The trader must therefore receive a cash payment in order to get the initial value (NPV) of the swap to equal zero. The investor must then pay for the bond (total proceeds) plus make a cash payment to the swap dealer to make the value of the trade on day 1 equal to zero.

If we assume a PAR asset swap structure, the investor makes an upfront cash adjustment in order to have the swap's NPV equal to zero. The total proceeds the investor pays for the bond on settlement day should be equal to the bond's PAR amount less this cash payment.

We can then calculate the clean bond price:

Total bond proceeds $\quad$ = Notional × Clean bond price
$\qquad\qquad\qquad\qquad$ + Accrued interest

(Bond details from Example 1)

US\$10,000,000 − US\$328,229 $\quad$ = US\$10 M × Clean bond price
$\qquad\qquad\qquad\qquad\qquad$ + US\$150,000

We can then solve for the bond's clean price

Clean price = 95.2177%

If we purchased the bond at a clean price of 95.2177% and then entered into a PAR Value asset swap structure the floating rate investor would receive a floating coupon of LIBOR + 150 bps. Normally when investors buy fixed rate bonds they purchase the bond on a relative spread over a similar term government benchmark bond. For example an investor may buy the fixed rate bond with a YTM (and thus an equivalent clean price) that is equal to 190 basis point over a benchmark UST. In this example we have solved for the clean price which we can then derive its YTM, which in turn is a relative spread over a similar term UST. If the clean price represents a YTM of 5.88% (derived from our bond calculator) and if the underlying 4-year UST is trading at 4.00%, then we need to purchase the fixed rate bond at a spread of 188 basis points over the UST.

CURVEßUILDER ASSET SWAP CALCULATOR

We can use a generic interest rate swap cashflow calculator to price an asset swap package or utilise the built in Curveßuilder Asset swap and bond calculators. This model automatically generates the required cashflows and underlying swap for a given fixed rate bond. The cashflows are from the interest rate swap dealer's perspective. The following numbers refer to the specific inputs in the model, which is illustrated in Exhibit 4.

1. Fixed coupon details, the underlying details   *(inputted)*
   of the fixed rate bond:
   > Settlement and maturity date
   > Fixed coupon rate, and the calculation basis
   > Clean price.

2. Fixed coupons accrued interest and total proceeds: *(given)*
   > Given the bond's details the
   > accrued interest and total proceeds are
   > calculated as of settlement date.

3. Bond's yield to maturity and equivalent yield   *(given)*
   to maturity:
   > Given the bond's details the model calculates
   > the yield to maturity as well as provides an
   > equivalent YTM (assuming a different basis).

4. Floating spread (in basis points, 0.01%):   *(inputted)*
   > Payable on the floating leg. Select how we
   > want to structure the underlying interest
   > rate swap, selecting either a PAR or market
   > value structure.

5. Breakeven analysis: *(given)*
   > The model provides a break-even analysis
   > for the underlying bond. It provides the
   > breakeven price, the clean price at which
   > you should purchase the bond
   > for a given floating rate margin (4). It also
   > provides a floating coupon margin for a
   > given clean bond price.

6. Bond sensitivity analysis: *(given)*
   > This section provides the risk characteristics
   > of the underlying bond such as duration,
   > and convexity.

7. Floating leg details: *(inputted)*
   > Details of the floating leg coupon associated
   > with the underlying interest rate swap,
   > calculation basis for the floating coupons.

8. Net cash payment: *(given)*

    Cash payment adjustment to be paid or received with respect to the underlying interest rate swap, paid upfront or at maturity. The payment amount and timing is based on the required structuring method (PAR or market value) and total proceeds of the underlying fixed rate bond.

A positive payment means that the swap dealer will make a payment to the client (total proceeds above PAR) while a negative payment indicates that a payment will be received from the client (total proceeds below PAR).

9. Cashflows for interest rate swap's fixed   *(given)*
   coupon leg:

    Which should mirror the cashflows associated with the underlying fixed rate bond.

10. Cashflows for the interest rate swap's   *(given)*
    floating coupon leg.

Exhibit 4 CurveBuilder asset swap and bond calculator

CurveBuilder: Asset Swap – Bond Calculator

1

Settlement date	19-Apr-05
Maturity date	19-Jun-09
Modified Maturity	19-Jun-09
Clean Price	100.416
Coupon	6.000
Fixed Cpn Freq	Semi-Annual
Roll convention	No Adjustment
Accrual method	30/360

Notional principal	10,000,000	
Curve	USD	

3

Yield To Maturity	5.883%	
Equivalent Yield	5.888%	Semi-Ann
Par Swap Rate	4.366%	

4

Floating Margin	150.0	bps
	PAR	Asset Swap

6 Bond Sensitivity Analysis

Duration	3.6778	
Modified Duration	3.5727	
Convexity	0.01150	
Price Value Change	0.03658	1
BPS yield change	0.2717%	100
		act/365

5 BreakEven Analysis

Floating Margin	150.0 bps	
Price	100.416	
	Break Even	

7 Floating Leg Details

Roll convention	No Adjustment
Accrual method	act/360
Floating Cpn Freq	Semi-Annual
First Coupon	Normal

2 Accrued Interest Details

Last Coupon Date	19-Dec-04
Accrued Interest	120 days
Accrued Interest	200,000 Cash
Total proceeds	10,241,600
As percentage	2.416%

8

Cash Payment	241,600	Payable UPFRONT

9 Cash Flow Tables

Fixed Leg — PVO1 4.117 — 2,469,973

Start Date	DCF	t	Cpn Value	CPN PV
19-Apr-2005	0.99969			
19-Jun-2005	0.99446	0.50000	300,000.0	298,337.4
19-Dec-2005	0.97624	0.50000	300,000.0	292,871.8

10 Floating Leg — PVO1 3.841 — -2,228,344

Start Date	DCF	FRA	Notional	Int	Int PV
19-Apr-2005	0.99969				
19-Jun-2005	0.99446	0.169	3.0855%	10,000,000.0	-77,716.1	-77,285.4
19-Dec-2005	0.97624	0.508	3.6712%	10,000,000.0	-262,870.8	-256,624.9

	Cash Payment	
	241,600	

LIABILITY SWAPS

A liability swap is an interest rate swap, which a client enters into in order to hedge a liability obligation. When a client raises funds, through a loan or bond issuance, the client may want to alter or hedge the associated coupon payments. A company many want to swap a fixed rate liability to floating rate interest payments, or a floating rate liability to a fixed rate of interest, given the company's view on interest rates and hedging objectives.

As a general rule banks manage their assets and liabilities on a floating rate basis. If all their assets earned LIBOR plus a spread and all the liabilities are paying interest linked to LIBOR the difference would be a (credit) spread profit regardless of the absolute level of interest rates or the term of either the asset or liability. Having matched assets and liabilities eliminates any interest rate exposure. A corporate on the other hand generally prefers to have all liabilities on a fixed rate basis, having a fixed coupon not only eliminates any interest rate exposure but the fixed interest cost makes it much easier to manage and plan within the business.

Interest rate swaps were initially used to take advantage of funding advantages. Most early literature on IRS discusses the comparative advantage firms have to fund on a fixed or floating rate basis. Each firm would fund on the basis that they had a comparative funding advantage and then enter into an interest rate swap with each other (with a commercial bank acting as an agent in the middle) in order to "swap" the funding into the desired basis (fixed or floating). Interest rate swaps are still used today to allow institutions to obtain the cheapest funding possible regardless of the coupon basis or currency of issuance and then overlaying the funding with a swap as required.

When a company issues a bond, and then enters into an interest rate swap there is generally a cash adjustment so that the swap's cashflows mirror that of the underlying funding. Most bonds are issued at a slight discount to PAR. Most liability swaps are structured as a PAR value structure rather than market value (see details under asset swaps). The interest rate swap will make a cash adjustment to take into account the discount bond pricing. For example let us consider a liability swap for the following fixed rate bond issue.

New issue:	*Fixed rate bond (FRB) details*
Notional:	US$10,000,000
Coupon:	5.00%
Frequency:	Annual
Basis:	30/360
Settlement date:	19-April-05
Bond maturity date:	19-April-10
Clean price:	98.50% *(price is at a discount to PAR)*
Days of accrued interest:	0 days
Assumed yield to maturity:	5.350%
Total proceeds from bond issue:	Notional × Price (no accrued interest)
	= US$10,000,000 × 98.50%
	= US$9,850,000

A client (ie, a bank) has just issued the above bond and now wants to enter into an IRS in order to change the coupon liability from a fixed rate basis to a floating rate basis.

Floating coupon details

Floating notional:	100% (PAR)
Upfront payment:	US$150,000 (US$ 10 M − US$9,850,000)
Coupon frequency:	Semi-annual frequency
Daycount basis:	Act/360
Floating rate index:	6-Month US$ LIBOR

An upfront payment is made by the swap counterparty to the client to adjust the total proceeds received upfront to equal PAR or 100% (US$10 M). The client therefore receives a total or 100% upfront (on settlement date) and then pays a floating rate coupon based on 100%.

PAR value liability swap: (adjustment upfront)

Principal and cash payments:

❏ Issuer receives total proceeds of US$9,850,000 for US$10 M notional of the FRB on settlement date, 19-April-05.

❏ On settlement date issuer receives (since the bond was issued at a discount) the difference between the initial market value (total proceeds paid upfront) and PAR, US$150,000 (US$10 M − 9,850,000), from the swap dealer.

❑ Total initial proceeds are therefore US$10 M or PAR.
❑ At maturity, the issuer pays back the full US$10 M to the investor.

Coupon flows
❑ Issuer pays a 5.00% fixed, semi-annual coupon, to the bondholder.
❑ Issuer receives the same fixed coupon from the swap dealer. The fixed coupon is received and paid based on the PAR amount of US$10 M.
❑ Issuer pays to the swap dealer 6 M LIBOR plus a spread, where the floating rate coupon is based on the bond's PAR value.
❑ The floating rate spread is calculated so that the floating leg's NPV equals that of the fixed leg's NPV, for a net NPV of zero. Solve for a zero NPV by changing the floating rate spread.

Figure 3 illustrates all the cashflows of the PAR value liability swap.

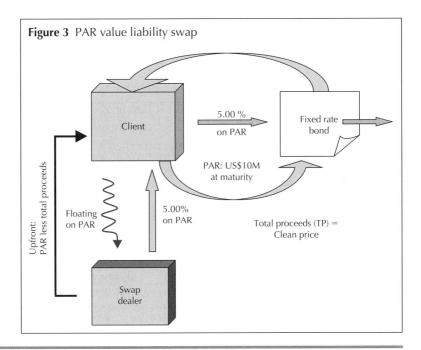

Figure 3 PAR value liability swap

We can use the pricing model within Curveßuilder to solve for the actual floating rate margin based on the bond's fixed rate coupons and the required cash payment required upfront.

Exhibit 5 Liability swap cashflows and pricing

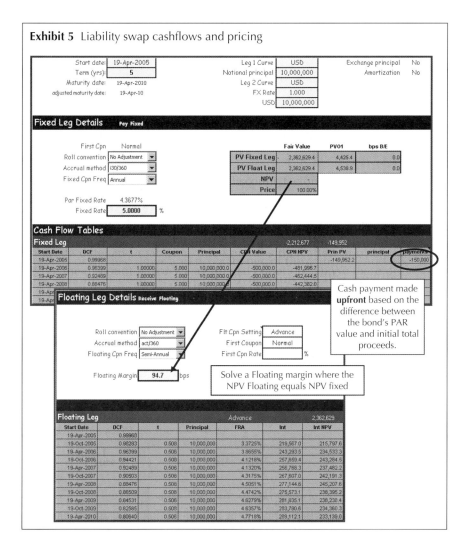

Rather than swap a given fixed rate issue we can use the calculations in reverse in order to determine the characteristics of a fixed rate bond for a given funding target on a floating rate basis. Assume that a bank wants to issue a 3-year fixed rate bond, and then swap the proceeds back into a floating rate obligation. They have an after hedge funding target which is 6 M US$ LIBOR + 25 bps which they want to achieve. We can solve for the fixed rate bonds price, and thus YTM by performing the above calculations in reverse order.

New issue:	*Fixed rate bond (FRB) details*
Notional:	US$10,000,000
Coupon:	4.00%*
Frequency:	Semi-annual
Basis:	30/360
Settlement date:	19-April-05
Bond maturity date:	19-April-08
Clean issue price:	Unknown
YTM:	Unknown

The company then wants to enter into an IRS in order to swap the fixed rate coupons for floating rate interest payments.

Desired floating coupon details

Floating notional amount:	100%/PAR
Frequency:	Semi-annual
Daycount basis:	Act/360
Floating rate index:	6-Month US$ LIBOR
Floating rate spread:	+25 basis points

In order to solve for the upfront payment we input the known bond details and the required details on the floating coupon leg into our swap pricing model. We input the target funding spread and then solve for a zero NPV by changing the upfront payment. The following example is from the swap dealer's perspective.

In this example, we calculated that the initial upfront payment required to make the initial NPV of the swap equal to zero is US$−99,170. This implies the swap trader requires a cash receipt (a negative amount on a pay leg is a receipt from the trader's point of view) on settlement date from the issuer in the amount of US$99,170 in order to have a zero NPV. The total new issue proceeds on

---

* Arbitrarily change the coupon so we achieve the desired new issue price for the bond.

settlement day will be US$9,900,830 (US$10 M − US$28,038) which provides an implied bond price of 99.7196% ($9,900,830/$10 M). This also gives an implied yield to maturity (YTM) of 4.356%, or an equivalent US treasury yield of 4.36%, which we have derived from the bond calculator, which is shown in Figure 4.

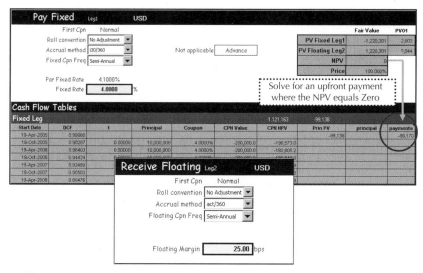

This yield to maturity can then be expressed as a spread over US treasuries. If the 3-year on the run US treasury is currently trading at a semi-annual YTM equal to 3.75%. This implies that this new bond issue will be issued at a spread of 61 bps over the 3-year UST (4.36% less 3.75%).

Figure 4 Curveßuilder bond calculator

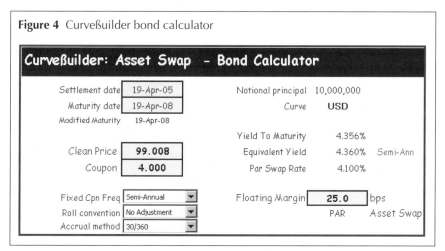

MARK TO MARKET (MTM) INTEREST RATE SWAPS

At any point in time we can value or mark to market (MTM) an interest rate swap. To MTM an existing swap we consider only the future cashflows and ignore any historic cashflows regardless of what was paid or which counterparty paid it. To value the IRS we update our market instruments used to derive our zero curve and then recalculate the NPV for each leg of the swap. The MTM is the updated combined NPV of the fixed and floating legs. In most cases we can value or MTM an existing swap using a mid-market curve as the fair valuation, rather than a bid or offer.

Example

Let us consider the interest rate swap example from the previous section, which we valued as of 15-April-2005. The initial swap had an NPV or MTM of zero. If we assume that we go forward in time by 2-years and value the swap as of 15-April-2007 and shift the curve by +100 bps (parallel curve shift) we can then revalue the existing swap. We value the remaining cashflows in NPV terms. Curveßuilder allows you to change the curve valuation date to any given date as well as shift the curve automatically by *100* bps, by using the curve shift function.

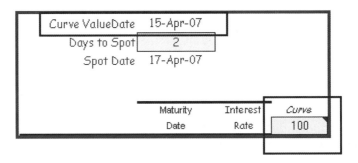

We can see that the MTM of the initial swap has increased in value by US$107,049,6. This is what we would expect given the fact that the initial swap is paying fixed. If we pay fixed as interest rates increase we are better off and thus a positive MTM. If we are receiving fixed we would be worse off (than current rates) and thus we would have a negative MTM. These valuations are from the dealer's perspective, and would have the equal value but opposite sign from the other counterparty's perspective. While this general valuation assumptions will hold, in some cases when there are mismatches in coupon payments (annual vs. quarterly) the valuation maybe positive or negative because of the valuation timing, rather then because of changes in underlying interest rates.

NPV as of 15-April-07	
PV fixed leg1	−586,308
PV floating leg2	689,281
NPV	102,973
Price	101,030%

> Changing the valuation or curve date from 15-April-2005 to 15-April-2007, with a parallel shift in the yield curve by 100 bps

We now examine in Exhibit 6 how the actual cashflows have changed. We will notice that for both the fixed and floating legs any previous coupons are no longer included in the valuation. Also the cash payment is no longer included in the cashflows.

When valuing an existing swap the first fixed coupon is normally a full coupon. Regardless of the valuation date the first fixed coupon is a full coupon payment. The coupon calculation is from the previous coupon payment date rather then from valuation date. For example the first coupon payment is calculated from 19-Oct-06 to 19-April-07, $t = 0.500$. The Curveßuilder cashflow calculator automatically derives a full first coupon for the fixed leg on any MTM valuation.

On the floating leg we need to consider the first interest rate fixing as well as make sure a first full coupon is included. The first coupon or LIBOR rate will have already been fixed at the beginning of the interest calculation period (for a set in advance fixings), rather than determined as of valuation date. While the swap below is valued on 15-April-07, we need the historic 6 M LIBOR fixing from 19-Oct-06. The first floating coupon is also a full coupon payment, calculated from the previous payment date rather than from valuation date, just as we did on the fixed leg. Curveßuilder allows you to input and fix the first FRA rate, as illustrated below, as well as calculate a full coupon payment.

FORWARD STARTING INTEREST RATE SWAP

Most new bond issues will normally have a settlement or start date, which is beyond a spot start. This delay allows the investment bank arranging the sale of the bonds time to sell the bonds as well as

Exhibit 6

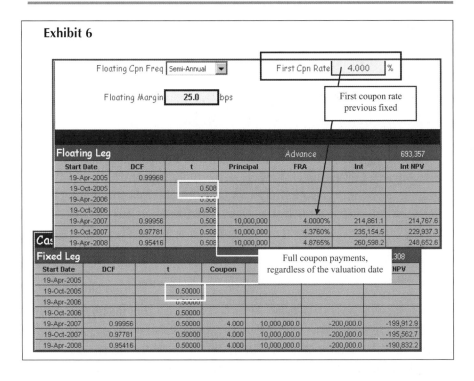

finalise any documentation prior to settlement date. It is common for a bond to have two to six weeks' delay, from the time of trade to settlement date. Settlement date is the actual day that the bond starts to accrue interest and when total proceeds for the bond are actually paid. Given this, the underlying swap associated with the new issue will also have a forward start date, matching that of the underlying bond.

If a 3-year spot start PAR fixed swap rate is 4.10%, what is the fixed rate for three years starting in one month's time? While the dealer enters into a delayed 3-year swap, which starts in one month with the client, as a hedge they enter into a spot start swap where the underlying term is three years and one month.

Manual delay calculation

Trade valuation date:	15-April-05	
Swap start date:	15-May-05	(1 month delay)
Swap maturity date:	15-May-08	(3-years' term)
1 M LIBOR	3.00%	

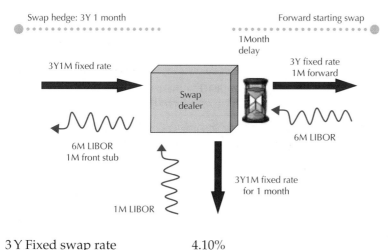

3 Y Fixed swap rate	4.10%
4 Y Fixed swap rate	4.22%

To approximate the 3-years swap rate one month forward we first interpolate the 3-year 1 month (3 Y1 M) fixed rate from the straight 3 Y and 4 Y swap rates. The fixed PAR swap rate, spot start, for 3 Y1 M is 4.110%. (4.10% + (4.22 − 4.10)/12). This is the fixed rate, which the swap dealer could receive for the full term of the swap, spot start. However, on the other side of the trade the delayed swap does not start for 1 month, therefore there needs to be an adjustment to the spot rate in order calculate the fair value (NPV = 0) fixed swap rate. After 1 month the hedge and the delayed swap will match one another, however for the first month there is a timing mismatch.

For the first month the fixed rate is received and 1-Month LIBOR is paid on the hedge, while there is no payment on the delayed swap. The dealer therefore will receive the fixed rate of 4.11% while paying away 1 M LIBOR, which is fixed in advance at 3.00%. The net difference is a benefit to the dealer, provided that the fixed rate is higher than the short term floating rate. In an upward sloping yield curve environment the delay will have a positive benefit and the forward fixed rate will always be higher than the spot rate. The net benefit in this example is 1.11% pa (4.11% received less 3.00% paid) but since the delay is only for 1 month and not a full year the delay is worth a total of 9.25 bps (1.11% × 30/360). In order to solve for the fair value fixed rate on the delayed swap we then need to incorporate this benefit. The 9.25 bps is amortised over the 3-year life of the delayed swap, which is worth approximately 3.1 bps per annum.

We then need to add this per annum benefit to the 3 Y 1 M fixed swap rate to get the fair value all in adjusted delayed swap rate of 4.141% (4.11% plus 0.031%). If we compare this rate to the straight 3 Y swap rate we see that the delay is worth 4.1 bps per annum (4.141% less 4.10%).

Using the Curveßuilder cashflow calculator we see that the actual fixed rate is 4.1406%, the difference as a result of slight timing mismatches and our assumption about the interpolated fixed rate (3 Y1 M rate).

What are the implications of this delay? For an entity that wants to issue a fixed rate bond, for the same equivalent floating rate margin, a fixed bond with a 4-week delay will give the investor an extra 4.1 bps in YTM, which is a relatively significant yield pick-up.

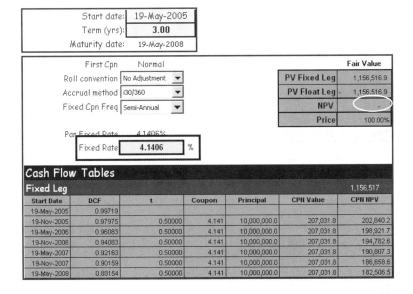

AMORTISING SWAPS

An amortising swap is again valued the same way as a plain vanilla swap however rather than having a fixed principal amount over the life of the swap the principal amount changes. The interest payments are based on the reducing notional amount rather than a fixed amount. While the principal amount can change it must be known in advance what the amount will be on any given date in order to be able to determine the amount of interest to be paid or received both on the fixed and floating legs.

The most common amortising structure is associated with an amortising loan. An amortising loan is where a counterparty makes a fixed payment on a periodic basis, where a portion of the payment is for interest expense while the remaining portion is for principal repayment. Provided that we know at inception of the swap what the principal amount is, we can calculate the interest payments and then PV the payments to trade date.

The Curveßuilder model allows you to select an amortisation (straight-line) schedule for a given initial principal, fixed coupon and a fixed maturity date. In the following example the fixed semi-annual payment amount is US$1,121,612, a portion of which is the interest expense and the remaining reduces the outstanding principal. While the fixed rate for a straight 5-year swap is 4.32%, the fixed rate for an amortising structure is 4.286%, this is a result of a shorter duration, which is a result of the earlier payments. (Note: both swaps have a floating leg where the floating margin is set at zero.)

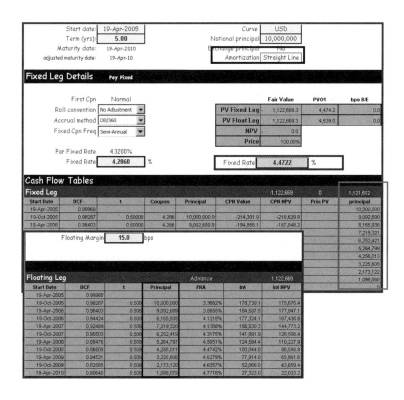

SHORT-TERM INTEREST RATE HEDGES

While interest rate swaps manage interest rate exposure over the long-term there are many applications when the interest rate risk is only short-term, while the exposure is to long-term rates. For example when a company plans to issue a fixed rate bond (or loan) in 30 days, normally the fixed rate bond is priced as a spread over an equivalent government bond. Until the bond is priced the company has exposure to changes in UST rates as well as changes in swap spreads. Depending on the companies' view on UST rates and swap spreads, and the required underlying long-term hedge they could apply several hedging techniques to manage this short-term exposure.

TREASURY LOCK

An entity that has exposure to movements in long-term treasury rates over a short period of time can hedge this exposure with the use of a treasury lock. A treasury lock is a synthetic forward sale of a US Treasury (or other government bond). The user enters into a contract, which fixes a forward starting treasury rate today (trade date) for settlement in a few months' time. On the contract's settlement date the difference between the contract rate and the actual treasury rate is cash settled. A treasury lock is a forward contract which means there is no premium to pay up front and there is no optimality within the structure, at expiry both parties are obliged to cash settle the contract, regardless of how rates have moved.

Assume that a company is planning to issue a US$10 million, 5-year bond in 30 days. The bond will be priced off the 5-year UST and thus the company has exposure to a change in UST rates from now until the time of pricing. The new issue pays a fixed coupon, which is equal to the 5-year UST rate (at the time of pricing) plus a credit spread applicable for the underlying issuer. If interest rates are higher (in 30 days) the coupon on the bond will be higher, therefore the company enters into a treasury lock to hedge the interest rate exposure. On trade date assume the client enters into the treasury lock while the current 5-year UST rate is 5.00%, and the 30-day 5-year UST lock rate is 5.05% (contract rate). The treasury lock allows the company to synthetically short the treasury, which will be cash settled in 30 days' time.

If, in 30 days, the UST rate is higher than the contract rate, say 5.50% then the company receives a cash payment equal to the difference between the contractual rate and the rate on settlement date. The cash settlement also takes into account the value of the 5-year basis point value (5-year PV01).

$$\text{Cash Received} = \text{PV01} \times (5\,Y\,\text{UST} - \text{Treasury Lock Rate}) \times 100$$

If the present value of a basis point associated with the underlying 5-year treasury is worth US\$4,200 per US\$10 million notional then the cash payment on settlement is worth:

$$\text{Cash Received} = \text{US\$4,200} \times (5.50\% - 5.05\%) \times 100 = \text{US\$189,000}$$

The cash gain compensates the borrower for the corresponding higher coupon on the new issue. The net result is an effective treasury rate of 5.05%, which is the treasury lock rate.

On the other hand if, in 30 days, the 5-year treasury rate is lower than the contract rate, say 4.55% then the company must make a cash payment to the dealer.

$$\text{Cash Payment} = \text{PV01} \times (\text{Treasury Lock Rate} - \text{UST Rate}) \times 100$$

$$\text{Cash Payment} = \text{US\$4,200} \times (5.05\% - 4.55\%) \times 100 = \text{US\$210,000}$$

This loss is a result of a corresponding lower coupon they need to pay on the new issue. Again the net result is an effective treasury rate of 5.05%.

Any gain or loss on the treasury lock can be amortised over the life of the corresponding funding transaction so that the net interest paid is equal to the treasury lock rate plus the applicable issuer's credit spread, regardless of the actual coupon being paid.

While the treasury lock provides a hedge against movements in US treasury rates for the corporate the hedge provider must hedge their position by physically shorting the US treasury as described on pp 3–50 (see shorting UST). The lock rate is a result of the financing of the UST short position, the difference between the repo rate earned on the proceeds from the UST borrowed position and the coupon payable on the short UST. The lock rate is the forward UST rate, which is equal to the spot yield plus the cost of carry on the short position.

SPREADLOCK

While a treasury lock fixes the underlying forward treasury rate, a spread lock fixes the forward swap spread. A spreadlock allows the user to lock in the forward differential between the fixed swap rate and the underlying treasury rate. A spreadlock is a forward contract, which means there is no optimality, and both parties are obliged to settle the contract, which is normally physically settled, at expiry.

Assume that a company is planning to issue a 5-year bond in 30 days. The new fixed rate issue pays will be priced with a YTM equal to the 5-year UST rate (at the time of pricing) plus a predetermined credit spread (88 bps). The company also plans (on pricing date) to enter into a simple IRS, receive fixed pay floating, in order to manage the long-term interest rate exposure (they have floating rate assets to fund). The corporate has exposure to decreasing swap spreads from now until the time of pricing in 30 days, given the fact that the spread they are paying on the new issue has already been fixed upfront. If swap spreads fall the floating margin they will have to pay on the floating leg of the swap hedge will be have to be higher. Assume that the current 5-year US$ swaps are trading at 5Y UST plus 40/45. A company hedges the swap spread exposure by entering into a receive spreadlock at +42 bps, for a period of up to 30 days. While they have hedged the swap spread risk they do not want to lock in the underlying treasury rate as any change in UST rates over the next 30 days are passed on to the investor, the company has no exposure to absolute UST rates. They enter into a receive spreadlock hedge which allows the issuer, at any time over the term of the spreadlock, to enter into a five year interest rate swap receiving a fixed rate which is equal to prevailing 5-year UST plus 42 bps vs. paying 6M US$ LIBOR. The net result is the company will end up paying 6M LIBOR plus 46 bps (88 bps less 42 bps) regardless of where UST or swap spreads are at the time of pricing.

While the company is hedged against movements in swap spreads for 30 days, the swap dealer must hedge their underlying position. To hedge the pay spreadlock the dealer enters into a 5-year 30-day fixed rate interest rate swap, this hedges the interest rate swap risk. They then need to short the underlying government bond, which effectively hedges the treasury risk associated with the spreadlock with the corporate.

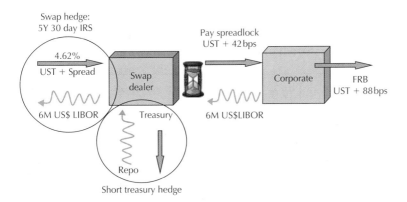

Short treasury hedge

From the dealers' perspective the net result of the underlying hedge is:

❑ Receive treasury rate plus spread
❑ Pay 6 M LIBOR
❑ Pay treasury rate
❑ Receive repo financing rate on short UST position.

$$\text{Net} = \text{Repo Rate} - \text{LIBOR} + \text{Spread}$$

The net difference is generally positive, which means there is a benefit associated with the underlying hedge, this benefit is passed onto the client in the form of a higher spread. In the above example the "forward spread" is 42 bps compared to the current spread of 40 bps.

7

Hedging and Trading
Interest Rate Swaps

When a dealer enters into an interest rate swap (IRS) with a client, they will have interest rate exposure until they can offset the trade with another counterparty. As interest rates change so will the net present value (NPV) of the initial swap transaction. A trader wants to minimise that risk, and manage the exposure until they can find an offsetting trade. Normally a trader will manage the risk in a portfolio of interest rate sensitive securities, which may include interest rate swaps, options or other fixed income instruments (such as government bonds). Even in the most liquid markets, a trader may need (or in some cases prefer for speculative reasons) to carry or warehouse a trade for a relatively short-term until they can find an offsetting long-term hedge. The trader may need a temporary hedge in order to manage the short term underlying interest rate exposure.

In order to manage the interest rate risk the first task of the trader is to measure the inherent risk of a security or portfolio of securities. The risk associated with changes in underlying interest rates is known as delta risk. Delta risk measures a sensitivity of a derivatives or portfolio's NPV to changes in interest rates. We measure delta as a change in NPV (ΔNPV) for a given change in interest rates (Δy).

$$Delta = \frac{\Delta NPV}{\Delta y}$$

RISK MEASUREMENT PV01

Normally delta is calculated with an assumed 1 basis point change in interest rate (Δy); therefore delta is also known as the positions present value of one basis point or PV01. PV01 is absolute measurement of how the NPV changes for a given 1 bp change in interest rates (sometimes also referred to as the dollar value of 1 bp or DV01).

For a PAR or at the money interest rate swap the initial NPV is zero, but as interest rates change the NPV of the swap changes. In order to manage the risk of an underlying swap (portfolio) we therefore need to calculate how sensitive the NPV is to changes in interest rates, so that we can apply an offsetting position to hedge the exposure.

For any interest rate swap we calculate the NPV using the current market yield curve (Figure 1); derive a zero curve and then calculate the appropriate DCF and FRAs which in turn calculates the NPV of our swap. We can estimate the PV01 of an IRS by manually increasing all inputs within our yield curve up by 1 bp (parallel shift up) and then recalculating the new adjusted NPV, the difference is the PV01. This is the macro-measurement of risk and can be broken down further by shifting not the entire curve but shifting each individual yield curve inputs and measuring how the underlying NPV changes as each input changes. A parallel shift in the entire yield fails to measure the effect of changes in the shape of the yield curve. We therefore need to measure not only how a shift in the entire curve effects the NPV but also how sensitive the NPV is to changes in each of the yield curve inputs.

The zero curve generating model within Curveßuilder allows us to apply a manual shift in the entire curve to see how a parallel shift in interest rates affects the NPV of any underlying instrument we are pricing.

As an example we can calculate the interest rate sensitivity of an individual swap, as outlined in Example 1 and Figure 2, by shifting each underlying instrument in our curve by 1 bp and calculate the change in the swap's NPV.

Figure 1 Initial curve

	Maturity Date	Interest Rate	Curve		CurveName	USD

	Maturity Date	Interest Rate	*Curve*		
DEPOSITS	No Adjustment	act/360			
ON	18-Apr-05	**2.8500**			
TN	19-Apr-05	**2.8500**			
1M	19-May-05	**3.0000**			
3M	19-Jul-05	**3.1500**			
6M	19-Oct-05	**3.3500**			

			ZERO Curve	
			zeroDT	**DCF**
			15-Apr-2005	1.000000
			18-Apr-2005	0.999763
			19-Apr-2005	0.999683
			19-May-2005	0.997190
			19-Jul-2005	0.991786
			15-Jun-2005	0.994798
			21-Sep-2005	0.985675
			21-Dec-2005	0.976542

SWAPS	No Adjustment	i30/360	Semi-ann		15-Mar-2006	0.967758
2.0	19-Apr-07	**3.9200**			21-Jun-2006	0.957308
3.0	19-Apr-08	**4.1000**			20-Sep-2006	0.947429
4.0	19-Apr-09	**4.2200**			20-Dec-2006	0.937427
5.0	19-Apr-10	**4.3200**			19-Apr-2007	0.924869
7.0	19-Apr-12	**4.5000**			19-Oct-2007	0.905026
10.0	19-Apr-15	**4.7000**			19-Apr-2008	0.884764
					19-Oct-2008	0.865089
					19-Apr-2009	0.845311
					19-Oct-2009	0.825850

FUTURES	Start Date	Future Price	Implied Rate		19-Apr-2010	0.806397
Include Futures					19-Oct-2010	0.787203
Jun-05	15-Jun-05	**96.600**	3.400		19-Apr-2011	0.768076
Sep-05	21-Sep-05	**96.300**	3.700		19-Oct-2011	0.749028
Dec-05	21-Dec-05	**96.110**	3.890		19-Apr-2012	0.730070
Mar-06	15-Mar-06	**95.990**	4.010		19-Oct-2012	0.711935
Jun-06	21-Jun-06	**95.875**	4.125		19-Apr-2013	0.693974
Sep-06	20-Sep-06	**95.779**	4.221		19-Oct-2013	0.676190
					19-Apr-2014	0.658588
					19-Oct-2014	0.641174
					19-Apr-2015	0.623950

Example 1

Trade/curve date:	15-April-05
Spot start:	19-April-05
Maturity:	19-Oct-07
Receive fixed:	4.35% s/a 30/360
Pay floating:	6-Month LIBOR Act/360
Floating spread:	51 bps

Figure 2 Swap cashflows and pricing

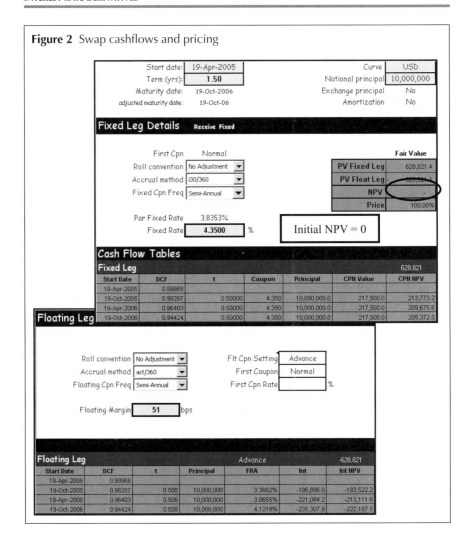

Figure 3 is the net or macro PV01 results, the initial NPV is US$0 and by shifting (Shift) the yield curve by +1 bp the NPV decreases by US$1,478.

Total PV01 is US$1,478, which means if all inputs increased by 1 bp (parallel shift in the curve) the NPV of the swap, would decrease in value by that amount. This is our macro measurement of the interest rate sensitively.

Within our pricing model there is a RISK simulator, which manually shifts each input within our curve by a fixed number of basis

points (1 bp). It shifts each individual instrument and then calculates the change in an underlying NPV.[1]

We can then break that sensitivity down further for each underlying component or yield curve instrument, as outlined in our initial curve Figure 1. Figure 4 show the NPV sensitivity to change in
deposit rates.

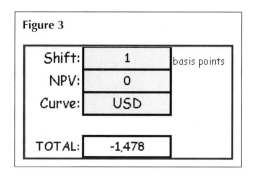

Figure 3

Shift:	1	basis points
NPV:	0	
Curve:	USD	

TOTAL:	-1,478

Figure 4 PV01 for deposit instruments

DEPOSITS	
ON	0
TN	0
1 M	-46
3 M	-111

For example if the 3 M-deposit rate increased by 1 bp the NPV of
the 1.5-year swap would change decrease by US$111. Given that the
first fixing on the floating leg is fixed today, the first LIBOR rate will
already be fixed. If we therefore fix the first FRA at the current 6 M
LIBOR Fixing rate of 3.41% the PV01 of the deposits should fall to
zero. For a spot start swap you should fix the initial FRA rate given
that it cannot and will not change from the current fixing rate
(assuming that it has already fixed). Curveßuilder allows you to fix
the first coupon to the current or already fixed rate.

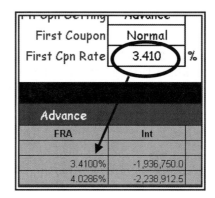

We continue the process of calculating the PV01 for the remaining curve instruments. Figure 5 shows the NPV sensitivities as the underlying futures prices change.

Figure 5 PV01 for future instruments

FUTURES	
Jun-05	-270
Sep-05	-247
Dec-05	-227
Mar-06	-261
Jun-06	-241
Sep-06	-76

If the first future (Jun-05 future) changed in price by 1 bp the NPV of the swap would decrease by US$270.

We have no interest rate exposure associated with the swap instruments, since the first swap input has a maturity of two years, and the underlying swap has a tenor of 1.5-years, therefore the NPV has no sensitivity to changes in swap rates. Our swap matures in Oct-06 and since the Sept-06 future provides a discount factor (DCF) to Dec-06 (3 months later) it is the last required instrument we need to price and therefore hedge the underlying swap.

Given that the Net PV01 is positive what can we determine about the underlying swap? If interest rates increased the NPV of the swap would also increase, which indicates that the underlying swap is a pay fixed IRS. Pay fixed swap's NPV acts similar to a short fixed bond position (in both cases you are paying a fixed coupon), as interest rates increase the price of the bond decreases, thus resulting in a profit. *A Pay fixed net position has a positive PV01.* A receive fixed IRS position is similar to a long fixed rate bond position (in both cases you are receiving a fixed coupon), as increase rates increase and the bond price falls the net result is a loss. *A Rec. fixed net position has a negative PV01.*

Table 1 Change in underlying NPV (net) for a given change in interest rates

	Pay fixed	**Receive fixed**
Increase in interest rates	Increase in NPV	Decrease in NPV
Decrease in interest rates	Decrease in NPV	Increase in NPV

HEDGING WITH EURODOLLARS

In order to hedge the underlying interest rate risk using futures we use the sensitivity measurements associated with each of the underlying futures we calculated in the previous example. In the above example we constructed our yield curve using Eurodollar futures out to Sept-06. This means any underlying swap, cash flow or portfolio with maturity less than Dec-06 can be priced and therefore hedged using Eurodollar futures and cash deposits.

The decision on how many Eurodollar futures to use is based on the underlying liquidity, and the efficiency to trade the underlying futures. US$ Eurodollar futures trade out to 10-years and are liquid out to 5-years. Therefore, it would be reasonable to construct a curve and underlying hedge using Eurodollar futures out to at least 5-years. However, to hedge a 5-year swap you would need to buy or sell a strip of futures out to 5-years, or 20 quarterly futures (4 qrts × 5-years). While you can trade packs and bundles of futures (see section on Eurodollar futures) it may not be efficient to trade so many futures and thus it maybe to using short term swaps or even US treasuries to hedge the underlying position.

In our analysis on risk or delta exposure we calculated that the PV01 associated with the Jun-05 Eurodollar future is US$−270. In order to offset this potential loss, we should hedge our position by selling the same underlying Eurodollar future. If you are short the future, as interest rates increase the price of the future falls, which results in a profit. The profit from the short future position offsets the loss on the swap. While the long future position will protect you from a loss associated with an increase in rates it will also mitigate any potential profit from a decrease in rates. The Eurodollar hedge therefore offsets both an underlying position's potential loss and gain, which ideally will result in a zero profit and loss scenario regardless of what happens to interest rates.

Underlying risk	Hedge: futures position
+ positive risk	Long futures
− negative risk	Short futures

In order to determine how many future contracts we need to short we use the generalised hedge ratio formula:

$$\frac{\text{PV01 risk}}{\text{PV01 per contract}}$$

In our example the PV01 of the underlying exposure is US$−270 while the PV01 or tick value is US$25 per contract (US$1,000,000 × 0.001 × (90/360)). The appropriate number of futures contracts we need to short is:

$$\frac{270}{25} = 10.8 \text{ Contracts}$$

But since we can only buy or sell full contracts you will need to round up or down to the nearest integer, say 11 contracts. While the rounding will result in a slight over or under hedging, the difference is not significant. We then continue the process for every future where we have interest rate exposure. Figure 6 calculates the required number of futures contracts we need to sell in order to hedge our underlying swap's interest rate exposure.

Figure 6 Futures exposure and underlying hedge

FUTURES			PV01 Hedge
		# Contracts	-1,325
Jun-05	-270	-11	-275
Sep-05	-247	-10	-250
Dec-05	-227	-9	-225
Mar-06	-261	-10	-250
Jun-06	-241	-10	-250
Sep-06	-76	-3	-75

The exposure goes out until the maturity of the underlying swap, Oct-06. Since the Sep-06 futures generates our DCF out to Dec-06, it is the last required instrument we would use to hedge the underlying swap. Remember that the future and the DCF that is derived from it have a DCF date not equal to the maturity of the future but instead the maturity date of the underlying instruments, which is three months later.

HEDGING WITH GOVERNMENT BONDS

A dealer enters into a swap with a client, see Figure 7, where they pay fixed receive floating and therefore have interest rate exposure until they can find an offsetting trade. In an ideal situation they would offset that with a back-to-back swap (mirror transaction). Until the dealer can find an offsetting trade they will need to manage the underlying interest rate risk, temporarily.

As an alternative to immediately covering your position, most swap traders will warehouse the risk until they can find a suitable offset to the original trade. Given that the risk or position is only temporary the trader needs to implement a short-term hedge to protect themselves from a change in interest rates.

From Figure 7 you see that the swap dealer is paying a fixed rate of 4.32% (rec. floating). If interest rates fall the fixed rate at which they could receive will be lower than the fixed rate they are paying and therefore a net loss would be incurred. In order to prevent this loss from occurring they will need a short-term hedge. Given that fixed swap rates are highly correlated with government rates (in

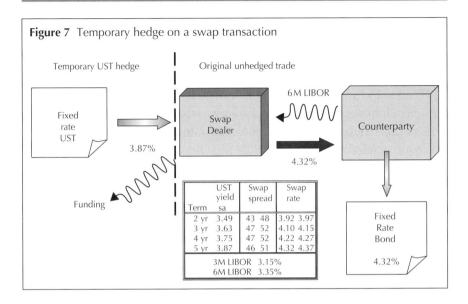

Figure 7 Temporary hedge on a swap transaction

Temporary UST hedge | Original unhedged trade

Fixed rate UST

3.87%

Funding

Swap Dealer

6M LIBOR

4.32%

Counterparty

Term sa	UST yield	Swap spread	Swap rate
2 yr	3.49	43 48	3.92 3.97
3 yr	3.63	47 52	4.10 4.15
4 yr	3.75	47 52	4.22 4.27
5 yr	3.87	46 51	4.32 4.37

3M LIBOR 3.15%
6M LIBOR 3.35%

Fixed Rate Bond

4.32%

the short term anyway) a good and efficient short term hedge would be to buy a fixed rate Government bond (US Treasury: UST).

In the above example the dealer is long the UST and funds the long position, paying LIBOR for the cash. In effect the fixed coupon that the swap dealer receives from the treasury will be the temporary fixed rate at which they will use as a hedge for the initial swap (a synthetic REC fixed swap).

How well does our UST hedge work?

❑ We notice that the fixed rate we receive is less than the fixed rate paid, which results in a negative carry on the fixed legs, for the time that you hedge using the UST. Even when we receive fixed and then short treasuries as a hedge there is generally a negative carry. The rate you earn on the cash (known as the repo rate) will normally be less than the LIBOR rate you need to pay on the swap transaction, and as a result a negative carry on the floating legs, which is generally more than the positive carry earned on the fixed legs.

❑ As long as swap rates and UST move in tandem (1 bp increase in UST results in a 1 bp increase in the fixed swap rates) the hedge will perform very well. However, there is still some residual or *basis risk*. If swap rates fall and UST yields increase, this implies that the swap spread have widened. In this situation a loss occurs on the initial swap as well as a loss on the UST position. A trader that hedges an interest rate swaps using government bonds therefore has *swap spread risk*. While they are not exposed to changes in interest rates they continue to have exposure to changes in swap spreads. In general on-the-run treasuries are the most appropriate hedge, and the end result would be slightly less basis risk than if you used off the run treasuries or even US bond futures.

To hedge a pay fixed swap a dealer would buy UST, while to hedge a receive fixed swap you would sell or short UST.

Underlying risk		Hedge: UST position
+ positive risk	Net pay fixed	Long UST
− negative risk	Net receive fixed	Short UST

We now need to know how many treasuries (notional amount) we need to buy or sell to hedge our position.

Assume a trader enters into the following 5-year, spot start swap, paying fixed, and receiving floating. The initial NPV of the swap is zero.

Example 1
Swap details
Spot date   19-April-05
Maturity date   19-April-10
Notional   US$10 million
Pay fixed   4.32%, 30/360, semi-annual
Rec floating   6 M LIBOR
Floating spread   0 bps

US Treasury details   (5-year on the run treasury)
Settlement date: 18-April-05
Maturity date: 15-Apr-10
Market price: 100.6073%
Coupon: 4.00%
YTM:[2]   3.865%
PV01:[3]   0.04520%

We run the Curveßuilder risk macro to see what the PV01 risk is on the swap, and as we expect all the risk is within the 5-year swap bucket. Ideally we would want to hedge the position with an offsetting 5-year swap (receive fixed), but instead we will temporarily hedge the position with a US Treasury.

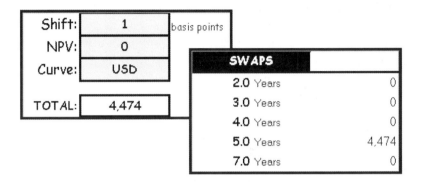

Shift:	1	basis points
NPV:	0	
Curve:	USD	
TOTAL:	4,474	

SWAPS	
2.0 Years	0
3.0 Years	0
4.0 Years	0
5.0 Years	4,474
7.0 Years	0

If the PV01 of the underlying 5-year swap is US\$ 4,472, and if the PV01 of the 5-year UST is 0.0452%, then we can then calculate our required hedge from our general hedging ratio.

$$Hedge = \frac{PV01_{exposure}}{PV01_{hedge}} = \frac{4{,}472}{0.0452\%} = US\$9{,}893{,}805$$

We therefore need to be long US\$ 9,893,805 (notional) of the 5-year on the run US Treasury. Given the notional hedge the overall PV01 of our treasury hedge is US\$−4,467 (\$9,893,805 × 0.0452%). The net PV01 (PV01 Swap US\$4,472 plus PV01 UST US\$−4,467) is now very close to zero. This infers that we no longer have outright interest rate exposure.

While the dealer has hedged against changes in interest rate they still have swap spread risk. If swap spreads decrease while interest rates remained unchanged, the fixed swap rate you could receive in the market decreases. As the market's fixed rate falls the trader's position incurs a loss. The potential loss is equal to the PV01 of the underlying treasuries you are using as a hedge. For every basis point that swap spreads decrease the PV01 of our net position decreases by US\$4,467. While this is still a significant risk, given that volatility of swap spreads is much less than that of underlying treasury rates, the overall exposure is significantly less (ie, swap spreads move less than absolute interest rates), even though the absolute PV01 risk measures is the same. The only way to reduce or eliminate this swap spread risk is to replace the UST hedge with an offsetting interest rate swap as a hedge.

PORTFOLIO RISK MANAGEMENT
While we could hedge each individual swap most traders will normally hedge and manage a portfolio of interest sensitive securities. In the table below we have a portfolio of simple interest rate swaps, there are five different swaps with an overall notional of US$150,000,000 with a current (as of curve date: 15-April-05) NPV

Start date	Maturity	Fixed pay/ rec	Fixed rate (%)	Flt spread	Notional 1,000,000	Fixed NPV	Flt NPV	Total NPV
					150			−5,922,513
2-Jun-04	2-Jun-10	Pay	5,000	10	10	−2,509,287	2,190,359	−318,927
15-Apr-05	15-Apr-08	Rec	4,000	75	60	6,829,611	−8,325,366	−1,495,755
2-Jun-03	2-Jun-07	Pay	5,000	50	50	−7,182,376	4,954,076	−2,228,300
23-May-99	23-May-08	Pay	3,000	0	15	−1,500,501	2,036,621	536,120
12-Apr-02	1-Apr-11	Rec	2,750	125	15	2,148,219	−4,563,869	−2,415,650

of US$−5,922,529. This total NPV is not the profit or loss on the portfolio it is only the current NPV. The figure does not take into account any gains or loss that would have been realised since the inception of each trade. The profit and loss on a daily basis will reflect the daily change in total NPV, plus any payments paid or received, plus any borrowing or lending costs associated with the trading book. For example if a trader receives a cash payment on 15-April-05. On 16-April, once the payment is received, the NPV would drop by the cash payment amount, while the cash account would increase by the same amount, resulting in a net P/L of zero.

We can now run the risk scenario on the portfolio to see how the NPV of the portfolio is sensitive to changes in interest rates.

CurveBuilder: RiskCalculator 44

Shift:	1	basis points
NPV:	-5,922,513	
Curve:	USD	

Run Risk

TOTAL: -2,486

DEPOSITS

ON	-17
TN	-16
1M	-67
3M	194
6M	-17

SWAPS

		PV01	Hedge
2.0 Years	7,014	193	36,257,324 Rec Fixed
3.0 Years	-8,056	285	-28,274,711 Pay Fixed
4.0 Years	618	371	1,664,533 Rec Fixed
5.0 Years	1,220	454	2,687,986 Rec Fixed
7.0 Years	-4,720	608	-7,764,448 Pay Fixed
10.0 Years	-17	830	-19,895 Pay Fixed

FUTURES

		PV01 Hedge	
		# Contracts	1,375
Jun-05	930	37	925
Sep-05	444	18	450
Dec-05	7	0	0
Mar-06	24	1	25
Jun-06	-29	-1	-25
Sep-06	0	0	0

Given the risk results we notice that the overall interest rate sensitivity is relatively small, with a net PV01 of US$−2,486. While we may not have significant exposure to a parallel shift in the yield curve we do have significant exposure to changes in the shape of the yield curve. For example, given the PV01 for the 2-year exposure of US$7,014 and the 3-year exposure of US$−8,056 the net curve risk is US$15,070. If the 2-year swap rate fell by 1 bp while the 3-year swap rate increased by 1 bp (a steepening of the yield curve by 2 bps) the net loss would be US$15,070. Curve risk

Table 2 Curve risk PV01

vs	3 Y	4 Y	5 Y	7 Y
2 Y	15,070	6,396	5,794	11,735
3 Y		−8,674	−9,276	−3,335
4 Y			−602	5,339
5 Y				5,941

is measured by the shorter term PV01 less the longer-term PV01 values associated with any two points on the curve.

Curve Risk = Short-term PV01 − Long-term PV01

A net positive PV01 calculation means that we have exposure to the yield curve steepening while a net negative PV01 calculation means we have exposure to a flattening of the yield curve. Table 2 summarises our curve risk for various parts of the curve. The calculations assume a 2 bps change in the yield curve; the short-term rate increases by 1 bp while the longer-term rate decreases by 1 bp.

The appropriate hedge to apply is more of an art rather than a science. We start by considering hedging with short-term interest rate futures. Since the majority of the short-term risk lies with only the first two futures we only hedge these two positions and ignore the other minor risks. Again since we have a net positive PV01 position we need to buy the appropriate number of futures as outlined in the earlier section. We buy 38 of the Jun-05 contract, and

Eurodollar	Futures hedges	Price	Position	
			56	**1,400**
1-Jun-05	ED	96,6000	38	950
1-Sep-05	ED	96,3000	18	450
1-Dec-05	ED	96,1100		

18 of the Sep-05 contract. The total PV01 of our hedge is US$1,400 while our underlying portfolio's PV01 is US$1,474. After we include the long futures position in our portfolio and then re-run the risk analysis we see that the short-term interest rate exposure is almost eliminated (net PV01 of US$74).

The after hedge PV01 risk analysis:

FUTURES	
Jun-05	-4
Sep-05	11
Dec-05	23
Mar-06	40
Jun-06	-13
Sep-06	17

We now look at managing the interest rate risk associated with our longer-term time buckets which are associated with the longer-term swap instrument. We decide that we have too much curve risk between 2 and 3 years; therefore we buy and sell the appropriate on the run UST to reduce this risk. We also decide that we want to reduce the outright PV01 risk at the 5- and 7-years time buckets, which we hedge by shorting the 5-year on the run UST. While this reduces our net PV01 risk (of the combined 5- and 7-year buckets) it does result in slightly more curve risk between the 5- and 7-year swap rates. The combined interest rate swap portfolio with the UST and Eurodollar hedges is as follows.

AddDeal		Curve	USD						**TOTAL**	**5,921,735**
				Fixed	Fixed	Flt	Notional	Fixed	Flt	Total
Deal ID		Start Date	Maturity	Pay/Rec	Rate	Spread	1,000,000	NPV	NPV	NPV
Total							150			**-5,922,513**
1001	IRS	2-Jun-04	2-Jun-10	Pay	5.000%	10	10	-2,509,287	2,190,359	-318,927
1002	IRS	15-Apr-05	15-Apr-08	Rec	4.000%	75	60	6,829,611	-8,325,366	-1,495,755
1003	IRS	2-Jun-03	2-Jun-07	Pay	5.000%	50	50	-7,182,376	4,954,076	-2,228,300
1004	IRS	23-May-99	23-May-08	Pay	3.000%	0	15	-1,500,501	2,036,621	536,120
1005	IRS	12-Apr-02	1-Apr-11	Rec	2.750%	125	15	2,148,219	-4,563,869	-2,415,650

UST Hedges			Maturity	Price	Coupon	YTM	Position	PV01 per 1M USD	Notional x PV01	NPV
							-2		**4,559**	**-1,666,252**
2Y	UST	18-Apr-05	31-Mar-07	100.4895	3.750%	3.488%	35	-188	-6,567	35,171,325
3Y	UST	18-Apr-05	15-Feb-08	99.3169	3.375%	3.630%	-30	-265	7,965	-29,795,069
5Y	UST	18-Apr-05	15-Apr-10	100.6073	4.000%	3.865%	-7	-452	3,161	-7,042,508
10Y	UST	18-Apr-05	15-Feb-15	98.0431	4.000%	4.245%	0	-787	0	0

EuroDollar Futures Hedges			Price				Position			NPV
							56		**1,900**	**13,510,500**
Jun-05	ED		96.6000				38		950	9,177,000
Sep-05	ED		96.3000				18		450	4,333,500
Dec-05	ED		96.1100							

After we include the Eurodollar and UST hedge positions in our portfolio and then re-run the risk analysis we see that indeed the curve risk between the 2Y and 3Y swap rates have been reduced (from US$15,070 to US$538).

After hedge PV01 risk analysis:

CurveBuilder: RiskCalculator				
Shift:	1	basis points		
NPV:	5,921,735			
Curve:	USD			
Run Risk				
TOTAL:	673			

DEPOSITS	
ON	-17
TN	-15
1M	-67
3M	194
6M	-17

SWAPS		PV01	Hedge
2.0 Years	447	193	2,311,887 Rec Fixed
3.0 Years	-91	285	-319,342 Pay Fixed
4.0 Years	618	371	1,664,533 Rec Fixed
5.0 Years	4,381	454	9,651,475 Rec Fixed
7.0 Years	-4,720	608	-7,764,448 Pay Fixed
10.0 Years	-17	830	-19,895 Pay Fixed

FUTURES		# Contracts	PV01 Hedge -25
Jun-05	-20	-1	-25
Sep-05	-6	0	0
Dec-05	7	0	0
Mar-06	24	1	25
Jun-06	-29	-1	-25
Sep-06	0	0	0

Once we combine all the hedges within our portfolio we calculate the overall PV01 risk, and see that it is now US$673 (positive), which has changed from our initial PV01 of US$−2,486. Initially we had a risk to interest rates increasing, we now have reversed that exposure to a loss if interest rates fall, however the net absolute exposure has been reduced.

As we mentioned earlier whenever we use government bonds as a temporary hedge, as we have done in this example, there will be residual basis risk or swap spread risk. The amount of swap spread risk is equal to the remaining or hedged PV01 calculation less the PV01 of the UST.

Swap Spread Risk = Hedged PV01 − PV01 UST
Swap Spread Risk PV01

	Hedged PV01	UST PV01	Swap spread risk PV01
2 Y	447	−6,567	7,014
3 Y	−91	7,965	−8,056
4 Y	618	0	618
5 Y	4,381	3,160	1,221
7 Y	−4,720	0	−4,720
Total swap spread risk			−3,923

In our example the net swap spread risk is equal to a PV01 of US$−3,940, which means if all swap spreads increased by 1 bp the value of our portfolio would decrease by US$3,940. This swap spread risk (PV01 calculation) is the same figure as we obtained from our risk analysis; swap spread risk is like there is no underlying hedge at all.

A trader of interest rate swaps is known as a "risk manager", since he or she is ultimately managing various risks in their portfolio. For a trader to make money on an underlying portfolio or position they need to consider several risks associated with their position, which can make or loose them money depending on how the market moves.

Interest rate risk

The interest rate risk for a single swap or a portfolio is derived from the overall PV01 as described earlier. The greater the absolute PV01 figure the greater our overall exposure is to changes in interest. A trader can take a view on the directional move in interest rates by increasing their absolute PV01 risk exposure. A positive PV01 means the trader has a view that interest rates will increase while a negative PV01 implies the trader has a view that rates will fall.

Curve risk

Curve risk is the risk that the curve does not shift parallel up or down which is what the macro PV01 figure assumes. While a trader can have a net zero PV01 figure which, infers that we have no exposure to a parallel shift in interest rates, the trader will still have risk to changes in the shape of the yield curve.

Swap spread risk

Most traders use treasuries as a temporary hedge, which reduces the overall interest rate exposure (PV01 value of the portfolio) but it also means that they still have swap spread risk. As swap spreads changes so will the underlying swap rates, which the trader ultimately wants to pay or receive in the market to fully, hedge their portfolio. This swap spread risk is equal to the hedged portfolio's PV01 less the PV01 of the UST. A net positive PV01 for a UST position means we are at risk if swap spreads decrease, while a net negative PV01 value means we are at risk is swap spreads increase.

1 This spreadsheet model provided allows you to run the RISK macro on any swap, option or portfolio. Simply link the NPV: cell to any underling's NPV, then run the macro to see how the NPV changes as each of the curve's inputs change by a given number of basis points (usually 1 bp in order to calculate the PV01).
2 Given that our 5-year swap rate is 4.32%, this is an implied swap spread of 45.5 bps.
3 If the YTM increased to 3.875% the price of the UST would increase to 100.5621%.

8

Cross-Currency Interest Rate Swaps

A cross-currency interest rate swap (CCIRS) is similar to an interest rate swap (IRS). Both are derivative contracts which help manage interest rate exposure as a result of an underlying asset or liability. While an interest rate swap manages interest rate risk a cross-currency interest rate swap manages both interest rates as well as foreign exchange exposure. Both are agreements between two counterparties to exchange cash flows over a period of time, and can be tailored to match the characteristics of an underlying asset or liability. The cashflows associated with an IRS are all in one currency and there is no exchange of principal. For a CCIRS each leg is in a different currency and there is an exchange of principal upfront and at maturity. The following diagram illustrates the exchange of cashflows within a cross-currency IRS.

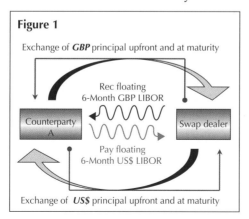

Figure 1

Exchange of **GBP** principal upfront and at maturity

Rec floating
6-Month GBP LIBOR

Counterparty A

Swap dealer

Pay floating
6-Month US$ LIBOR

Exchange of **US$** principal upfront and at maturity

The exchange of principal occurs upfront and at maturity at the same FX rate, regardless of how the FX rate has changes during the life of the transaction, or where the rate is at maturity. Normally the principals are exchanged, upfront and at maturity, at the transaction's initial spot rate.

For most major currency pairs there is a very liquid and transparent market for CCIRS. While swap dealers can quote fixed for fixed CCIRS it is more common to quote a floating for floating CCIRS. A swap where both legs are floating is called a *basis swap*, and when the legs are in different currencies we refer to this as a cross-currency basis swap, which is what we have illustrated above with the US$-GBP example. For a dealer to quote and hedge a fixed for fixed cross-currency swap interest rate swap they would need to combine a basis swap with simple fixed for floating IRS. We will discuss the pricing and structuring of a fixed for fixed swap later in this chapter.

WHAT IS THE VALUE OF A CROSS-CURRENCY BASIS SWAP?

You would assume that there must be a significant value to a CC basis swap given the fact that you are exchanging coupons, which have a significant interest rate differential. However if we consider the value of each of the individual legs you will realise that the value of a CC basis swap should have an initial NPV of zero.

If we examine the cashflows and NAV of the US$ floating leg in Table 1, you will notice that the net NPV is zero. This should not be a big surprise given the fact of how we constructed our zero curves and thus how we estimate our floating rate interest. If we assume to get paid LIBOR and then effectively discount the cashflows at LIBOR the net present value should be zero. If a floating leg (with no additional margin) has an NPV of zero, which holds regardless of the underlying currency, the value of a cross-currency basis swap (initially) should have a net NPV of zero.

Table 1 US$ Floating leg, with exchange of principles

Dates	t	DCF	LIBOR (%)	Coupon value	NPV coupons	NPV principal
19-Apr-05		0.99969				99,968,827
19-Oct-05	0.5083	0.98261	3.418	−1,737,554	−1,707,346	
19-Apr-06	0.5056	0.96300	4.029	−2,036,690	−1,961,336	
19-Oct-06	0.5083	0.94249	4.282	−2,176,581	−2,051,400	
19-Apr-07	0.5056	0.92346	4.076	−2,060,778	−1,903,040	−92,345,705
					−7,623,122	7,623,122

ZERO NPV VALUATION

Another way to look at the valuation of a CCIRS is to consider the trade as two transactions:

1. an exchange of floating rate coupons;
2. an off-market foreign exchange forward.

Individually the value of each component has a positive or negative NPV, but combined the NPV is zero. The value of the coupon exchange depends on whether or not you are paying or receiving.

Pay high yielding currency   Rec low yielding currency NPV < 0
Rec high yielding currency   Pay low yielding currency NPV > 0

Along with this off market exchange of coupons the second component of a CC basis swap is similar to an off market FX forward trade. There is an exchange of principal at maturity, but rather than exchange the principal at the appropriate forward rate, it is done at the initial spot rate. Given that the fair value FX forward rate is a simple function of the interest rate differential between two currencies, the value of the off market FX forward transaction is equal but opposite (same amount but opposite sign) to the NPV of the exchange of coupons.

CROS- CURRENCY BASIS SWAPS QUOTES AND PRICING

While the economic value of a CC basis swap is zero, there is generally a quoted market rate for such a trade. CC basis swaps are quoted as a spread, in basis points, from one floating currency to another. Cross-currency basis swaps are normally quoted against US$ (6M US$ LIBOR). The basis points quoted are generally relative to the underlying quoted currency *vs.* paying or receiving US$ LIBOR (flat).

Figure 2

CAD Basis Swaps	Pay	Receive
1) 1 Year	8.0000	10.0000
2) 2 Year	10.0000	12.0000
3) 3 Year	11.2500	13.2500
4) 4 Year	12.7500	
5) 5 Year	14.2500	

GBP Basis Swaps	Pay	Receive
1) 1 Year	-1.1000	0.9000
2) 2 Year	-0.4000	1.6000
3) 3 Year		2.0000
4) 4 Year	0.2000	2.2000
5) 5 Year	0.2000	2.2000

Source: Bloomberg

For example the swap dealer's quote for a 2-year Canadian dollar (C$) cross-currency basis swap is Pay 10 bps *vs.* receiving 12 bps. The swap dealer will:

Pay C$ floating + 10 bps *vs.* Rec US$ LIBOR flat
Rec C$ floating + 12 bps *vs.* Pay US$ LIBOR flat

In the previous section we discovered that the value of a CC basis swap should be zero, so why is the market quoting a basis point value to swap from one currency to another? In general the basis swap quote is market driven in order to maintain equilibrium in supply and demand of the underlying basis swaps. The quoted rate can be positive or negative and is derived from the overall market's supply and demand for specific currencies. From time to time the basis swap markets becomes unbalanced, and the only way to balance or establish equilibrium is to provide a premium or cost for those who want to enter into the basis swap.

Example
In a balanced market there would be an equal number of counterparties wanting to rec Floating Canadian dollars as there are willing to pay Canadian dollars, *vs.* US$. In this situation every time a dealer enters into a CC basis swap, they can offset it with an opposite transaction, with another counterparty. However, the market becomes unbalanced when there are more counterparties wanting to pay C$ than rec C$. In this situation the swap dealer can balance

the books in one of two ways. They can encourage more counter-parties to rec C$ by paying a premium on the Canadian dollars, a dealer will pay C$ + 10 bps. The other way to establish a balance is deter those that want to pay C$ by adding a basis cost to the C$ floating leg, a dealer will rec C$ floating + 12 bps. Therefore, the value of the basis swap market comes from the market's "Balances" for specific currency and has nothing to do with the interest rate differential or FX volatility of an underlying currency pair.

Figure 3 shows a graph of the JPY/US$ (3 and 5 years) basis swap levels since June 1996, and you see that during 1997 the basis swap market went significantly negative.

> Pay ¥ floating less 30 bps *vs.* Rec US$ LIBOR flat
> Rec ¥ floating less 28 bps *vs.* Pay US$ LIBOR flat

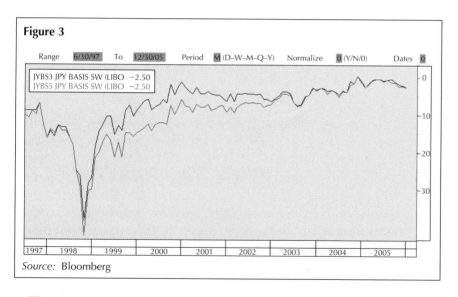

Figure 3

| Range | 6/30/97 | To | 12/30/05 | Period | M (D–W–M–Q–Y) | Normalize | 0 (Y/N/0) | Dates | 0 |

JYBS3 JPY BASIS SW (LIBO −2.50
JYBS5 JPY BASIS SW (LIBO −2.50

Source: Bloomberg

This was a result of a huge flow of foreign denominated assets into Japan, and investors swapping the assets from US$ into JPY. As a result there was demand for banks to pay JPY and rec US$, and since there was no offsetting flow of JPY this pushed the basis market to historically low levels. Given that the fair economic value of the basis should be zero, it was understandable that many market players (in particular hedge funds and bank proprietary traders) took advantage of this bias and started to pay JPY. These trades caused the market to sharply adjust (balance) in early 2000.

SYNTHETICALLY CREATE A CC BASIS SWAP

We can synthetically create a basis swap if no market is available or if the underlying market is inefficient. A dealer enters into a pay CAD Rec US$ cross-currency basis swap (as illustrated below) and they want to hedge it, but if no offsetting basis swap is available to cover the position a hedge can be created synthetically.

A synthetic CC basis swap can be created by synthetically replicating each of the two legs in US$ and CAD (from a dealer's perspective).

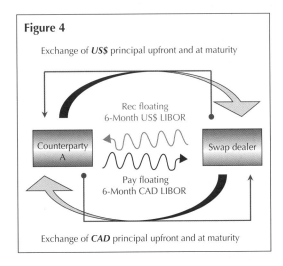

Figure 4

Exchange of *US$* principal upfront and at maturity

Rec floating
6-Month US$ LIBOR

Counterparty A

Swap dealer

Pay floating
6-Month CAD LIBOR

Exchange of *CAD* principal upfront and at maturity

US$ leg
1. Upfront, exchange of principal, receive US$ from client.
2. We invest the US$ in a money market deposit earning US$ LIBOR.
3. The interest earned covers the US$ LIBOR payment on the swap.
4. At maturity, the investment pays US$ which then is paid to client.

CAD leg
1. Upfront, you borrow C$ and pay C$ LIBOR.[1]
2. You give the C$ to the client, for the exchange of principal upfront.
3. The C$ LIBOR you receive from client pays the interest cost.
4. At maturity, you get the C$ back from client and then payback loan.

While the cashflows work well in practice it is not as easy to implement. Where a trader can borrow and invest cash may be significantly different to LIBOR flat. The US$ funds invested will bear the credit risk of the borrower, and therefore is not considered a risk free investment. While you could invest in risk free instruments, such as US treasuries, normally UST earn a rate of return, on an asset swap basis, significantly below LIBOR, depending on where swap spreads are at the time of purchase. So as the borrowing and lending rates deviate from LIBOR flat and once you consider the credit and capital implications of any investment, it is generally not practical to synthetically create a basis swap. In some less developed markets it may be practical if the basis swap benefit is more than enough to compensate for any loss on the bid offers of borrowing or lending. It is import for a trader to know where they can borrow or lend cash. It is common that as a matter of internal practice the cash surplus and deficits from a derivatives trading book are funded or credited at the overnight (ON) LIBOR. In some cases LIBOR is paid on cash borrowed, while any cash surplus earns LIBID (LIBOR less 1/8) is paid on cash lent to the trading book.

BASIS POINT CONVERSION

When we enter into a cross-currency basis swap, where we exchange floating rate coupons and principal amount the economic value of such a trade is zero (NPV = 0).

It would then be natural to assume that if we arbitrarily add X basis points to one leg of the swap we can add the same X basis point on the other leg, and the NPV should still be zero. The following diagram illustrates the coupon flows of a basis swap without and then with a floating rate margin (principal exchange is not included).

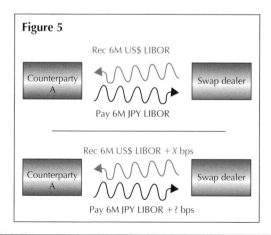

Figure 5

Rec 6M US$ LIBOR

Counterparty A — Swap dealer

Pay 6M JPY LIBOR

Rec 6M US$ LIBOR + X bps

Counterparty A — Swap dealer

Pay 6M JPY LIBOR + ? bps

When adding or subtracting basis points from one swap leg, it normally is not equal and offsetting on the opposite leg; why? Because one basis point in one currency does not equal one basis point in another. This is when the interest rate differential has an impact on the pricing of a cross-currency swap. The PV01 values will be different as a result of interest differentials as well as the coupons basis and payment frequencies. In order to determine what the value of an X basis point margin on one leg is worth on another we need to determine a conversion ratio. A conversion ratio is a factor (ratio) that makes the value of both bps margins equal, and the NPV equals zero, as it would be without any spreads on either leg.

We can then approximate[2] the PV01 of each leg using simple bond math, assuming that the initial value of the underlying bond is 100% or par, at the current YTM. The following example uses an HP17B calculator functions to calculate the PV01 for each leg.

Example

Term	5-years
US$ rates	5.00%, semi-annual, 30/360
JPY rates	0.50%, semi-annual, 30/360

		US$	JPY
N	(Number of coupon payments)	10	10
Swap rate	(YTM)	5.01%	0.51%
PMT	(Coupon payment)	2.5	0.25
FV	(Future value)	+100	+100
Solve for PV	(Present value)	−99.9563	−99.9507
	PV01 (100 − New PV)	0.0437	0.0493

The PV01 for US$ is 0.0437 while for JPY it is 0.0493. The lower the interest rate the more a basis point is worth on a relative basis. We can calculate the appropriate basis point conversion ratio from US$ to JPY, given the two PV01s.

$$\text{Conversion Ratio} = \frac{\text{PV01}_{US\$}}{\text{PV01}_{JPY}} = \frac{0.0437}{0.0493} = 0.8810$$

(Converting from top currency to bottom currency)

Therefore, 1 US$ basis point is worth approximately 0.881 JPY basis points. For every basis point added or subtracted from one floating leg we need to convert that spread into an equivalent spread on the opposite leg using the conversion ratio. Given the conversion ratio of 0.881, we can calculate the JPY equivalent spreads, for a given US$ spread (no basis swap charge is included). The conversion ratio is only applicable to the margin and not to the floating rate (LIBOR) itself.

Table 2

US$ LIBOR flat	=	JPY LIBOR flat
US$ LIBOR + 50 bps	=	JPY LIBOR + 44.05 bps
US$ LIBOR − 50 bps	=	JPY LIBOR − 44.05 bps
US$ LIBOR + 100 bps	=	JPY LIBOR + 88.1 bps
US$ LIBOR − 100 bps	=	JPY LIBOR − 88.1 bps

While this is only an approximation, when we price a CC basis swap with a margin on one leg, the zero curve pricing model automatically takes the implied conversion ratio into account.

While we know that the fair value of a cross-currency basis swap should be zero, there is normally a charge or a benefit for entering into a CC basis swap, which makes the initial NPV positive or negative. We also know that when we want to increase or decrease the floating rate spread from zero we must also take into account the basis point conversion ratio. We will now look in more detail at the application and structuring of cross-currency interest rate swaps.

HEDGING USING BASIS SWAPS

A corporate can apply a cross-currency interest rate swap to hedge foreign exchange and interest rate risk. As an example; a UK corporate has been offered a loan in US$ (paying US$ LIBOR flat) but prefers to have GBP interest payments given that all their income is in GBP. The corporate wants to obtain the US$ loan and then hedge the loan by entering into a cross-currency swap where they, pay 6 month GBP LIBOR *vs*. Rec 6-Month US$ LIBOR.

Illustration of hedged cashflows (from the corporate perspective)

Current market rates

Current spot GBP/US$:	1.75
Current 5-year basis swap quote:	0.2/2.2 (Pay/Rec)

	Cross currency interest rate swap			US$
	GBP leg	US$ leg		Loan
Initially	+£10,000,000	−US$17,500,000		+US$17,500,000
6M	−6M £ LIBOR + 2.2 bps	+6M US$ LIBOR		−6M US$ LIBOR
12M	−6M £ LIBOR + 2.2 bps	+6M US$ LIBOR		−6M US$ LIBOR
			Hedge ⇒	
54M	−6M £ LIBOR + 2.2 bps	+6M US$ LIBOR		−6M US$ LIBOR
60M	−6M £ LIBOR + 2.2 bps	+6M US$ LIBOR		−6M US$ LIBOR
60M	−£10,000,000	+US$17,500,000		−US$17,500,000

£ Interest: £10,000,000 × (6M £ LIBOR + 2.2 bps)
US$ Interest: US$17,500,000 × (6M US$ LIBOR)

You can see from the cashflow example that the US$ leg of the cross-currency swap hedges the US$ cashflows on the loan, the coupons and principal flows. As a result, the corporate, has no further exposure to either £/US$ exchange rates or to changes in US$ interest rates. The corporate, on a net basis, receives GBP principal upfront, pays 6M GBP LIBOR + 2.2 bps, and then at maturity pays back the GBP principal. They have a US$-based loan, but all the corporate (net) cashflows are in GBP.

While the initial NPV of a PAR IRS is normally zero, the value a cross-currency IRS generally has a positive or negative NPV at inception. That value is equal to the premium or cost associated with the cross-currency basis swap which we enter into in order to swap from one currency to another. When we price an interest rate swap we are normally solving for an NPV of zero, but for any cross-currency swap we solve for an NPV equal to the basis swap's NPV.

For the example above we can calculate the NPV of the basis swap, from the corporate point of view.

If the NPV of the base case basis swap is zero:

❑ Rec US$ floating + 0 bps Pay GBP Floating + 0 bps NPV = 0

Then we calculate the NPV of the basis swap using our zero curve pricing model:

❑ Rec US$ floating + 0 bps Pay GBP floating + 2.2 bps
NPV = US$6,094

Figure 6

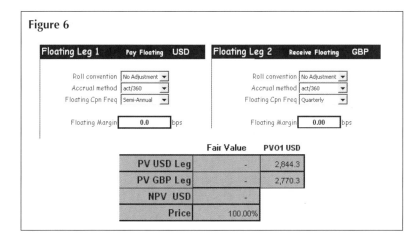

The initial fair market value of a 5-year CCIRS is US$6,094.

The Initial NPV with no margin is zero.

The NPV of the basis swap will reflect the premium or cost of the basis swap:

Figure 7

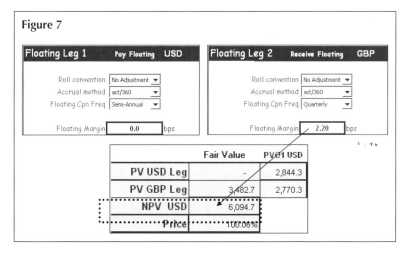

Both swaps are based on identical underlying swap characteristics:

Figure 8

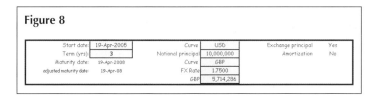

FIXED FOR FIXED CROSS-CURRENCY SWAP

Generally there is no visible market for fixed (US$) or fixed (CAD) cross-currency swap. In order for the swap dealer to price and hedge a fixed (US$) for fixed (CAD) CCIRS they must break the trade down into separate individual legs as seen in Figure 9 (the figure ignores any exchange of principal for the sake of simplicity).

If we assume we have an investor (counterparty A based in Canada) which wants to buy a US$ fixed rate asset, which they want to swap the fixed US$ to fixed CAD. Counterparty A will pay the dealer the fixed coupon in US$ (4.50%), the dealer then enters into a series of "legs" in order to swap the fixed US$ coupons into a fixed CAD rate, which the dealer pays to the investor.

From the dealer's perspective:

Leg 1: Pay fixed US$ Rec floating US$,   solve for floating rate spread

Leg 2: Pay floating US$ Rec floating CAD,   solve for CAD floating rate spread Including any basis swap

Leg 3: Pay floating CAD,   Rec dixed CAD,   solve for CAD fixed rate

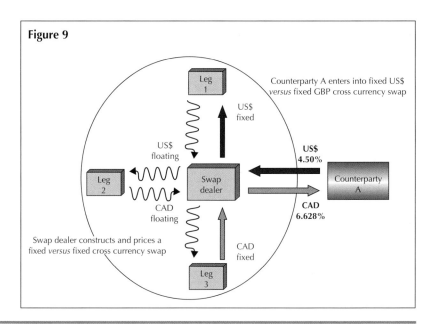

Figure 9

Leg 1
Fixed floating US$

For a given 4.50% fixed rate, we solve for a floating rate margin where the NPV is equal to zero.

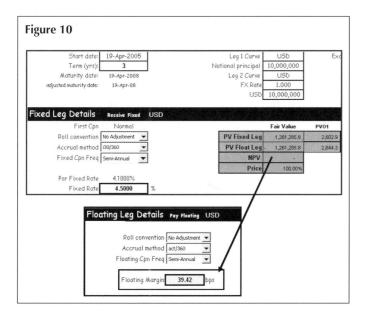

Figure 10

We can apply a simple, fixed for floating IRS to swap a fixed 4.50% coupon to a 6M LIBOR + 39.42 bps.

Leg 2

For a given market quoted CAD/US$ basis swap (Rec floating CAD +11.25 bps pay 6M US$ LIBOR) solve for the fair value NPV:

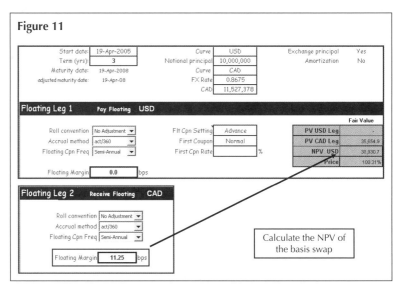

Figure 11

Then solve for the floating rate margin, where the NPV of the swap is equal to the NPV of the above basis swap. The US$ floating rate margin is +39.4 bps while the NPV of the required basis swap is US$ 30,930.

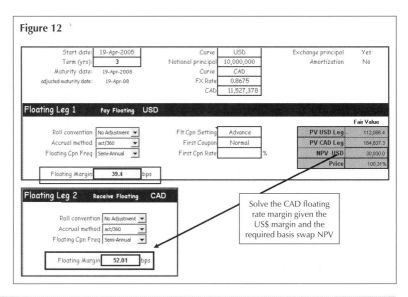

Figure 12

Leg 3 Converts the floating CAD leg into a fixed rate CAD

CAD fixed for floating interest rate swap

Given the floating rate margin (+52.01 bps) on the floating CAD leg we can now solve for the equivalent (zero NPV) CAD fixed rate.

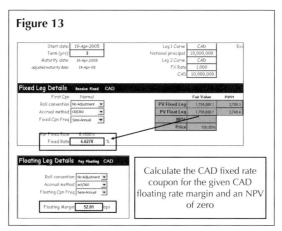

Figure 13

We could solve the fixed for fixed swap so that the NPV is equal to the required basis swap NPV. It provides the same result but from it would not fully reflect the underlying components required to hedge the trade, and we would still need to solve for the applicable fair value of the trade, which is equal to the NPV of the underlying basis swap (US$30,930).

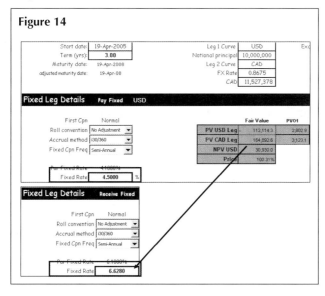

Figure 14

CROSS-CURRENCY ASSET SWAPS

We can apply a cross-currency swap to a foreign denominated asset in order to convert the foreign cashflows into domestic cashflows and thus eliminate any foreign exchange exposure. Using the same fixed rate bond example as we used in the previous chapter on interest rate swaps, we can illustrate how we can swap the bond's cashflows from one currency into another. Just as we did with an interest rate swap there is a cash adjustment to the cashflows in order to take into account a bond price premium or discount. Most cross-currency asset swaps are done as a PAR structure rather than as a market value structure.

Fixed Rate Bond (FRB) details

Notional:	US$10,000,000
Settlement date:	19-April-05
Bond maturity date:	19-Jun-09
Coupon:	4.50%
Frequency:	Semi-annual
Basis:	30/360
Clean price:	96.66% *(price is at a discount to PAR)*

Days of accrued interest:	120 days *(based on 30/360)*
Amount of accrued interest:	4.50% × (120/360) × US$ 10,000,000
	US$150,000

Total proceeds to purchase:	Notional × Clean price + accrued interest
	US$10,000,000 × 96.66% + 150,000
	US$9,816,000

If we assume we have an investor that wants to convert the US$ FRB into a GBP floating rate asset.

Floating coupon details

Notional amount:	GBP 17,500,000 (1.75 × US$10,000,000 (PAR))
Floating index:	6M GBP LIBOR
Coupon basis:	Semi-annual, Act/360

Assuming current market rates:

Spot FX US$/GBP: 1.75
Basis swap: +5/+7 (Pay/Rec)

There is a cash adjustment made upfront so that the client pays a spot equivalent of PAR or 100% upfront (in domestic currency, on settlement date) and then receives a floating rate coupon based on the equivalent PAR amount.

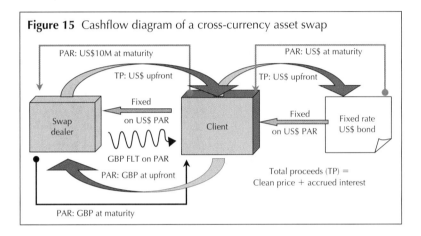

Figure 15 Cashflow diagram of a cross-currency asset swap

PAR value asset swap: (adjustment upfront)

Principal cashflows

❑ On settlement date:
 – Investor pays the total proceeds of US$9,816,000 for US$10M notional FRB.
 – Investor receives total proceeds from the swap dealer.
 – Investor pays the swap dealer GBP equivalent to the US$ PAR amount of the US$ FRB, converted at the current spot rate of 1.75; GBP 17.500,000.

❑ At maturity:
 – Investor receives US$10M from the maturing bond, which they pay to the swap dealer.
 – Investor receives from the swap dealer GBP 17.5M.

Coupon cashflows

❏ Investor earns from the FRB a 4.50% fixed, semi-annual coupon, which they pay to the swap dealer. The fixed coupon is received and paid based on the PAR amount of US$10M. The initial fixed coupon received is a full coupon and the entire coupon is passed on to the swap dealer, regardless of the settlement date.

❏ Swap dealer pays client GBP 6M LIBOR plus a spread, where the floating rate coupon is based on a GBP equivalent US$ PAR value. The initial floating interest period starts on settlement date and matures on the first floating coupon roll (first coupon payment date), which may result in an initial coupon period shorter than the remaining periods. For very short coupon periods it may be preferred to have an initial long first coupon, which combines the initial short stub to the first full coupon.

❏ The floating rate spread on the GBP floating leg is calculated so that the net NPV of the cross-currency swap is equal to the NPV of the required basis swap.

The trade between the client and the swap dealer can be broken down into further components in order to solve for the appropriate floating spread on the GBP leg.

❑ a fixed for floating interest rate swap, denominated in US$
❑ a CC basis swap, US$/GBP, to convert the US$ cashflows into GBP.

Fixed for floating interest rate swap

This includes an upfront cash adjustment so that we have a PAR asset swap structure (cash adjustment to take into account the bonds price at a premium or discount). The cash adjustment will be netted out (dropped) in the final cashflow but is required initially to price the overall structure.

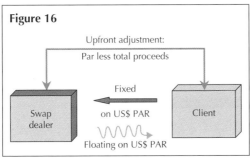

Figure 16

Cross-currency basis swap

We exchange floating rate coupons as well as principal upfront and at maturity. The US$ and GBP principals exchanged are based on PAR converted at the initial FX spot rate. We net the upfront cash adjustment with the PAR amount we deliver on the trade settlement date. We will also need to include the required basis swap in the overall structure, which is not included in the following illustration.

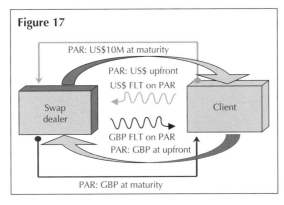

Figure 17

The initial leg is the fixed for floating (US$) IRS. Calculate the US$ floating margin that generates a zero NPV, taking into account the upfront fee received of US$184,000, to take into account the bond is priced at a discount.

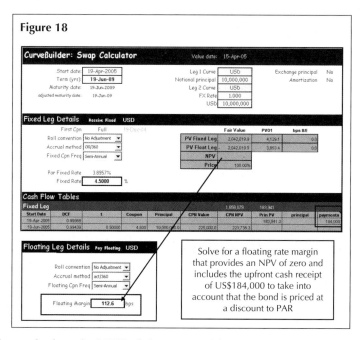

Figure 18

Then calculate the NPV of the required basis swap, which is being quoted as +5 bps to receive GBP floating.

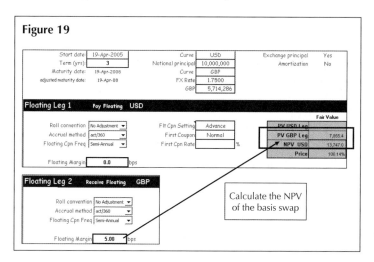

Figure 19

Finally, solve for the required GBP floating rate margin given the US$ floating rate margin (112.6 bps) and the required NPV (US$13,747) derived from the basis swap above.

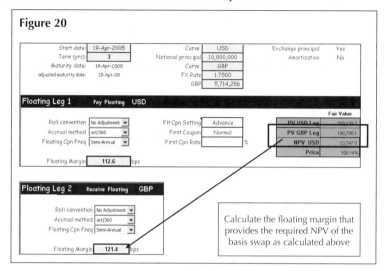

Figure 20

A UK investor buy a 4+ year fixed rate US$ bond, paying a fixed coupon of 4.50%, with a clean price of 96.66%, and total proceeds for US$10M notional of US$9,816,000. The investor then overlays a CC swap to swap the US$ proceeds and coupons into GBP (pay fixed US$ receive floating GBP), eliminate the FX and US$ interest rate risk and receiving a GBP floating rate coupon of 6M GBP LIBOR + 121.4 bps.

LIABILITY SWAP

A company can issue a foreign denominated bond (or loan) and then hedge the liability using a cross-currency interest rate swap. Most bonds are issued at a slight discount to PAR, therefore some cash adjustment will need to be done. Most liability swaps are structured on a PAR value structure rather than market value (see details under the asset swap section). A PAR value structure implies that a cash adjustment is done upfront and thereafter all coupon flows are based on PAR. For example consider a liability swap for the following newly issued fixed rate bond.

New issue: Fixed Rate Bond (FRB) details
Notional: US$10,000,000
Coupon: 5.00%

Frequency:	Annual
Basis	30/360
Settlement date:	19-April-05
Bond maturity date:	19-April-10
Clean price:	98.50% *(price is at a discount to PAR)*
Days of accrued interest:	0 days
Assumed yield to maturity:	5.350%

Total proceeds from bond issue:	Notional × Price (no accrued interest)
	US$10,000,000 × 98.50%
	US$9,850,000

A bank has just issued the above FRB and now wants to overlay a CCIRS in order to hedge the coupon liability from a foreign fixed rate basis to a domestic floating rate basis.

Required floating GBP coupon details

Floating notional amount:	GBP 100% (PAR)
Floating rate index:	6-Month GBP LIBOR
Coupon basis:	Semi-annual, Act/360

Assuming current market rates:

Spot FX US$/GBP:	1.75	
Basis swap:	+5/+7	(Pay/Rec)

There is a cash adjustment made upfront so that the client receives a spot equivalent of PAR or 100% upfront (in domestic currency, on settlement date) and then pays a floating rate coupon based on that PAR amount.

PAR value liability swap: (adjustment upfront)

Principal cashflows

❑ On settlement date:
  ❑ Issuer receives total proceeds of US$9,850,000 for US$10M notional FRB, which they pay to the swap dealer.
  ❑ Issuer receives from the swap dealer an equivalent GBP amount based on the full US$ PAR amount converted at the current spot rate, GBP17,500,000 (US$10M × 1.75 GBP/ US$).
❑ At maturity:
  ❑ Issuer pays back the full GBP 17.5M to the swap dealer.

❏ Issuer receives the US$ PAR amount (US$10M) which they then payback to the bondholders.

Coupon flows

❏ Issuer pays a 5.00% fixed, semi-annual coupon, to the bondholder.
❏ Issuer receives the same fixed coupon from the swap dealer. The fixed coupon is received and paid based on the PAR amount of US$10M.
❏ Issuer pays to the swap dealer 6M GBP LIBOR plus a spread, where the floating rate coupon is based on the bond's equivalent GBP PAR value.
❏ The floating rate spread is calculated so that the net NPV is equal to the NPV of the required basis swap, which is used to swap the cashflows from one currency to another.

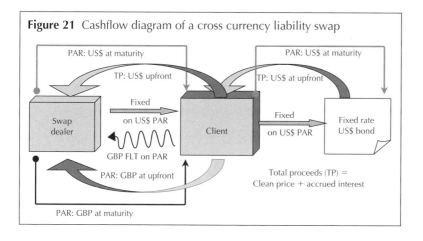

Figure 21 Cashflow diagram of a cross currency liability swap

In order to price and hedge the net cashflows the trade must be broken down into its individual components: a vanilla IRS, plus a cross-currency basis swap.

The initial IRS leg makes an upfront cash adjustment so that the total proceeds are grossed up to PAR. A floating rate spread is solved for in order to have a net NPV of zero. We then take these PAR proceeds and enter into a cross-currency basis swap.

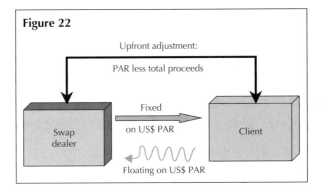

The second leg of the trade is a cross-currency basis swap in order to swap the proceeds from US$ to GBP.

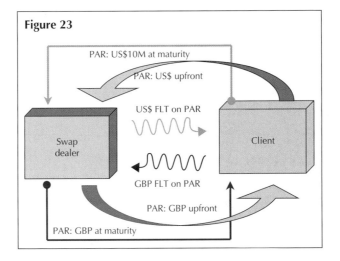

While there is an explicit cash adjustment upfront, and exchange of PAR equivalent notional amounts, normally these payments are netted out and thus no separate upfront adjustment is actually paid.

Initial fixed for floating IRS, including upfront cash adjustment on the fixed leg to take into account the initial discount pricing on the new issue. The discount will bring the total proceeds to a PAR amount. Normally the hedging counterparty will not receive this cash payment but it is required in order to bring the total proceeds to PAR (assuming we do a PAR structured swap).

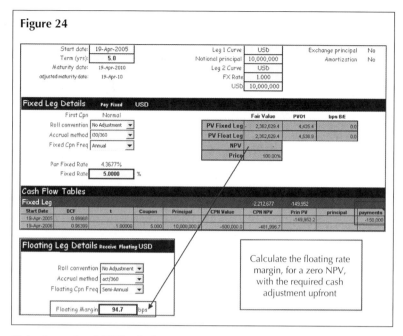

Figure 24

Calculate the NPV of the required basis swap, which is being quoted at +7bps to pay GBP and receive US$.

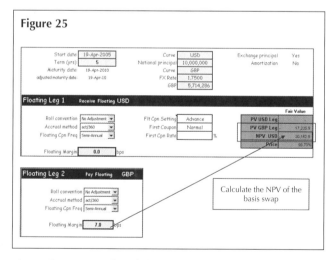

Figure 25

Then given the required US$ floating margin received of +94.7bps we calculate the GBP floating rate margin, solving for a margin that provides the equivalent NPV as a vanilla BGP/US$ basis swap, as calculated above (US$30,162).

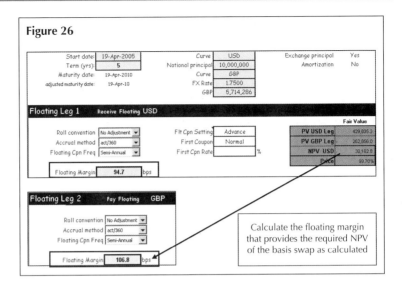

Figure 26

A UK corporate issues a fixed rate US$ bond, paying a fixed coupon of 5.00% for five years, at an all in issue price of 98.50%. They can swap the US$ proceeds and coupons into GBP by entering into a cross-currency swap (rec fixed US$, pay floating GBP), eliminate the FX and US$ interest rate risk and pay a GBP floating rate coupon of 6M GBP LIBOR + 106.8 bps.

CASE STUDY: RELATIVE BORROWING COSTS

You work for an investment bank as a derivative salesperson covering corporate clients, you advising them on hedging interest rate and foreign exchange exposure. One of your clients, who works for the treasury department of a US corporate (and is responsible for funding) has called you for some advice. The corporate has decided to issue foreign currency debt provided that they do not incur any additional foreign exchange or interest rate risk. They have instructed your friend to manage this through the use of Interest rate and cross-currency swaps.

Another investment banker has told your friend the following:

Given the low level of interest rates in Japan at the moment you would be crazy NOT to borrow in Japanese Yen. With five year interest rates below 1.00% in JPY and over 4.00% in US$, you are silly not to take advantage of the preferable interest rates in Japan.

You have confirmed with your debt capital markets (DCM) team the following facts:

❑ Given comparable bond sales into Japan, a new issue for this corporate would need to offer a spread of 50 basis points over the similar term government bond in order to attract investor demand (you and the other investment bank agree on this new issue spread).
❑ You have also confirmed with your loan syndication team that your bank could offer the corporate a fixed rate US$ loan for five years at a rate of 4.40%.

Given that the corporates income is in US$ and they are uncertain about the direction of future interest rates they want to have all funding swapped back into fixed rate US$.

What advice do you give your client?
Current market rates as of today, for JPY and US$:

US$/JPY spot exchange rate	105
JPY basis swap	−10/−8 (Pay JPY/Rec JPY)
Conversion ratio[4]	0.9182

Figure 27

Term	JPY Yield sa	Swap Spread	Swap Rate	Term	UST Yield sa	Swap Spread	Swap Rate
3 yr	0.40	5 10	0.45 0.50	2 yr	2.50	35 45	2.85 2.95
4 yr	0.45	10 15	0.55 0.60	3 yr	2.80	40 50	3.20 3.30
5 yr	0.60	15 20	0.75 0.80	4 yr	3.10	45 55	3.55 3.65
				5 yr	3.40	50 60	3.90 4.00
				3M LIBOR	1.81%		
				6M LIBOR	1.98%		

We need to solve for an after hedge equivalent US$ fixed rate for the JPY issue. To determine the equivalent US fixed rate we would need to work backward from the known fixed JPY leg. Given that there is no direct market for a fixed JPY *vs.* fixed US$ we will need to structure the cross-currency swap in order to derive the after hedge fixed US$ rate.

Figure 28 Cross Currency IRS Hedge: JPY into US$

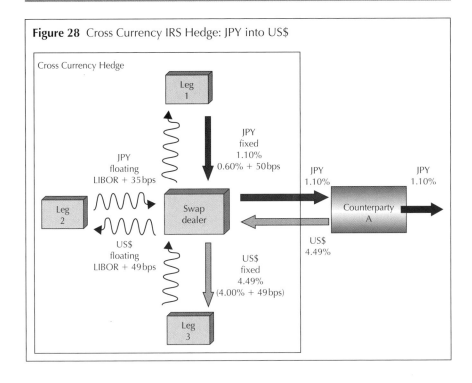

Solution

Without using any pricing models we can calculate a very close approximation of the US$ fixed rate from the given information. Given that the new issue would have to be sold with a yield to maturity of 50 basis points over the equivalent government bond (or Japanese Government Bond JGB) our first step is to calculate the required fixed JPY coupon for the new bond issue (assuming PAR bond pricing).

Required JPY coupon/YTM

5-year JGB yield	0.60%
New issue spread	50 bps
Required coupon/YTM	1.10%

We can now combine a series of legs to calculate the equivalent (after hedge) US$ fixed rate they would need to pay. Figure 28. illustrates the required legs to hedge a fixed rate JPY new bond issue into a fixed rate US$ liability.

Leg 1: Interest rate swap: JPY fixed to JPY floating

Fixed JPY rate: 1.10%

5-year JPY swap rates: 0.75/0.80% (Pay/Rec)

Equivalent JPY floating: JPY LIBOR + 35 bps (1.10% less 0.75%)

We now have the fixed JPY leg into floating JPY

Leg 2: Cross-currency basis swap: JPY floating to US$ floating

The US$ to JPY basis swap is equal to

Pay JPY LIBOR − 10 bps = Rec US$ LIBOR + 0

But we need to receive JPY LIBOR + 35 bps (not JPY − 10 bps), the difference on the JPY leg is 45 bps. We use the US$/JPY basis point conversion ratio to calculate the equivalent US$ basis point spread:

45 JPY basis points are equivalent to 49 US$ basis points.[3]

Therefore after taking into account the basis swap and conversion ratio:

JPY LIBOR + 35 bps = US$ LIBOR + 49 bps

We now have the floating JPY leg into floating US$.

Leg 3: Interest rate swap: US$ floating to US$ fixed

Floating US$ spread: US$ LIBOR + 49 bps

5Y US$ swap rates: 3.90/4.00% (Pay/Rec)

5Y US$ fixed: 4.49% (4.00% + 49 bps)

We now have the floating US$ leg into Fixed US$.

For a US corporate to issue a 5-year fixed rate bond in JPY they would need to offer a coupon (or YTM) of 1.10% in JPY. In order to hedge the foreign exchange and JPY and US$ interest rate exposure they would need to enter into a received fixed JPY, paying fixed US$ cross-currency interest rate swap.

From our analysis we see that the US$ fixed rate the would need to pay in US$ on their hedged JPY denominated bond, is 4.49%, which is more expensive than the funding they could achieve if they obtained a plain vanilla fixed rate US$ loan from your bank (4.40%). The low interest payments available in JPY may look attractive initially, but *on a relative after hedge cost* it is cheaper to obtain a vanilla loan in the domestic market.

1   Most C$ floating interest is linked to BAs (Bankers Acceptance Rates), which is essentially the same as LIBOR; both are interbank interest rates for borrowing and lending cash.
2   In order to get the exact conversation rate we would need to know the accurate PV01 calculations from our swap pricing model, but this method provides a very close and quick approximation.
3   JPY 45 bps $\times$ 1/0.9182 = US$ 49 bps.
4   US$ 1 bp = .9182 bps JPY.

9

Interest Rate Options

The following chapter is not an in-depth mathematical explanation of interest rate options, nor does it cover the derivation of the option models. What we will examine is the common formulae used to price interest rate options and then explore the applications of these models. For a more in-depth analysis to option pricing refer to the references provided at the end of this book.

If we assume that the forward interest rates follow a lognormal distribution, with a constant volatility (σ) we can use the Black '76 model to price European interest rate options:

$$\text{Black European Call option} = F \times N(d_1) - K \times N(d_2) \qquad (1)$$

$$\text{Black European Put option} = K \times N(d_1) - F \times N(d_2) \qquad (2)$$

where F is the implied forward interest rate and K is the strike rate, and $N(\cdot)$ is the cumulative normal distribution function. The Black '76 model is a slight variation of the original Black-Scholes model, where the latter prices an option on the current spot rate while the Black '76 model is an option price relative to the forward rate.

OPTION FUNDAMENTALS

An option gives the right but not the obligation to buy or sell an underlying security at a fixed price either on or before maturity date. For this right the buyer of the option pays a premium. The right to buy the underlying is a *call* while the right to sell the underlying is a *put*. The right to exercise any time up to and including the maturity date is an American option, while the right to exercise only at maturity is a European option. The buyer of the option is long the option, while the writer (seller) is short the option.

The payoff of a European option is given by a fixed payoff formula, where K is the strike price of the option and S is the settlement price of the underlying asset, these are the payoffs at expiry and do not include any premium paid or received.

	Long	Short
Call	$\text{Max}(S - K, 0)$	$\text{Min}(0, K - S)$
Put	$\text{Max}(K - S, 0)$	$\text{Min}(0, S - K)$

We can graphically illustrate the payoffs of the four basic options, upon exercise, given a strike (K) and a settlement price of the underlying (S), which is shown in Figure 1. The buyer of the option (a long position) has unlimited potential gains, with a minimum return of zero, for this benefit the buyer pays a premium (limited loss with unlimited potential gains). The writer of the option (a short position) is exposed to downside losses, since they must meet the obligations of the buyer if the option is exercised. For this risk the writer receives an upfront premium (limited gains, unlimited

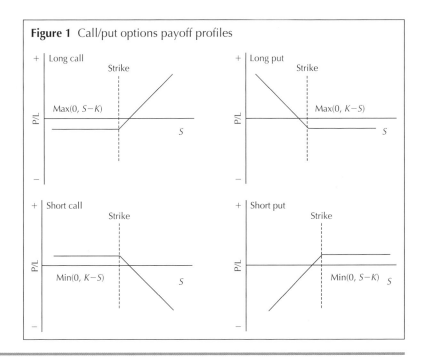

Figure 1 Call/put options payoff profiles

losses). While the writer of an option has unlimited exposure to an adverse movement in the underlying asset price, a market maker or trader of options normally manage this exposure by buying and selling the underlying cash asset. This hedging technique is called delta hedging. We will explore delta hedging in more detail later on.

The value or premium of an option is comprised of two components, time value and intrinsic value. *Intrinsic value* is the difference between the market price and the strike rate, with a minimum value of zero. The intrinsic value is what the option is worth if it was exercised immediately. *Time value* is the difference between the option premium or price and the intrinsic value. Time value is considered to be the price of optionally in the premium; it represents the value of "what can happen" between now and the maturity of the option.

An *at-the-money (ATM)* option is where the strike is equal to the price of the underlying ($K = S$). There is no intrinsic value and the entire option premium is composed of time value.

An *in-the-money (ITM)* option is where the strike (K) is more favourable than the current price of the underlying (S). An ITM option has positive intrinsic value and will always be exercised at maturity. The further the strike is in the money, the more intrinsic value, and thus the more expensive the option.

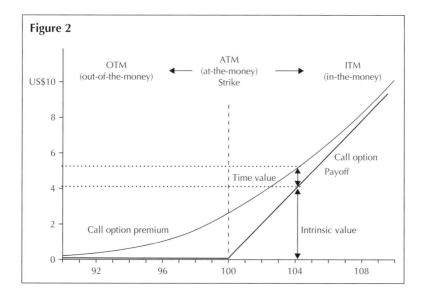

Figure 2

219

An *out-of-the money (OTM)* option is where the strike price is less favourable than the price of the underlying (S). There is no intrinsic value and the entire option premium is composed of time value. At expiry, if the option is OTM it expires worthless. The further the strike is out of the money, the less likely the option will expire in the money and therefore the cheaper the option.

Example
A *call* option, with a strike of 100 has an option premium of US$5. The current price of the underlying asset is 104 (as illustrated in Figure 2):

Intrinsic value $= S - K = 104 - 100$		$= \text{US\$4}$
Time value $=$ Premium $-$ time value $= \text{US\$5} - \text{US\$4}$		$= \underline{\text{US\$1}}$
Option premium		$= \text{US\$5}$

Example
A *put* option, with a strike of 100 has an option premium of US$5. The current price of the underlying asset is 101:

Intrinsic value $= K - S = 100 - 101$		$= \text{US\$0}$
Time value $=$ Premium $-$ time value $= \text{US\$5} - \text{US\$0}$		$= \underline{\text{US\$5}}$
Option premium		$= \text{US\$5}$

Given the fact that there is always some time value within an option it makes no economic sense to exercise an American option early, if exercised you would capture the intrinsic value of the option, but give up the time value. Rather than exercise an American option early you should instead sell the option and receive the premium which should be worth more than it would be if exercised.

The value of any option is derived from the present value of the expected return.

Example
You buy an option, on a coin flip, heads you win, tails you lose. You receive US$1 for heads, and US$0 for tails, what is the expected payoff on this option? Given the fact that the probability of getting a head or a tail is 50% for either then the expected return (ER) is:

$$ER = \Sigma \ (payoff \times probability\ of\ payoff)$$

$$ER = 50\% \times US\$1 + 50\% \times US\$0 = US\$0.50$$

If the expected return on this simple option is US\$0.50 then the fair price of the option should be US\$0.50 also.

$$Option\ Premium = PV\ (Expected\ return)$$

The Black '76 option pricing formula is a mathematical model to determine the expected payoff of an option. For a given forward rate and under the assumption that the realized rate follows a random lognormal distribution we can calculate the probability that the option will end up in the money. If we know the probability of a certain price (S) at maturity and for any given price there is a fixed payoff ($\max(S - K, 0)$) we can then estimate the expected return. This is essentially what the Black '76 formula is calculating.

OPTION RISK CHARACTERISTICS: THE GREEKS

An option's premium or price changes as the underlying variables that determine the price change. Figure 3 illustrates how the option premium changes as the underlying asset price changes (or as interest rates change for interest rate options). It also illustrates how the premium changes for different underlying option terms. The sensitivity of the option's price to changes in underlying variable, such as price, volatility and time, is summarised and quantified in the risk parameters, which we refer to as the Greeks. While the

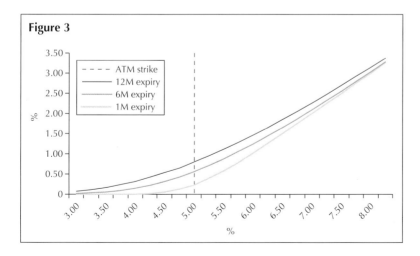

Figure 3

Greeks tells us how sensitive the option's price is to changes in the underlying variables it is only a "mathematical snapshot" at a given point in time, the Greeks continuously change.

OPTION'S PRICE SENSITIVITY TO A CHANGE IN THE UNDERLYING PRICE: DELTA AND GAMMA

The *delta* of an option is defined as the rate of change of the option premium with respect to a change in the price of the underlying asset. The delta measures how the price of the option will change as the price of the underlying asset changes. The delta will change as the underlying variables changes.

$$\text{Delta Call} = \frac{\text{Change in the option price}}{\text{Change in the underlying}} \qquad (3)$$

For a long call option the delta is positive, as the price of the underlying asset increases the price of the option also increases. For a European call option the maximum value of delta is 1, while the minimum value is zero. A call option that is deep in the money will have a delta close to 1, while an option that is deep out of the money will have a delta close to zero. Figure 4 show the delta for a call options and shows how delta changes as the time to expiry changes. A short call option has the opposite signs.

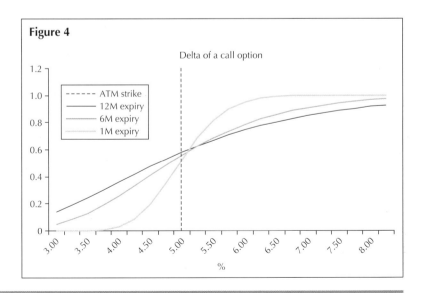

Figure 4

Delta of a call option

- ATM strike
- 12M expiry
- 6M expiry
- 1M expiry

For a long put option the delta is negative, as the price of the underlying asset increases the price of the option decreases. For a European put option the maximum value of delta is 0, while the minimum value is -1. A long put option that is deep in the money will have a delta close to -1, while a put option that is deep out of the money will have a delta close to zero. A short put option has the opposite signs.

The higher the delta the more sensitive the option price is to changes in the underlying price. The time to expiry and the relative strike are the major determinants that affect the value of an option's delta.

High delta risk: (Option price changes significantly for small changes in underlying)

Short dated maturities

ATM strikes

Low delta risk: (Option price does not change significantly for small changes in underlying)

Long dated maturities

OTM or ITM strikes

The delta also measures the relative probability that the underlying will expire in the money. Again, an option that has a high delta (close to 1) has a very high chance of ending up in the money. An ATM option with a delta of 0.50 or 50% implies an approximate 50% chance that the option will expire in the money.

An option trader's portfolio will have exposure to changes in the price of the underlying cash market. They can use delta to derive an appropriate cash position to manage and hedge the price risk. The writer of the option can hold an appropriate delta hedge in the underlying cash market; any change in the option's price as a result of a change in the underlying asset will be offset (hedged) by an equal and opposite change in value of the cash position.

A *delta neutral* position is where the delta position of the option or portfolio of options combined with a cash position is equal to zero. The value of the portfolio is immune to changes in the underlying cash price. The delta of an underlying cash position is always 1 for a long position or –1 for a short position.

Delta can be calculated at any given point in time but as the underlying spot price changes the delta value will change. A position that was originally delta neutral would become unhedged as delta changes. In order to remain delta neutral a trader needs to dynamically hedge their position, continuously re-hedging as delta changes. If we hold an appropriate cash position equal to the option's delta, and adjust the hedge as delta changes we should be immune to price changes of the underlying asset. Any gain (loss) on the option's price will be offset by a loss (gain) in the underlying cash position.

For a written call option as the price of the asset increases, the delta also increases, as illustrated in Figure 4. As delta increases the trader needs to buy more of the underlying cash position. As the price falls and delta decreases the trader will sell their cash position to reflect the change in delta. The simple rule for delta hedging a short call option is to "buy high and sell low". Delta hedging a short option will always cost money, buying high and selling low, which the trader is compensated for in the form of an option premium. On the other hand delta hedging a long option will always make money, buying low and selling high, which the trader pays an upfront premium for this privilege. The amount of loss or gain on the underlying delta hedge will be a result of how the underlying actually changes, the more volatile the underlying price the greater the cost or benefit, while the lower the volatility in the underlying the less the cost or benefit.

When short of options (written options)
❑ Hedging adjustments cost money
❑ Premium received upfront as some compensation.

When long of options (bought options)
❑ Hedge adjustments make money
❑ Premium is paid out upfront.

The following examples[1] illustrate how delta hedging works.

Assume an option trader has written a 7-month (0.575-years) call option with an ATM strike of 100. If the call option were exercised at maturity they would have to sell or deliver 100,000 units of an underlying at the fixed (strike) price of 100. The delta tells you how many units of the underlying you should hold given the probability that you will have to deliver the underlying. At maturity the option is either; ITM and the delta is equal to 1 (deliver 100,000 units) or the option is OTM and the delta is zero (deliver no units). Assume (for sake of simplicity) that the option trader adjusts their delta hedge at the end of each week.

Scenario 1: If at maturity the option expires out of the money, with a delta of 0, the final position in the underlying units should be zero (since no need to deliver anything). The net loss as a result of the hedging strategy is US$−1,172,303. This is close to the value of the option using the BS formula. The difference is a result of time value, the formula value is the present value while the delta hedging cost is a future value. We can also run the scenario through many simulations, on average the value of the delta hedging should be very close to the cost of the option.

Table 1

	Price	100				Simulations
	Strike	100		Avgerage Hedge Cost		1,070,133
	Volatility	30%		Number of Simulations		1,000
	Interest Rate	5.00%				
	Units	100,000				
	Term	0.575	years			
Daily/Weekly (d/w)		w		Payoff		-
	Put/call	Call		Cumulative Cost		1,172,303
	BS Premium	1,041,891		Total Payoff		1,172,303
	FV of Premium	1,072,299				
						Cumulative
Term	Price	Delta	Units	Cost	Int Cost	Cost
0.000	100.00	0.595	59,491	5,949,108		5,949,108
0.019	99.79	0.590	-518	-51,730	5,707	5,903,085
0.038	96.43	0.527	-6,320	-609,380	5,663	5,299,368
0.058	95.26	0.501	-2,534	-241,379	5,084	5,063,073
0.077	90.60	0.404	-9,686	-877,581	4,857	4,190,349
0.096	93.78	0.464	5,984	561,167	4,020	4,755,537
0.115	94.14	0.467	328	30,876	4,562	4,790,975
0.134	101.77	0.617	14,983	1,524,774	4,596	6,320,345
0.153	93.58	0.446	-17,101	-1,600,212	6,064	4,726,196
0.173	96.05	0.496	4,955	475,906	4,534	5,206,636
0.192	99.34	0.564	6,793	674,774	4,995	5,886,405
0.211	93.90	0.438	-12,599	-1,183,020	5,647	4,709,032
0.230	91.71	0.380	-5,760	-528,239	4,518	4,185,311
0.249	83.63	0.194	-18,608	-1,556,119	4,015	2,633,207
0.268	79.89	0.120	-7,417	-592,578	2,526	2,043,155
0.288	82.48	0.152	3,223	265,816	1,960	2,310,931
0.307	82.42	0.140	-1,204	-99,218	2,217	2,213,930
0.326	82.02	0.122	-1,804	-148,000	2,124	2,068,054
0.345	75.48	0.036	-8,633	-651,619	1,984	1,418,419
0.364	77.36	0.043	723	55,941	1,361	1,475,720
0.384	78.28	0.042	-71	-5,529	1,416	1,471,607
0.403	74.82	0.014	-2,819	-210,884	1,412	1,262,135
0.422	79.45	0.033	1,930	153,305	1,211	1,416,651
0.441	81.96	0.045	1,181	96,790	1,359	1,514,800
0.460	79.47	0.016	-2,941	-233,685	1,453	1,282,569
0.479	74.26	0.001	-1,480	-109,920	1,230	1,173,879
0.499	78.91	0.003	191	15,091	1,126	1,190,096
0.518	79.94	0.001	-166	-13,302	1,142	1,177,935
0.537	75.16	0.000	-120	-9,002	1,130	1,170,063
0.556	77.35	0.000	0	-6	1,123	1,171,180
0.575	80.11	0.000	0	0	1,124	1,172,303

Scenario 2: If at maturity the option is in-the-money, with a delta of 1, the final position in the underlying is 100% (we will be holding 100,000 units in order to deliver when the ITM option is exercised). The cumulative cost of the delta hedging is US$11,072,028. The option will be exercised and the 100,000 units are sold at the strike price of US$100. The net cost at maturity is US$1,072,795 (total cost less the proceeds from the sale of the units at 100), again a value similar to the BS formula.

Table 2

	Price	100				Simulations	
	Strike	100			Avgerage Hedge Cost	1,071,779	
	Volatility	30%			Number of Simulations	1,000	
	Interest Rate	5.00%					
	Units	100,000					
	Term	0.575	years				
Daily/Weekly (d/w)		w			Payoff	2,799,983	
	Put/call	Call			Cumulative Cost	(1,727,955)	
	BS Premium	1,041,891			Total Payoff	1,072,028	
	FV of Premium	1,072,299					

Term	Price	Delta	Units	Cost	Int Cost	Cumulative Cost
0.000	100.00	0.595	59,491	5,949,108		5,949,108
0.019	101.79	0.624	2,895	294,735	5,707	6,249,550
0.038	104.96	0.674	5,063	531,385	5,996	6,786,931
0.058	111.54	0.768	9,393	1,047,688	6,511	7,841,130
0.077	118.70	0.849	8,074	958,349	7,522	8,807,002
0.096	122.25	0.882	3,307	404,292	8,449	9,219,743
0.115	127.28	0.919	3,704	471,434	8,845	9,700,022
0.134	126.81	0.920	35	4,430	9,306	9,713,757
0.153	118.02	0.855	-6,509	-768,163	9,319	8,954,913
0.173	121.26	0.888	3,300	400,185	8,591	9,363,690
0.192	118.85	0.870	-1,767	-210,054	8,983	9,162,618
0.211	114.18	0.822	-4,779	-545,620	8,790	8,625,789
0.230	117.88	0.868	4,640	546,903	8,275	9,180,967
0.249	118.00	0.874	587	69,242	8,808	9,259,017
0.268	123.26	0.924	4,986	614,572	8,883	9,882,472
0.288	128.96	0.960	3,578	461,385	9,481	10,353,338
0.307	122.81	0.931	-2,866	-351,975	9,933	10,011,295
0.326	132.02	0.978	4,660	615,199	9,604	10,636,099
0.345	127.91	0.969	-920	-117,676	10,204	10,528,627
0.364	118.11	0.912	-5,671	-669,781	10,101	9,868,947
0.384	121.02	0.944	3,216	389,167	9,468	10,267,583
0.403	118.90	0.936	-833	-99,073	9,850	10,178,360
0.422	117.14	0.929	-652	-76,376	9,765	10,111,749
0.441	112.05	0.875	-5,420	-607,250	9,701	9,514,200
0.460	117.52	0.955	7,973	936,949	9,128	10,460,276
0.479	116.45	0.959	399	46,451	10,035	10,516,762
0.499	121.34	0.992	3,332	404,248	10,089	10,931,100
0.518	124.94	0.999	709	88,596	10,487	11,030,182
0.537	131.80	1.000	76	10,038	10,582	11,050,802
0.556	126.04	1.000	0	12	10,602	11,061,416
0.575	128.00	1.000	0	0	10,612	11,072,028

The sensitivity of delta to changes in the underlying price (how delta changes as the underlying price changes) is known as the option's *gamma*. While delta is the first derivative of the Black formula with respect to the underlying asset price the gamma is the second derivative. The general formula to calculate the gamma of a European call or a put is equal to:

$$\text{Gamma} = \frac{\text{Change in the option delta}}{\text{Change in the underlying}} \qquad (4)$$

Gamma is always positive for a net long or bought option position, while gamma is always negative for a net short or written option position.

High gamma risk: (delta changes quickly)
  Short dated maturities
  ATM strikes

Low gamma risk: (delta does not change quickly)
  Long dated maturities
  OTM or ITM strikes

Figure 5 illustrates the change in gamma for different terms to maturity as well as for different spot rates relative to the ATM strike.

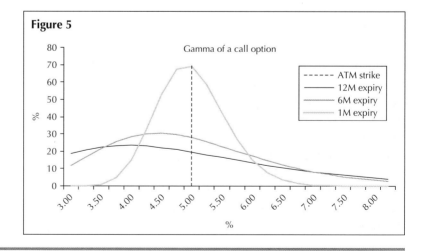

Figure 5

An option trader hedges the price risk of an option through delta hedging. When they are delta neutral they have no price risk. However, as delta changes they are no longer hedged and thus face price risk, until they rebalance their portfolio. The more sensitive the change in delta is to changes in the underlying asset price the more risk the trader has of becoming unhedged. Gamma quantifies this risk so that it can be monitored and managed. Gamma therefore measures the riskiness of a portfolio, or the risk that they become unhedged.

While an option's delta can be hedged using a position in the underlying asset, given the fact that the gamma of the underlying cash is zero, we can only hedge gamma risk using offsetting options.

A high gamma indicates that the underlying delta is unstable, which means it will change dramatically for a small change in the underlying asset price. A low gamma indicates that the underlying delta is stable, which means delta will not change significantly for a small change in the underlying asset price. When close to expiry, spot movements have a greater impact on the probability of exercise of an option (ie a high gamma), for example a call option with a strike 100 on an underlying asset:

Table 3

Spot	1 Second to expiry		1-Year to expiry	
	Exercise?	Delta	Exercise?	Delta
99.99	No	0	Unknown	0.501
100.01	Yes	1	Unknown	0.499
	High gamma position		Low gamma position	

An option trader that is delta hedging a short option position wants the cost of the hedging to be less than the premium received, and therefore prefers to have a low gamma. While a trader hedging a long option wants to earn back the premium paid, and therefore wants a high gamma. Table 3 shows the relative option positions and what the implications are for a volatility trader. For positions where they have "risk", delta hedging could result in an unlimited loss or at least the risk that the loss is greater than the premium earned. While for positions that provide "opportunities", delta hedging allows the trader to earn more than the premium paid.

Table 4 Implications for a volatility trader

	Long options (positive gamma)	Short options (negative gamma)
High gamma	Opportunities	Risk
Low gamma	Less opportunities	Less risk

OPTION'S PRICE SENSITIVITY TO A CHANGE IN THE UNDERLYING VOLATILITY: VEGA

The *vega* of an option is defined as the change of the option's premium with respect to a change in implied volatility. Vega is defined and calculated as follows:

$$Vega = \frac{\text{Change in option premium}}{1\% \text{ Change in implied volatility}} \qquad (5)$$

As volatility changes so does the distribution of possible outcomes. The higher the underlying volatility, the greater the uncertainty and thus the higher the option price. Figure 6 compares the vega of an option for different expiry dates and for different underlying asset prices (or interest rats in this case).

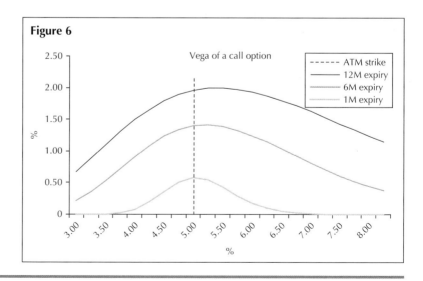

Figure 6

A long or bought option has a positive vega. As the underlying implied volatility increases so will the value of your call or put. For a short or written position the vega is always negative. As the implied volatility increases the value to buy back the option to cover your short position becomes more expensive, while a decrease in implied volatility decreases the price of the option, making it cheaper to cover your short position.

The relative value of vega is affected by the term of the option as well as the relative strike to the underlying cash price.

High vega risk: (Option price changes significantly for change in underlying implied volatility)
  Long dated maturities
  ATM strikes

Low vega risk: (Option price does not change significantly for change in underlying implied volatility)
  Shorter dated maturities
  OTM or ITM strikes

The *theta* of an option is defined as how the option price will decrease as time to expiry decreases by one day (all other factors being equal). Also known as time decay. As time passes the value of the option declines (the distribution of possible outcomes shrinks). OTM options become less likely to be exercised, while ITM options become more likely to be excised. Time decay occurs slowly at first but then accelerates as expiration approaches. Theta is high (option loses value quickly) for short dated options with ATM strikes. Theta is low (option loses value slowly) for longer dated options with OTM/ITM strikes.

The following table summarises the signs of the different Greeks for long and short calls and puts.

Table 5

Position	Delta	Gamma	Vega
Long call	+	+	+
Short call	−	−	−
Long put	−	+	+
Short put	+	−	−
Long cash	+	0	0
Short cash	−	0	0

For example

A long call will have a positive delta and vega, which means the option price will increase as the price of the underlying increases, or as the underlying implied volatility increases. The gamma is also positive which means that the option delta will increase as the price increases.

As we buy or write an option within a trading book it will either increase or decrease the underlying risk parameters. It is these parameters (delta, gamma, vega) which a trader is "risk managing" on a continuous basis.

When managing the risk of an option portfolio we use long or short cash positions to manage the delta risk. For gamma and vega exposure we need to hedge the risk with other (European) options. A trader manages their net Greek positions, first by hedging the vega and gamma risk using other "hedging options", then hedge the residual delta risk using cash. In order to hedge both gamma and vega we will need to solve for an appropriate hedge using two hedging options, a combination of the two options can hedge both risk parameters.

In the following example we start with a portfolio of eight options, a combination of long and short calls and puts. We calculate the net Greeks for the portfolio then solve for an appropriate combination of hedging options (HOTC1 and HOTC2) that will have an equal but opposite gamma and vega values. The combined positions will then be gamma and vega neutral. But again as the underlying variables change and as time passes the Greeks will change and the hedge will need to be rebalanced. Once we have hedge vega and gamma we are left with a net delta position of US$12,778, which we can now hedge away using the underlying cash market without any affect on the neutrals (gamma/vega).

Table 6

Option Portfolio

Value Date	15-Apr-05								Cash			
Option	Call/Put	Strike	Notional*	Vol	Expiry	Term	FWD	dcf	Premium	Delta	Gamma	Vega
OTC1	Call	5.00%	(100,000,000)	17%	15-Apr-06	1	4.75%	0.9644	106,138	(1,997)	(232.7)	(8,926)
OTC2	Call	5.25%	(100,000,000)	17%	15-Oct-05	0.5	4.75%	0.9833	33,447	(1,081)	(254.9)	(4,888)
OTC3	Put	4.50%	50,000,000	17%	15-Jul-05	0.25	4.50%	0.9920	(37,832)	(1,453)	258.4	2,224
OTC4	Put	4.25%	(75,000,000)	17%	15-May-05	0.083	4.25%	0.9975	31,122	2,918	(715.3)	(1,830)
OTC5	Put	5.25%	(170,000,000)	17%	15-Apr-06	1	4.75%	0.9644	529,206	3,960	(356.7)	(13,683)
OTC6	Call	4.25%	(75,000,000)	17%	15-Oct-05	0.5	4.75%	0.9833	203,429	(3,089)	(158.5)	(3,040)
OTC7	Call	4.00%	100,000,000	17%	15-Jul-05	0.25	4.50%	0.9920	(254,761)	4,580	186.6	1,606
OTC8	Call	5.00%	100,000,000	17%	15-Oct-07	2.500	4.50%	0.90546	(141,524)	1,857	143.9	12,683
	Net Notional	**5.00%**	**(270,000,000)**	**17%**		**2.500**	**4.50%**	**0.90546**	**(141,524)**			
							Net Greeks of Portfolio		469,224	5,694	(1,129.3)	(15,856)

Hedging Options

Option	Call/Put	Strike	Notional*	Vol	Expiry	Term	FWD	dcf	Cash Premium	Delta	Gamma	Vega
HOTC1	Call	4.75%	84,653,606	17%	15-Oct-05	0.500	4.75%	0.9833	189,490	4,361	581	11,133
HOTC2	Call	4.50%	53,086,220	17%	15-Jul-05	0.250	4.50%	0.9920	80,334	2,722	549	4,723
	Net Notional		**137,739,827**				Net Greeks of Hedge		269,825	7,084	1,129.3	15,856
							Net Greeks			12,778	-	-

* + Notional Long option, - Notional Sold option

233

CAPS AND FLOORS

An interest rate *cap* is made up of a series of individual European *call* options on the implied forward or FRA rates. Each individual option is known as a caplet. The price of the cap is the sum of the individual caplet prices.

$$Cap = \sum_{i=1}^{n} Caplet_i$$

At expiry if the option is in-the-money the writer of the option pays to the buyer a cash payment equal to:

$$\text{Cash payment} = (S - K) \times \frac{days}{basis}$$

where

S is the LIBOR fixing on fixing date;
while K is the cap or strike rate of the caplet.

An interest rate *floor* is made up of a series of individual interest rate European *put* options on the implied forward or FRA rates. Each individual option is known as a floorlet. The price of the floor is the sum of the individual floorlet prices.

$$Floor = \sum_{i=1}^{n} Floorlet_i$$

At expiry if the option is in-the-money the writer of the option pays the buyer a cash payment equal to:

$$\text{Cash payment} = (K - S) \times \frac{days}{basis}$$

where

S   LIBOR on fixing date;
K   the floor or strike rate of the floorlet.

Each individual caplet or floorlet option starts on trade date (t_0) and expires at the beginning of the interest rate calculation period (when the interest is set in advance and paid in arrears).

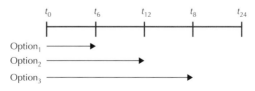

For a spot start cap and floor normally there is no option on the first fixing, since it is already fixed as of trade date, therefore no uncertainty. The first option expires 6 months (whatever the interest period rolls are) forward and then paid at then end of the interest calculation period to coincide with the actual interest payment. There are $N - 1$ individual options to cover the exposure of an underlying floating rate exposure, where N is the number of floating rate interest rate payments.

We expand the Blacks '76 model to take into account the time to expiry of the underlying option, and term of the underlying interest period. The value or premium of each individual caplet/floorlet is derived using the following formulas.

$$\text{Caplet Value} = \text{dcf}_{\text{expiry}} \times \tau \times [F \times N(d_1) - K \times N(d_2)] \quad (6)$$

$$\text{Floorlet Value} = \text{dcf}_{\text{expiry}} \times \tau \times [K \times N(-d_2) - F \times N(-d_1)] \quad (7)$$

where

$\text{dcf}_{\text{expiry}}$ Discount factor to expiry of the option;
τ term of underlying (days/basis);
F Forward or FRA Rate;
K Strike Rate or Caplet/Floorlet level.

$$d_1 = \frac{\ln\left(\frac{F}{X}\right) + \left(\frac{\sigma^2 \times T}{2}\right)}{\sigma\sqrt{T}} \qquad d_2 = \frac{\ln\left(\frac{F}{X}\right) - \left(\frac{\sigma^2 \times T}{2}\right)}{\sigma\sqrt{T}} = d_1 - \sigma\sqrt{T}$$

where

σ Volatility of the forward rate;
T Time, in years, to option expiry;
$N(\cdot)$ Cumulative normal distribution function.

Example
Assume you have a caplet, on 6-Month LIBOR, which expires in 2.5-years, the implied Forward (FRA) Rate is 4.501%,[2] the annual volatility is 17.4%, $\text{dcf}_{\text{expiry}}$ is 0.90546, and the Cap's Strike rate is 5.00%.

$$d_1 = \frac{\ln\left(\frac{4.501\%}{5.000\%}\right) + \left(\frac{0.174^2 \times 2.5}{2}\right)}{0.174 \times \sqrt{2.5}} = -0.2446$$

$$N(d_1) = 0.403424$$

$$d_2 = -0.2446 - 0.174 \times \sqrt{2.5} = -0.51969$$

$$N(d_2) = 0.30164$$

$$Caplet = 4.501\% \times 0.403424 - 5.00\% \times 0.30164 = 0.003076$$

This is the value of the option as at option expiry date. We now need to discount the value to trade date, and also take into account the term of the underlying interest period (6 months or 183 actual days).

$$Caplet = 0.90546 \times \frac{183}{360} \times 0.003076 = 0.1416\%$$

To buy an interest rate cap on an interest payment (on a floating interest rate to be fixed in 2.5-years) on a loan with a notional amount of US$100,000,000, it would cost an upfront premium of US$141,600 (0.1416% × US$100M). The cost of this cap implies a breakeven rate of 5.2832%.

Break Even Rate = Strike Rate + Premium Paid (in per annum bps)
Break Even Rate = 5.00% + 0.1416 × 360/180
Break Even Rate = 5.2832%

If LIBOR fixes greater than the breakeven rate they are better off as a result of the cap anything under the breakeven they would be worse off, all be it with no hedge.

We can also use the built in Cap/Floor pricing model and see that the individual caplet price is 0.14158% and see that the entire cap is worth 0.306% of the notional amount.

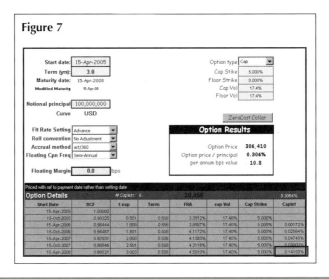

Figure 7

Start date:	15-Apr-2005		Option type	Cap
Term (yrs):	3.0		Cap Strike	5.000%
Maturity date:	15-Apr-2008		Floor Strike	0.000%
Modified Maturity	15-Apr-08		Cap Vol	17.4%
			Floor Vol	17.4%
Notional principal	100,000,000			
Curve	USD		ZeroCost Collar	
Flt Rate Setting	Advance		**Option Results**	
Roll convention	No Adjustment			
Accrual method	act/360		Option Price	306,410
Floating Cpn Freq	Semi-Annual		Option price / principal	0.306%
Floating Margin	0.0	bps	per annum bps value	10.8

Priced with ref to payment date rather than setting date

Option Details		# Caplets: 6		28,456			0.3064%
Start Date	DCF	t-exp	Term	FRA	cap Vol	Cap Strike	Caplet
15-Apr-2005	1.00000						
15-Oct-2005	0.90325	0.501	0.508	3.3512%	17.40%	5.000%	
15-Apr-2006	0.96444	1.000	0.506	3.0597%	17.40%	5.000%	0.00172%
15-Oct-2006	0.94467	1.501	0.508	4.1172%	17.40%	5.000%	0.02564%
15-Apr-2007	0.92531	2.000	0.506	4.1383%	17.40%	5.000%	0.04745%
15-Oct-2007	0.90546	2.501	0.508	4.3118%	17.40%	5.000%	0.09002%
15-Apr-2008	0.88521	3.003	0.508	4.5010%	17.40%	5.000%	0.14158%

A caplet provides protection or a financial benefit if interest rates increase. A corporate, which borrows on a floating rate basis, paying 6M LIBOR, is exposed to rising interest rates. To hedge this exposure they could enter into a simple interest rate swap to lock in a given fixed rate. However, if the corporate has the view that the realized LIBOR will not be as high as the implied forward rates they would prefer to leave the floating rate exposure. However, rather than leave themselves totally exposed they may decide to buy a cap. Caps allow the buyer the flexibility to benefit from lower short-term interest rates but the insurance or protection from increasing rates.

Example
A corporate has a floating rate loan, paying 6M LIBOR. For the corporate to hedge the interest rate exposure, they purchase a cap. They have a view that short term rates will fall over the next 2.5-years, so they want to keep their interest exposure floating. However, in case their view is wrong they buy a cap with a strike of 5.00%, which they decide on given their view on rates and the relative cost. In 2.5-years if the actual LIBOR fixing is 6.00%, the option expires in the money and the corporate receives a cash compensation for the higher interest payments they have to make on the loan. The corporate would receive a cash payment of US$5,083 ((6.00 − 5.00%) × 183/360 × US$1M). The settlement is made at the end of the interest calculation period, to correspond with the underlying interest payment date. The net payment made by the corporate is then equal to the cap or strike rate of 5.00% (ignoring the cost of the cap).

CAP PREMIUM IN SWAP FORM
In the above example the client pays for the option premium upfront, then pays the realised 6M LIBOR rate on the loan, and receives compensation if the realised rate is higher than the strike rate.

Rather than pay the option premium upfront the premium can be structured in *swap form*, as a basis point margin payable on a periodic basis. The floating rate, which the client receives, matches the interest payment required on the underlying loan, while the floating payments the corporate pays reflects the periodic cost of the cap.

Client receives: 6M LIBOR

Client pays: 6M LIBOR plus X bps, subject to a cap rate.

In the above example the option premium is expressed as a basis point (X) margin, payable every 6 months. Given the price of the cap is 0.0306% we can calculate this premium as a margin on the floating coupon is:

$$\text{bps margin premium} = \frac{\text{Cap Premium}}{\text{PV01}} \qquad (8)$$

If the cap premium is worth US\$306,410 (per US\$100M) and the PV01 for the 3-year term is US\$28,456,[3] then the bps per annum margin is 10.8 bps.

Client receives: 6M LIBOR

Client pays: 6M LIBOR + 10.8 bps, subject to a Cap Rate 5.108%

COLLAR

Caps provide protection against rising interest rates while leaving the potential benefit from lower rates, many corporates do not like paying the upfront premium. One way to reduce the amount of premium payable is to purchase an OTM cap (increase the strike rate), while this will reduce the premium it will also increase the exposure to higher interest rates (as a result of a higher cap rate). Another premium reducing strategy is to offset the premium paid by selling (and thus receiving premium) a floor. A combination of a long cap and a short floor is called a Collar. In fact we can structure a collar, by adjusting the strikes of the cap and floor, so that the premium received from the short floor equals the premium paid for the long cap. A zero cost collar provides the client with free[4] protection from increasing interest rates, and some, but not all the benefit from lower than implied forward rates. Figure 8 illustrates how a collar functions over 10-years, with a simulated LIBOR path.

A corporate with interest rate exposure from a floating rate loan can eliminating the risk, and any upside benefit from lower interest rates, with the application of a fixed rate IRS. If however they have a view that short term rates will be lower than the forward rates are predicting, they could leave the floating rate exposure and then

Figure 8

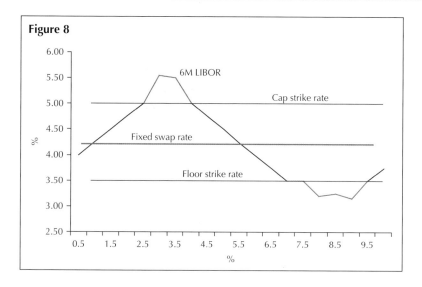

manage the risk using a zero cost collar. A collar provides protection (all be it at a slightly higher fixed rate than the swap) but also retain some of the benefit from lower rates.

A *long collar* (long cap plus short floor), caps the maximum amount of interest payable while establishing a floor or minimum interest payment regardless of how low interest rates fall. The long cap provides protection from increasing interest rates while the premium payable is subsidised by the short floor, which gives up the benefit of interest rates falling below the floor rate.

A *short collar* (long floor plus short cap), floors the minimum of interest received on a floating rate asset, while the maximum of interest earned is capped. The long floor provides protection from falling interest rates while the premium payable is subsidised by the short cap, which gives up the benefit of interest rates increasing above the cap rate.

A corporate treasury with floating rate exposure (on the back of a floating loan) needs to have a view on short-term rates, before they decided an appropriate hedging strategy. They need to have a view on short-term rates relative to what the implied forward rates are predicting. If the corporate treasury has a view that short-term rates will be higher than the forwards imply then they should enter into a fixed floating IRS thereby locking in a fixed rate and eliminating any risk. If the view was that short-term interest rates are probably going to be lower than the forward rates are predicting, they should leave the floating rate exposure open and then use interest rate options to manage the potential risk of higher rates.

CAPS AND FLOORS APPLIED TO FLOATING RATE ASSETS

A cap or a collar can also be used to create a structured asset. A combination of a cap and a floating rate note (FRN) an investor can create a yield enhanced security provided that short-term interest rates do not rise above a fixed strike rate.

Example

An investor holds a 3-year floating rate note (FRN), with a floating coupon paying 6M LIBOR flat. The investor has the view that LIBOR will not increase above 5.00% over the next three years. The investor sells a cap with a strike equal to 5.00%, earns the premium, and the premium is then amortised and paid over the life of the FRN on each coupon date.

Investor pays: 6M LIBOR
Investor receives: 6M LIBOR + 10.8 bps subject to a Cap Rate 5.108%.[5]

INTEREST RATE SWAPTION

An interest rate swaption is an option on a forward interest rate. While caps and floors are options on short-term rates, a swaption is an option on longer-term (swap) rates. The buyer of the option has the right but not the obligation to enter into an underlying interest rate swap with the swaption seller.

While in basic option terminology we have calls and puts, which are called caplets and floorlets for short-term options, for swaptions we classify the options as:

Payer swaption: The right but not the obligation to enter into an interest rate swap; pay fixed and receive floating (IR call).
Receiver swaption: The right but not the obligation to enter into an interest rate swap; receive fixed and pay floating (IR put).
European swaption: This can only be exercised at the maturity of the option.
American swaption: This can be exercised at any time, up to and including maturity.

Bermudan swaption: This can be exercised on any one of multiple discrete exercise dates, which normally correspond with the underlying coupon payment dates.

When you talk about swaptions there are two relevant underlying terms (time frames), the term to maturity of the option and the term of the underlying IRS. A 3-year European swaption on a 5-year IRS allows the buyer with the right, but not the obligation, in three years' time, to enter into a 5-year IRS. Normally swaptions are quoted and settled assuming a floating leg with no additional spread (3M LIBOR flat).

Most swaptions are physically settled, where the buyer of the swaption exercises their option and enters into a fixed floating IRS with the writer of the swaption. Unlike a cap or floor where it is more common and practical to cash settle. While it is more common to physical settle, a cash settlement mechanism can be used in order to determine the appropriate cash payment upon exercise.

We can value a European swaption using the Black '76 model as discussed earlier, and adjust the valuation to take into account the term of the underlying swap. We make the adjustment using the PV01 of the underlying forward starting IRS ($PV01_F$).

$$\text{Payer swaption} = PV01_F \times (F \times N(d_1) - K \times N(d_2)) \tag{9}$$

$$\text{Receiver swaption} = PV01_F \times (K \times N(-d_2) - F \times N(-d_1)) \tag{10}$$

where

$\quad PV01_F \quad$ PV01 of the forward starting swap;
$\quad N(\cdot) \quad$ Cumulative normal distribution function;
$\quad F \quad$ Forward swap rate;
$\quad K \quad$ Strike Rate.

As before d_1 and d_2 are calculated using the following formulas:

$$d_1 = \frac{\ln\left(\frac{F}{X}\right) + \left(\frac{\sigma^2 \times t}{2}\right)}{\sigma\sqrt{t}} \qquad d_2 = d_1 - \sigma\sqrt{t}$$

Example
Assume you purchase a European Payer Swaption on 15-April-2005, the swaption has a one-time exercise date on 15-April-2010,

where you have the right but not the obligation to pay fixed at 5.25% and receive 6M US$ LIBOR for 3-years, a 5 into 3 payer swaption. The implied forward starting swap rate is 5.1271%,[6] volatility is 20% and the $PV01_F$ of the 3-year forward rate is 2.19335:

$$d_1 = \frac{\ln\left(\frac{5.1271\%}{5.25\%}\right)+\left(\frac{0.20^2 \times 5}{2}\right)}{0.20\sqrt{5}} = 0.17064$$

$$d_2 = 0.17064 - 0.20\sqrt{5} = -0.2766$$

Payer swaption $= PV01_F \times (F \times N(d_1) - K \times N(d_2))$

Payer swaption $= 2.19335 \times (5.1271\% \times N(0.17064)$
$\qquad\qquad\qquad - 5.25\% \times N(-0.2766))$[7]

Payer swaption $= 1.8816\% \times Notional$

For a swaption on a notional amount of US$100,000,000 would cost the buyer an upfront premium of US$1,881,600. Assume a corporate has a floating rate liability paying 6M LIBOR. The corporate has a view that short-term rates will fall over the next 12 months so they do not want to lock in a fixed rate. Rather than lock in a fixed rate with an IRS they instead purchase a payer swaption to provide protection from higher rates. If in five years their view turns out to be wrong and interest rates are higher, the corporate could exercise the swaption and pay the fixed strike rate of 5.25%. If instead rates are lower the corporate has the choice to continue paying floating or lock in the lower rates.

The Curveßuilder model calculates the value of the swaption using the method outlined above. Curveßuilder can price a payer or receiver, European or Bermudan swaption.

Figure 9

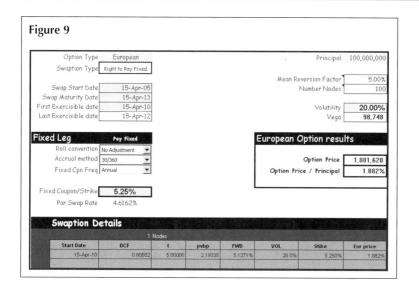

Option Type	European					Principal	100,000,000
Swaption Type	Right to Pay Fixed						
					Mean Reversion Factor		5.00%
Swap Start Date	15-Apr-05				Number Nodes		100
Swap Maturity Date	15-Apr-13						
First Exercisible date	15-Apr-10				Volatility		20.00%
Last Exercisible date	15-Apr-12				Vega		98,748

Fixed Leg — **Pay Fixed**

Roll convention	No Adjustment
Accrual method	30/360
Fixed Cpn Freq	Annual

Fixed Coupon/Strike	**5.25%**
Par Swap Rate	4.6162%

European Option results

Option Price	1,881,620
Option Price / Principal	1.882%

Swaption Details

1 Nodes

Start Date	DCF	t	pvbp	FWD	VOL	Stike	Eur price
15-Apr-10	0.80682	5.00000	2.19335	5.1271%	20.0%	5.250%	1.882%

The vega risk of the swaption is given within the model and is equal to US\$98,748, for the given notional size of US\$100 million. For a 1% change in the implied volatility the price of the swaption would change by US\$98,748, everything else being equal. To reduce the vega exposure we need to trade an offsetting option, an option with negative vega. We calculate the delta risk of the option by running the "risk simulation" within the Curveßuilder model. We see that the overall PV01 of the swaptions is US\$11,917, however the sensitivity at different points of the curve is significant, as a result of the optionality. To reduce the delta risk you could enter into an offsetting delta risk using plain vanilla interest rate swaps. We reduce negative PV01 risk by entering into a pay fixed IRS, while we reduce positive PV01 by entering into a receive fixed IRS.

Swaption Delta Risk
Total = \$11,917

SWAPS	
2.0 Years	-10
3.0 Years	-18
4.0 Years	-279
5.0 Years	-25,481
7.0 Years	25,133
10.0 Years	12,572

Using the Curveßuilder model we can calculate the value of a Bermudan option and see that it is worth marginally more, than a European swaption, given the fact that there are several more possible exercise dates. The Bermudan is worth 2.042% vs. 1.882% for the one time call European swaption. The Bermudan is worth less than the sum of the individual European option prices, since there is a chance that the option will exercise early and the later options would automatically expire worthless. There is no close form solution to price Bermudan swaptions, since the expiry is path dependent we therefore need to value a Bermudan swaption using a more complex one factor no arbitrage models. The output from the model provides the individual prices of the European options on various exercise dates for comparative purposes only; they do not factor into our Bermudan pricing.

Figure 10

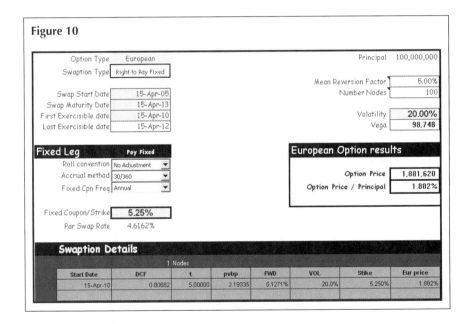

Option Type	European
Swaption Type	Right to Pay Fixed
Swap Start Date	15-Apr-05
Swap Maturity Date	15-Apr-13
First Exercisible date	15-Apr-10
Last Exercisible date	15-Apr-12

Principal	100,000,000
Mean Reversion Factor	5.00%
Number Nodes	100
Volatility	20.00%
Vega	98.748

Fixed Leg — Pay Fixed

Roll convention	No Adjustment
Accrual method	30/360
Fixed Cpn Freq	Annual

Fixed Coupon/Strike	5.25%
Par Swap Rate	4.6162%

European Option results

Option Price	1,881,620
Option Price / Principal	1.882%

Swaption Details

1 Nodes

Start Date	DCF	t	pvbp	FWD	VOL	Stike	Eur price
15-Apr-10	0.80682	5.00000	2.19335	5.1271%	20.0%	5.250%	1.882%

We run the risk simulation to calculate the delta of the Bermudan swaption. The overall PV01 of the swaptions is US$9,573.

Table 7

	Swaption Delta Risk Total PV01: $12,197		

SWAPS		PV01	Hedge
2.0 Years	-9	191	-46,525 Pay Fixed
3.0 Years	-17	280	-60,081 Pay Fixed
4.0 Years	-237	366	-648,428 Pay Fixed
5.0 Years	-25,151	447	-56,213,548 Pay Fixed
7.0 Years	22,539	599	37,619,184 Rec Fixed
10.0 Years	15,079	799	18,861,788 Rec Fixed

CALLABLE BONDS

Swaptions can be used to structure callable bonds. A callable bond is where the issuer has the right but not the obligation to redeem the bond before the final maturity date.[8] A bank issues a 5-year fixed rate bond and has the right to call the bond back after three years, this bond is a 5-year non-call 3-year, referred to as a 5NC3. The investor has a fixed rate bond but has the risk that the bond will be called early. The bond will be called when interest rates are low, which means the investor will have to reinvest at a lower rate. For this re-investment risk the investor receives a higher than normal fixed coupon. In most cases, the issuer will monetize this call option by selling a swaption to a interest rate option trader. In essence the investor is selling a call option to the issuer which the issuer turns around and sells to a swap dealer, the benefit or premium received from the option (swaption) is then shared between the issuer (cheaper than normal funding) and the investor (a higher than normal coupon).

Example
A corporate funds at 6M LIBOR flat, they issue a 5-year non-call 3-year bond paying a fixed rate of 4.577%. Rather than retaining the call feature they monetise the swaption by selling it to a swap dealer. The premium they receive for the swaption compensates the corporate for the higher fixed rate payable on the bond. In this example the corporate enters into a 5-year initial hedge and then sells a 3- into 2-year receiver swaption.

The initial interest rate swap hedge is for five years. The current 5-year PAR rate is 4.3677% (IRS has a fair value of zero) but rather than receive the PAR rate they receive a higher fixed rate of 4.577%. This hedge will thus have a negative NPV (we need to pay cash in order to receive a higher than PAR fixed rate). At the same time they sell a receiver swaption, for which they will receive an upfront premium. We derived the fixed rate of 4.577% by solving for a fixed rate that a net or combined NPV of zero. We need to solve for this fixed rate through an iterative process since the price of the swaption is dependent on the fixed rate and the value of the combine package is dependent on the applicable fixed rate.

Cost of initial 5-year hedge:	−US$926,500	per US$100 Mil
Premium of receiver swaption:	+US$926,071	per US$100 Mil
Net cost of structure	−US$429	per US$100 Mil

The net cost of the callable structure is now close to zero, which implies that the initial (fair value) price of the callable bond is PAR/100%.

If in three years' time the current 2-year PAR swap rate is lower than 4.577%, the swaption expires in the money and the swap dealer exercises the swaption. The corporate is then obligated to pay the fixed rate to the swap dealer rather than to the Bond holders, which results in the note being called[9] (as there is no underlying hedge). It is not so much that the bond is called but more that the underlying hedge is called. If the initial hedge and swaption were done with the same counterparty they can effectively cancel the two swaps at no cost.

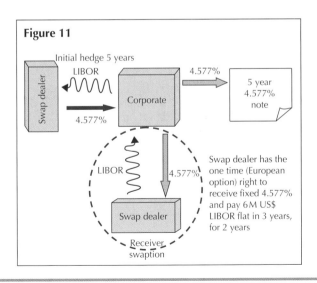

Figure 11

We can also structure a callable bond using a payer swaption. In this structure (a combination of the fixed rate bond and a swaption) the initial hedge is three years, where the corporate receives a higher fixed rate than the current 3-year PAR swap rate. This initial hedge will have a negative value. The corporate then sells a payer swaptions (3-year option on a 2-year swap) which they receive an upfront premium.

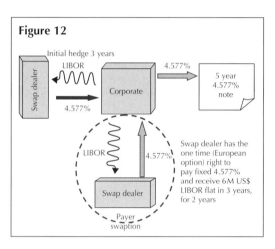

Figure 12

Cost of initial 3-year hedge: −US$1,203,500   per US$100 Mil
Premium of payer swaption: +US$1,203,074   per US$100 Mil
Net cost of structure   −US$426   per US$100 Mil

Regardless of how the callable bond is structured the net results (price and mechanics) are the same.

While the investor has the risk of an early call if interest rates are low (reinvestment risk) they are compensated in the form of a higher coupon. The issuer on the other hand also has the risk that they have shorter term funding. Instead of 5-year funding they may only have 3-year funding, which is a risk to the corporate. While they may not have any "economic" risk they do run term risk with callable bonds. Generally an entity will issue a callable bond provided that the after hedge cost of funding is lower. In this example the corporate may have a general funding level of LIBOR +0bps, but through the issuance of a callable bond they maybe able to fund at LIBOR −15bps, saving 15bps per annum on their net funding cost (albeit they have the risk of an early call).

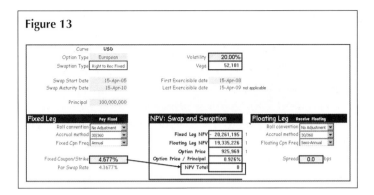

Figure 13

We can use the built in callable bond calculator in Curvebuilder which combines the initial interest rate swap hedge with an appropriate receiver swaption. For a given level of Funding (LIBOR flat in this case) we solve for a NPV of zero by changing the bonds FIXED rate.

VOLATILITY

The most important input into our Black's option pricing model is the level of volatility. Volatility (σ) measures the uncertainty about the return of underlying interest rates. For a given forward rate the higher the volatility the greater the uncertainty of the actual rate. Volatility can be defined as the standard deviation of the distribution of returns around the forward rate over a one-year period. The graph below shows the distribution probability of interest rates over a period of time given a high volatility and a low volatility.

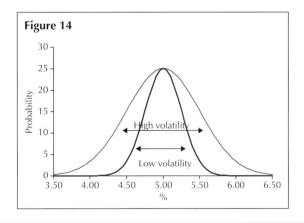

Figure 14

While we can measure the standard deviation of an underlying asset or interest rate using historic data, to price an option we require the volatility going forward, called the option's implied volatility. Implied volatility is the market's estimate of volatility for the underlying asset from now until expiry. The implied volatility is the volatility that is implied from the option's current market price. While historic volatility is a good indication of what implied volatility should be, in practice they will be different. Implied volatility is an independent market driven variable, readily observable through the interbank or broker market. In fact the interbank market trades option volatility rather than the option premium itself. When asking for a bid and offer on a 5-year cap with a strike of 6.00%, rather than quote a cash premium a dealer would quote the dealing volatility levels.

Below is a typical broker screen, which provides implied volatilities for caps and floors. For a 5-year cap or floor with a strike of 6.00% the implied volatility is 18.90%. One noticeable characteristic about implied volatility from the broker's indication is that the level of volatility is not only time dependent it is also strike dependent. An ATM strike for a cap or floor is equal to the equivalent term fixed swap rate.

Table 8

20:16 USD CAP/FLOORS IMPL VOLS										PAGE 1 / 3	
Strike Levels:										■ ICAP	
	Strike		ATM		3.0		4.0		5.0		6.0
1 Year	1) 4.74	14)	11.59	1)	17.30	14)	12.80	27)	11.40	40)	10.80
2 Year	2) 4.65	15)	15.68	2)	21.20	15)	18.20	28)	15.40	41)	15.80
3 Year	3) 4.62	16)	17.75	3)	23.40	16)	19.90	29)	17.40	42)	17.80
4 Year	4) 4.63	17)	18.74	4)	24.20	17)	20.70	30)	18.50	43)	18.60
5 Year	5) 4.66	18)	19.20	5)	24.60	18)	21.10	31)	18.90	44)	18.90
6 Year	6) 4.67	19)	19.48	6)	24.80	19)	21.40	32)	19.20	45)	19.10
7 Year	7) 4.69	20)	19.63	7)	24.80	20)	21.50	33)	19.40	46)	19.20
8 Year	8) 4.70	21)	19.65	8)	24.80	21)	21.50	34)	19.40	47)	19.10
9 Year	9) 4.72	22)	19.57	9)	24.50	22)	21.50	35)	19.30	48)	19.00
10 Year	10) 4.74	23)	19.46	10)	24.40	23)	21.40	36)	19.20	49)	18.80

Source: Bloomberg/ICAP

The following typical broker page shows the implied volatility for a US$ ATM swaption. The rows refer to the option tenor while the columns refer to the underlying swap tenor. A 1-year option on a 5-year ATM swap rate has a market-implied volatility of

18.9%. An ATM strike is equal to the forward rate, the 5-year swap rate one year forward. This table only provides the implied volatility for ATM strikes there will be an entire volatility surface that reflects the implied volatilities for different terms and strikes.

Table 9

USD ATM SWAPTION STRADDLES - IMPLIED VOLATILITIES									
	1Y	2Y	3Y	4Y	5Y	6Y	7Y	8Y	9Y	10Y
1M OPT	12.6	15.1	16.3	16.0	15.6	15.5	15.4	15.3	15.2	15.1
3M OPT	13.6	15.7	16.3	16.4	16.6	16.5	16.4	16.3	16.2	16.0
6M OPT	14.9	16.8	17.3	17.5	17.6	17.5	17.4	17.3	17.1	17.0
1Y OPT	17.7	18.7	18.8	18.8	18.9	18.7	18.6	18.4	18.2	18.1
2Y OPT	20.2	20.1	19.9	19.7	19.6	19.4	19.2	19.0	18.8	18.6
3Y OPT	20.4	20.2	20.0	19.8	19.7	19.4	19.2	19.0	18.7	18.5
4Y OPT	20.3	20.1	19.9	19.7	19.5	19.2	19.0	18.7	18.5	18.2
5Y OPT	20.3	20.2	19.9	19.5	19.2	18.9	18.7	18.4	18.2	17.9
7Y OPT	19.6	19.3	18.9	18.5	18.2	17.9	17.6	17.4	17.1	16.9
10Y OPT	18.2	17.9	17.5	17.1	16.8	16.6	16.3	16.1	15.9	15.7

Source: Bloomberg/ICAP

While the basic assumptions of option pricing assumes a flat volatility (same volatility regardless of the strike rate), in reality we know that this assumption does not hold. Rather than try to develop more complicated models the market instead implements a volatility surface to take into account market imperfections.

In most market securities (stocks, foreign exchange, interest rates) the actual distribution patterns show a few anomalies that force us to alter the volatility assumption of the basic model. The most obvious is a volatility smile.

Volatility smile. Historical data shows that while the lognormal assumption is reasonably accurate, we notice that outliers or moves far out or in the money will occur more than statistically predicted. This implies that options that are far in or out of the money are under-priced given the assumption of constant volatility. In order to take this "fat-tail" anomaly into account we increase the implied volatilities (and thus price) for strikes that are out or in the money.

The following graph illustrates the probability distribution given the markets implied volatility vs. the distribution with a fixed volatility under a lognormal distribution.

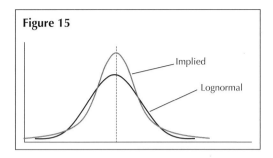

Figure 15

VOLATILITY STRIPPING

The implied volatility for a cap is normally given as a flat vol for a series of options. The volatilities for a cap or floor are "equivalent" volatilities and do not reflect the term structure of volatility. From the market quote we see that the 2-year cap volatility is 15.4% (for an ATM strike) which assumes the same vol regardless of the underlying caplet maturity. In order to value each caplet with the correct implied volatility we need to performance a procedure called caplet stripping in order to extract the market information regarding the volatility for each caplet.

Assume that the underlying period for each caplet is 6M, a 1-year cap vol is thus applicable for the 6-month FRA 6 months forward, so there is no further stripping required. However the 2-year vol of 15.4% is the applicable volatility for three caplets starting in 6 months. But if we already know that the vol for the first FRA should be 11.4% then we will need to solve (or strip out) the applicable vol rates for the other 2 caplets so that the total price of the 2-year cap remains the same (equivalent).

Table 10

Maturity Years	Caplet Volatility	1Y Cap Vol	2Y Cap Vol	3Y Cap Vol	4Y Cap Vol	5Y Cap Vol
0.50	11.4%	11.4	15.4	17.4	18.5	18.9
1.00	13.5%		15.4	17.4	18.5	18.9
1.50	16.5%		15.4	17.4	18.5	18.9
2.00	17.5%			17.4	18.5	18.9
2.50	19.1%			17.4	18.5	18.9
3.00	19.3%				18.5	18.9
3.50	20.1%				18.5	18.9
4.00	19.7%					18.9
4.50	19.9%					18.9

The price of a 2-year cap with a 5.00% strike and a constant implied vol of 15.4% for all three caplets is equal to the sum of the three caplets priced with the same strike, but each caplet priced with different implied volatilities. We price the first caplet with the known implied vol of 11.4%, the second caplet with a vol of 13.67%[10] and the final caplet has an applicable vol of 16.6%.

Pricing a cap with a flat vol of 15.4%, with a price of US$60,652.

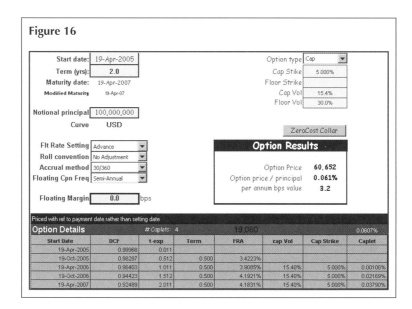

Figure 16

Pricing a cap with term specific implied volatility's, with a same price.

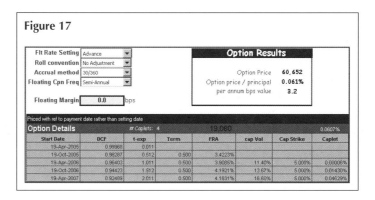

Figure 17

The stripped vol curve now provides the applicable vols for caplets and floorlets depending on when they expire. The caplet volatility now reflects the term structure of volatility. Given that the volatility rates are equivalent it makes no difference when we are pricing spot start caps or floors, however when we are risk managing a portfolio of options or pricing forward starting options, the term structure of volatility becomes important and we should use the stripped vol rather than the flat vol.

The most difficult aspect to pricing and trading European options is not the underlying calculation but more importantly how we obtain market volatilities and how we implement a robust volatility surface given the term structure and smile/skew effects that exist within the market.

DIGITAL OPTIONS

A European digital[11] option provides a discontinuous or fixed payoff if it expires in the money. The amount of payoff is fixed and it is irrelevant how much the underlying is in the money. The payoff profile below compares the payoffs of a European cash-or-nothing digital call option along with that of a European call option.

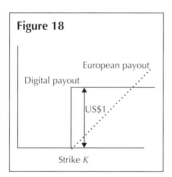

Figure 18

European payout

Digital payout

US$1

Strike K

Rubinstein and Reiner explain in a 1991 paper[12] how to value binary options using Black's '76 model. Since the payoff is not path dependent on the underlying reference rate all we need to know is what the probability that the option ends up in the money. Similar to flipping a coin, payoff if heads = US$1, tails = US$0. Given that the probability of a head is 50% then this simple digital option is worth US$0.50 (50% × US$1). Digital options where the underlying is an interest rate are called digital caps and digital floors. The formula for valuing a digital cap is:

$$\text{digital cap} = \text{dcf}_{\text{expiry}} \times \tau \times N \left(\frac{\ln\left(\frac{F}{K}\right) - \frac{\sigma^2 \times T}{2}}{\sigma \times \sqrt{T}} \right) \quad (11)$$

And the value of a digital floor:

$$\text{digital floor} = \text{dcf}_{\text{expiry}} \times \tau \times N \left(\frac{-\ln\left(\frac{F}{K}\right) + \frac{\sigma^2 \times T}{2}}{\sigma \times \sqrt{T}} \right) \quad (12)$$

where

$\text{dcf}_{\text{expiry}}$	Discount factor at option expiry date;
τ	Period covered by the underlying caplet;
F	Forward rate;
K	strike;
σ	Volatility;
T	Time to maturity;
$N(.)$	Cumulative normal distribution function.

Example
Assume a 1-year European digital cap, where the implied forward rate is 4.75%, where the strike is 5.00%. 1-year volatility is 30%, and the discount factor to the expiry date ($\text{dcf}_{\text{expiry}}$) of the option is 0.9710. The option payout US$1 if in the money and US$0 is out of the money at maturity.

$$d_2 = \frac{\ln\left(\frac{4.75\%}{5.00\%}\right) - \frac{0.30^2 \times 1}{2}}{0.30 \times \sqrt{1}} = -0.3210$$

$$N(d_2) = 0.3741$$

$$\text{Digital cap} = 0.9710 \times 0.3741 = 0.3633$$

The value of a digital cap is therefore US$0.3633 per US$1 payout.

While the fair value of a digital option can be obtained using the above formula most traders will find it very difficult to delta hedge the underlying risk. ATM digital options very close to expiry will have a very large gamma, which means delta can change from 0 to 1 very rapidly as the strike moves in and out of the money with a very small move in the underlying asset price. Rather than price and manage the underlying risk using the above formula, we can synthetically replicate and thus hedge the digital option using a call (caplet) spread.[13] A digital option with a strike of K and a payoff of US$1 has the same payoff at expiry, if in the money, as the long call with a strike of K_1 combined with a short call with a strike of K. The resulting cap spread (S_1) provides the same payoff required as the digital option upon expiry, if in the money.

Table 11

Spot at maturity	Digital payoff	Call spread payoff
$S > K$	US$1	US$1
$K_1 < S < K$	US$0	$S - K_1$
$S < K_1$	US$0	US$0

The only difference in payoffs, and thus pricing, is when the spot rate at expiry is between K_1 and K, the caplet spread option will provide a positive payoff while the digital payoff is equal to zero. So while the true value of a digital option can be obtained using the above formula, the fair or market value will use the more conservative approach of a caplet spread.[14] Once we have the value of the spread option we then need to scale the notional amount of the caplet spread so that the difference in strikes (net payoff) would be equal to that of the digital option of US$1.

$$\text{SpreadPayoff} = \text{LongCap} - \text{ShortCap}$$
$$\text{SpreadPayoff} = (\tau_1 \times (K - S) - \tau_2 \times (S - K_1)) \times \text{Notional}$$

where

$\tau_{1,2}$	term of underlying caplet, in years;
K	Higher strike (strike of digital option);
K_1	Lower strike;
S	Spot or reference rate at expiry.

If we assume that we want a spread payoff equal to US$1, and the capped payoff to occur when $S = K$, we then simplify the formula in order to determine the required notional amount for the long and short cap positions (which will be equal);

$$US\$1 = \tau \times (K - K_1) \times Notional$$

$$Notional = \frac{US\$1}{\tau \times (K - K_1)}$$

If we assume that the digital strike is 5.00% ($K = 5.00\%$), a forward rate of 5.00%, implied volatility of 30% and the term of the underlying interest period is one year, we can examine what notional amounts we require for different cap spreads. The more aggressive the pricing, the tighter the spread and the more volume and liquidity required in order to hedge the trade. The width of the strike spread we choose (difference between the high strike and the low strike, $K - K_1$), therefore depends on the liquidity of the underlying market.

Table 12

$K = 5.00\%$ $K_1=$	Notional of Hedge (per US$1 payoff)	Price Per US$1
4.50%	US$200	0.5089
4.85%	US$666	0.4604
4.95%	US$2,000	0.4470
4.999%	US$100,000	0.4405
Digital formula (11) Price		0.4404

DIGITAL OPTION APPLICATIONS
Range accrual swap
We can use digital options to construct a range accrual swap. A range accrual swap is where the payment or coupon is paid, provided that underlying interest rate index, such as 6M LIBOR, stays within a predefined range.

Example of a range accrual swap

Term   5 years
Client pays   6M LIBOR
Client receives 8.00% $\times n/N$, payable annually
n Number of days in the period where the index fixes within range
N Total number of days in the period, 365 days
Index   6-Months US$ LIBOR
Range   3.50–6.50%

Figure 19

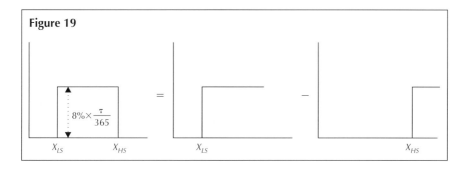

A range accrual swap can be priced as a series of daily corridor or collar options. For every business day (three days for a Friday to include weekends) we buy a corridor options. A corridor option is a long digital call option with the strike equal to the lower range, and a short digital call option with a strike equal to the upper range. The long call earns a fixed payoff if the index (6M LIBOR) is greater than the lower bound, and the short call options pays the fixed payoff away if the index is above the upper range. The digital payoff is equal to cash payment required for the one day of a fixed accrual coupon of 8%.

$$\text{Daily payoff} = 8.00\% \times 1/365 \times \text{Notional}$$
$$= \text{US\$219.18 per US\$1 million}$$

Each day that the underlying index is within the given range we need a corridor option to pay off US\$219.18 per US\$1 million notional in order to provide a return equal to the accrual coupon rate of 8.00%.

While the each individual daily corridor option is priced to the individual expiry date, the payoff accrues and then is paid on each coupon roll date. While there is a theoretical mismatch in timing of the options payout and the coupon payment dates, this effect is generally insignificant and is not considered in the pricing. When the coupon payment period is extended to 12 months the timing effect will have a more significant impact.

In this example we are pricing the range accrual in swap form rather than charging an upfront premium. When we structure an asset we price options in swap form to reflect the fact that the issuer will be paying a floating rate of interest which is swapped into a structured coupon and then paid to the investor. An issuer of a struc-tured note has vanilla floating rate funding while the investor earns a "structured" coupon, which is based on the options payoff. Regardless of how much the investor earns (0% or 8%) the issuer pays the same level of funding,[15] since the issuer hedges the coupon payment. Range accrual swaps are a popular structured asset, as they are relatively easy to price, and understand from an investor's point of view.

In a range accrual swap we structure the range accrual variables (fixed accrual coupon and the applicable range) in order that:

$$\text{NPV (Funding: 6M US\$ LIBOR)} = \text{NPV (SUM: Daily corridor options)}$$

The amount of interest we expect to receive, as determined by the forward rates, equals the sum of the daily corridor options we have purchased. If they do not equal then we can adjust either the fixed coupon or adjust the applicable index range. In some case we can have multiple, bullish or bearish ranges to better reflect an investors view on interest rates.

Multiple ranges: Year1 3.00–5.00%, Year2 3.50–5.50%
Bearish range: 4.00–99%
Bullish range: 0.00–4.50%

Regardless of the view on interest rates we need to structure the desired range around a fixed coupon so that the expect sum of money received (on the issuer's funding) equal to the sum of the required options.

For a 5-year structure there are many options to risk manage (from a writer's point of view) and it is generally done on a portfolio basis rather than by individual options. For a 5-year swap we would need to structure, price and risk manage approximately 1130 daily corridor options (5y × 260 days).

Again we can price the fair value of the daily corridor options using the digital formula provided or we can use a more realistic and conservative approach and price each digital option as a call spread. While the computation is more involved, from a risk management perspective it is more practical.

Periodic knock-in cap

We can combine options to structure a knock-in or knock-out cap (barrier caps). A knock-in (KI) cap is when the cap does not become active or live unless a barrier rate is reached. We structure this periodic knock-in (or knock-out) feature, where the barrier is applicable for the current interest rate period, not for the entire term of the structure (a periodic knocked-in). Initially the barrier rate is set in the money, and since the barrier rate may never be reach, and the option may never become active, the price of the option will be lower than a plain vanilla European cap.

Under a knock-in (KI) cap the payoff profile is similar to that of a regular cap, the only difference is that the payment is conditional on the barrier rate being reached before expiry. The payoff of a KI cap is:

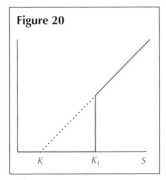

Figure 20

$(S - K)$ subject to the barrier rate, K_1 being reached, where S is the LIBOR rate at maturity.

A KI cap is structured using a combination of a long cap with an out of the money strike of K_1, and a long digital option with a strike equal to K_1 with a payoff equal to $(K_1 - K)$. If the barrier is reached the vanilla cap provides the upside payoff while the digital options increases all payoffs by the required fixed payment.

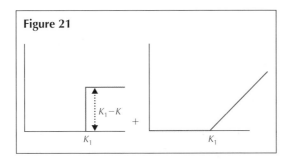

Figure 21

Example

In our initial cap pricing example where the FRA was 4.501%, vol = 17.4%, strike = 5%, term = 2.5y, dcf = 0.90546, the value of the option was US$1,415 per million. If we structure it as a knock-in cap with a barrier rate of 5.50% the options combination is worth $1,078 ($853 for European option plus US$284 for the digital option).

A table of the price of a knock-in cap with a strike of 5.00% and various barriers, compared to a plain vanilla option that is worth US$3,049 per US$1 million.

Table 13

KI barrier	Price
Vanila	US$1,415
5.25%	US$1,386
5.50%	US$1,078
6.00%	US$638

As an alternative we could purchase an out of the money option which would be even cheaper. For a vanilla European cap with a strike of 6.00%, the cost would be US$500, compared to the value of a KI cap with a strike of 5.00% and a barrier of 6.00%: US$638.

Application

A hedger of a floating rate obligation may decide to enter into a KI cap if they had the view that short term interest rates were going to be lower than the forward rates. In this case they would prefer to remain in floating and then buy protection in the event that their view was wrong. A KI cap provides the required protection but at a cheaper premium than a same strike European cap, albeit with slightly more risk.

A knock-out (KO) cap is similar to a vanila cap, however if a higher (in the money) barrier rate is reached then the underlying cap is knocked out, but only for that specific interest period (a periodic KO cap). If the cap is knocked out the hedger is then forced to pay the (higher) vanila LIBOR rate. While the cost of the underlying cap will be cheaper, compared to a European cap, there is the aditional risk that the cap will be knocked out if rates are too high. The further the strike is set out of the money the less value the KO feature will have and the closer the price will be to a vanila European cap. While the cost of the option maybe cheaper this hedging strategy is only a partial hedge as the hedger still faces the risk of paying higher rates if the cap is knocked out.

Periodic knock-out swap

We can also use a combination of an interest rate swap and options to subsidise the fixed rate payable. A corporate issues floating rate debt and decides to swap the proceeds into a fixed rate obligation. In this scenario the corporate has the view that short-term rates will be higher than the forwards are predicting. They also have a view that while short-term rates will remain high they probably will not increase too dramatically over the term of their loan. Rather than just pay the fixed swap rate, the corporate can take a strategic view on rates and through the use of an option strategy reduce the fixed rate payable. In a PAR vanilla swap the corporate would pay a fixed 4.32% and receive floating (to pay the underlying loan). A knockout swap is a hedge where a counterparty pays a lower fixed (swap) rate, receive floating, and on each fixing date as long as a higher barrier rate has not been reached the corporate pays the subsidised fixed swap rate. If the barrier is reached the underlying IRS knocks out, and the client is left with an unhedged floating rate exposure, for that period only. The hedger pays the lower fixed rate as long as short-term rates do not reach the barrier rate. If LIBOR reaches the barrier level the hedge is knocked out and the corporate ends up paying the higher LIBOR rate, but only for that period (periodic knock-out). If LIBOR falls below the barrier rate thereafter, the lower fixed rate continues. The biggest risk to the hedger is that LIBOR increases above the barrier rate immediately and remains very high.

Example
5-year swap

Client pays fixed:	4.10%
Receive floating:	US$ 6M LIBOR reset every 6 months
Knock-out condition:	If 6M LIBOR $\geq 7.00\%$ at reset date no cash flow would be exchanged in that period: swap resumes if LIBOR is below 7.00% on any subsequent reset rate.

We can structure this swap with the use a vanilla IRS, and a series of European and digital interest rate caplets. This swap is optional on both legs of the IRS, so each leg must be structured in order to get the desired payoff profile.

Under a normal IRS the fixed leg is a simple fixed rate payment for the life of the swap. Under a periodic KO swap the fixed leg is structured as a fixed rate payment plus a long digital option.

Knock Out Swap: Fixed leg components: (from the swap dealer's point of view)

❑ receive a subsidised fixed rate 4.10%
❑ short a digital cap, payout 4.10% barrier at 7.00%

The corporate pays the fixed rate of 4.10% for the life of the swap, and buys a European digital cap, where they pay a fixed payment equal to 4.10% if LIBOR reaches the target rate of 7.00%. This combination essentially knocks out (cancels) the fixed payment once the barrier rate is reached.

Pay fixed leg (from dealer's point of view)

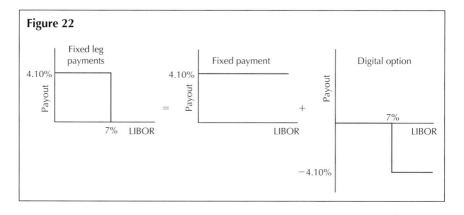

Figure 22

On the floating leg, normally LIBOR is received for the life of the swap, while under a KO swap the floating leg is structured with the combination of receiving LIBOR, and a short cap and a short digital option.

Knock Out Swap: Floating leg components: (from the customer's point of view)

❑ receive US$ LIBOR
❑ short a vanilla cap, strike rate 7.00%
❑ short a digital cap, payout 7.00% barrier at 7.00%

Receive floating leg: (from the customers point of view)

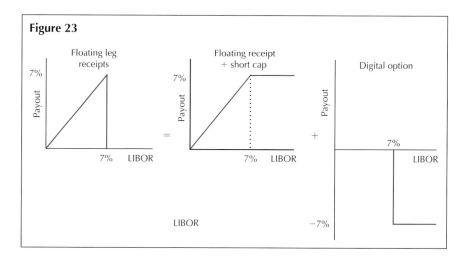

Figure 23

The premium received from the short options allows us to subsidise the fixed coupon (on the fixed leg) even further. The corporate will receive LIBOR up to a maximum rate of 7.00%, the short cap limits the amount received. This combination essentially knocks out the floating payment by paying away the capped LIBOR rate.

We price the structure so that the sum of components equals zero:

NPV (fixed leg) less NPV (floating leg) = 0 NPV
NPV (fixed payment + long digital cap)
  − NPV (LIBOR – short caplet, short digital) = 0

We adjust the subsidized fixed rate and the barrier until this zero NPV condition is true.

The further the barrier rate is away from the forward rates the less value the knock-out option will have. A barrier set far out of the money will have little optional value and as such the fixed rate will be very close to the vanilla swap rate. However if the barrier rate is close to the LIBOR rate, the fixed rate will be very close to the initial

LIBOR fixing and the probability that the structure is knock-out will be very high, thus leaving the corporate with no hedge.

1   Example from Hull, J., "Options, Futures and other Derivatives", page 307.

2   The FRA or implied forward rates are obtained from our zero curve models.

3   The margin is applicable to all coupon periods including the initial period, where no caplet applies.

4   No premium is paid upfront, the cap premium is paid for by giving up some of the upside potential.

5   Spread will be different given the bid/offer spread on the cap.

6   The forward rate, dcf_{expiry} and $PV01_F$ are obtained from our zero curve models.

7   The value $N(\cdot)$ can be done using the excel function = NORMSDIST (.)

8   Sometimes these bonds are referred to as early redeemable or extendible bonds. A 5-year bond callable after 3-years is the same as a 3-year bond where the issuer has the right to extend the issue for an additional 2-years.

9   The issuer is not forced to call the note but if the fixed rate payable on the existing bond were higher than the current cost of funding they would be better off by calling the note.

10 We need to interpolate the 1.5y, 2.5y, 3.5y and 4.5y vol points in order to fully strip the curve.

11 Also known as a binary option.

12 Binary options "unscrambling the binary code" *Risk* October 1991.

13 Also in some less developed (currency) options markets where there may not be a liquid market for digital options, they can be created synthetically using a call spread.

14 In many cases you will notice that the fair value of an underlying option or derivative is not equal to the true or market value. When the underlying risks cannot be quantified or hedged away effectively or when traders build up a significant unwanted position, they will need to "adjust" their prices in order to compensate for this unwanted position. The true price will reflect the fact that they may need to hedge a position in a more conservative or expensive manner.

15 Institutions will issue structured to achieve cheaper financing compared to a regular fixed bullet coupon or an FRN.

10

Further Interest Rate Swaps and Options

Whenever there are variations from a vanilla swap or FRA rate there requires pricing adjustments to the vanilla rates. Typical adjustments include the timing of coupon payments, for example an in arrears fixing FRA or a constant maturity swap (CMS). We will also need to make adjustments when the payment is in another currency, for example in a differential or quanto swap.

While we can hedge these instruments using vanilla products, but because of the slight variations there will always be a pricing differential. This implies there is an arbitrage profit to be made after hedging the interest rate risk using vanilla products. The existence of arbitrage profit means the pricing is not fair value and therefore we need to make an adjustment to our variant product pricing in order to eliminate this arbitrage profit. While we can calculate the expected forward rates from our zero curve, in order to calculate the fair value forward rate we need to make an adjustment to the derived rate to reflect the pricing differential.

In general the underlying pricing differential is caused by convexity and the adjustments made to the pricing are known as convexity adjustments. A bond or interest rate swap's price has a price yield relationship that is convex rather than linear. Figure 1 illustrates this convex relation that exists between the swaps value and changes in underlying interest rates, the same as we see with a fixed rate bond. So when we price derivatives based on the forward rate we need to include an adjustment to take into the underlying convexity.

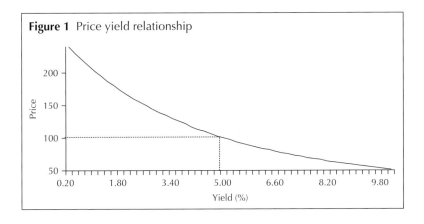

Figure 1 Price yield relationship

CMS

A constant maturity swap (CMS) rate is the PAR swap rate for a constant term. The CMS rate is a floating index, which changes on a daily basis while the term of the swap remains constant. A CMS swap is when the floating leg fixing index is equal to a (CMS) swap rate rather than a short-term index, such as LIBOR.

Vanilla IRS example

Swap term:	5-years
Client rec:	4.32%, semi annual 30/360
Client pays:	6 M US$ LIBOR, payable every 6 month, 30/360
	Set in advance of the interest calculation period, paid in arrears.

CMS IRS example

Swap term:	5-years
Client rec:	4.594%, semi annual 30/360
Client pays:	3-year CMS rate, payable every 6 month, 30/360
	Set in advance of the interest calculation period, paid in arrears.

The mechanics behind the CMS rate fixing is similar to that of any floating rate index. Every business day a group of relevant banks are polled, asked what they are quoting as their 2, 3, 4, 5...30 year fixed swap rates. The results are averaged and then posted on a relevant fixing page via an electronic data feed service. The most commonly used CMS fixing page is ISDAFIXING1, which is available via Reuters.

We value a CMS swap using the same method as a conventional IRS. We estimate the expected floating rate coupons, calculate the NPV of the floating interest payments and then solve for a fix rate so that the net NPV is zero. The only difference is that the floating rate coupons are based on the implied forward long-term swap rate rather than short-term FRA rates. We can use the zero curve to calculate the expected forward rates, for example the 3-year fixed swap rate 6, 12, 18, 24…54 months forward.

Where t_0 is today and t_1 is 6 months forward then the coupon payments at t_i on the floating leg is equal to:

Vanilla swap $=$ Notional $\times$ $(t_6 - t_0)/360 \times 6\,\text{M LIBOR as at } t_0$
CMS swap $\quad=$ Notional $\times$ $(t_6 - t_0)/360 \times 3\,\text{Y Swap rate as at } t_0$

For a CMS swap the coupon fixings are similar to that of a forward starting swap so we can hedge a CMS swap with a series of a forward starting vanilla IRS. However the CMS coupon is a linear function of the swap rate, while the value (NPV) of a swap is a convex function of the same swap rate. Given the convexity, if we hedge a long (receive) CMS rate with a forward starting swap the net result for a move in rates will always be a profit. The existence of arbitrage profit implies that the calculated forward rate is not a fair rate, where the expected NPV equals zero. We therefore need to adjust the implied forward rate for the explicit convexity present in our vanilla hedge.

The convexity adjustment for the forward rate has been proven to be worth[1]:

$$S\_cvx = -\frac{1}{2}\sigma^2 S^2 t \frac{P''(S)}{P'(S)} \tag{1}$$

where

S	forward swap rate;
σ_S	volatility of the forward swap rate;
t	time to payment date (in years);
$P'(S)$	first derivative of swap price with respect to the swap rate (S);
$P''(S)$	second derivative of swap price with respect to the swap rate (S).

A swap with a coupon of S, a payment frequency of f, and a yield to maturity of y, has a price $P(S)$ of

$$P(S) = \Sigma \frac{S/f}{\left(1+\dfrac{y}{f}\right)^{ft}} + \frac{1}{\left(1+\dfrac{y}{f}\right)^{fT}}$$

$P(S)$ is the price of the forward starting swap which is a function of the forward rate S, $P'(S)$ is the first derivative or the duration of the price, while $P''(S)$ is the second derivative which is the convexity of the price. Given that duration is always positive and convexity is always negative the convexity adjustment will always be positive. CMS convexity adjusted forward rates will be higher than vanilla forward starting swap rates. Rather than derive the first and second partial derivative we can approximate the convexity adjustment where[2]:

$$\frac{1}{2}\sigma^2 S^2 t \times \frac{P''(S)}{P'(S)} = S\sigma^2 t \left(\frac{S_T}{\left(1+\dfrac{S}{f}\right)\left[\left(1+\dfrac{S}{f}\right)^t - 1\right]} - 1 \right) \tag{2}$$

Therefore the convexity adjusted forward rate is the implied forward rate plus the convexity adjustment.

$$S\_cvx = S - S\sigma^2 t \left(\frac{S_T}{\left(1+\dfrac{S}{f}\right)^{(Tf+1)} - \left(1+\dfrac{S}{f}\right)} - 1 \right) \tag{3}$$

where

S	forward swap rate;
σ_S	volatility of the forward swap rate;
T	term of underlying rate;
t	time to payment date (in years).

While the above formula takes into account the convexity adjustment we also need to consider a timing adjustment. Under a CMS swap the payment is made at the reset date while for a normal swap the payment is made at the end of the reset period. We therefore have to make an additional timing adjustment to the implied forward rate. The convexity timing adjusted forward rate is equal to:[3]

$$S\_cvx\_t = S\_cvx \times \exp\left(\frac{-\rho\sigma_S\sigma_R t S\tau}{1+S\tau}\right) \tag{4}$$

where

S	forward swap rate;
σ_S	volatility of the forward swap rate;
σ_R	volatility of the FRA (caplet);
ρ	correlation between FRA (R) and the swap rate S;
t	time to payment date (in years).

Normally the timing adjustment is negative, as long as short-term and long-term rates are positively correlated which is generally the case, as you would expect. We can now calculate the time and convexity adjusted forward rates so we can fairly value the CMS floating leg.

Example
The 3-Year (semi-annual) swap rate 4.5-years forward is 5.0043%, the swap rate volatility (σ_s) is 20% (swaption vol) and the FRA (σ_R) volatility is 30% (caplet vol) and the correlation between short-term rates and longer term 3y swap rates is 75%. Using Equation (3) we approximate the convexity and time adjusted forward swap rate:

S	5.0043%
σ_S	20%
σ_R	30%
T	3
t	4.5

First solve for the convexity adjusted forward rate:

$$S\_cvx = 5.0043\% - 5.0043\% \times 0.2^2 \times 4.5 \times \left[\frac{5.0043\% \times 3.0}{\left(1+\frac{5.0043\%}{2}\right)^{(3\times2+1)} - \left(1+\frac{5.0043\%}{2}\right)} - 1\right]$$

$$S\_cvx = 5.0797\%$$

And the time adjusted, convexity adjusted rate is:

$$Si\_cvx\_t = 5.0797\% \times \exp\left[\frac{-0.75 \times 0.2 \times 0.3 \times 4.8248\% \times 4.5 * 0.5}{1 + 4.8248\% \times 0.5}\right]$$

$$S\_cvx\_t = 5.0555\%$$

We now have the convexity and time adjusted fair value forward swap rate (3-years swap rate) 4.5-years forward, which is the expected rate for our coupon payment in 5-years time. We can continue this process for all expected coupon payments. We can then solve for a fair value CMS fixed rate where:

We can use the Curveßuilder pricing model to complete the calculations for all coupon fixings, and then calculate the fair value CMS fixed rate of 4.617%. The pricing difference, compared with a vanilla 5-year IRS, is 29.7 bps higher (4.617% less 4.32% 5 Y vanilla PAR swap rate).

Table 1

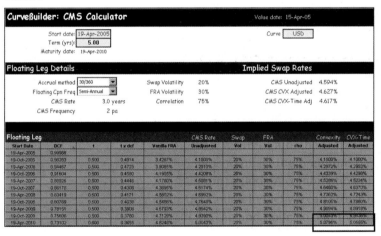

CurveBuilder: CMS Calculator								Value date: 15-Apr-05		
Start date: 19-Apr-2005							Curve	USD		
Term (yrs): 5.00										
Maturity date: 19-Apr-2010										

Floating Leg Details					Implied Swap Rates					
Accrual method 30/360		Swap Volatility	20%		CMS Unadjusted	4.594%				
Floating Cpn Freq Semi-Annual		FRA Volatility	30%		CMS CVX Adjusted	4.627%				
CMS Rate	3.0 years	Correlation	75%		CMS CVX-Time Adj	4.617%				
CMS Frequency	2 pa									

Floating Leg					CMS Rate	Swap	FRA		Convexity	CVX-Time
Start Date	DCF	t	t x dcf	Vanilla FRA	Unadjusted	Vol	Vol	rho	Adjusted	Adjusted
19-Apr-2005	0.99968									
19-Oct-2005	0.98283	0.500	0.4914	3.4287%	4.1000%	20%	30%	75%	4.1000%	4.1000%
19-Apr-2006	0.94467	0.500	0.4723	3.9085%	4.2910%	20%	30%	75%	4.2972%	4.2953%
19-Oct-2006	0.91604	0.500	0.4580	4.1905%	4.4208%	20%	30%	75%	4.4339%	4.4296%
19-Apr-2007	0.88926	0.500	0.4446	4.1780%	4.5081%	20%	30%	75%	4.5286%	4.5234%
19-Oct-2007	0.86170	0.500	0.4308	4.3895%	4.5174%	20%	30%	75%	4.6460%	4.6370%
19-Apr-2008	0.83419	0.500	0.4171	4.5802%	4.6992%	20%	30%	75%	4.7362%	4.7243%
19-Oct-2008	0.80769	0.500	0.4038	4.5488%	4.7640%	20%	30%	75%	4.8105%	4.7980%
19-Apr-2009	0.78151	0.500	0.3908	4.6793%	4.8542%	20%	30%	75%	4.9094%	4.8918%
19-Oct-2009	0.75606	0.500	0.3780	4.7129%	4.9390%	20%	30%	75%	5.0043%	4.9836%
19-Apr-2010	0.73102	0.500	0.3895	4.8248%	5.0043%	20%	30%	75%	5.8796%	5.0655%

While the pricing of a CMS swap is relatively straightforward the estimation of the pricing parameters is slightly more complex. In order to get the fair value we need accurate estimations of the appropriate forward cap and swaption volatilities and if possible incorporate any volatility smile information. We also need to estimate the correlation between short-term and the CMS term rate, which we can estimate from historical analysis. While the estimation of these parameters is important the effect on the pricing is not very significant so as a reasonable approximation we can use the spot starting vols, provided that the underlying terms (term to payment date and the underlying FRA term) are not too long.

CMS APPLICATIONS
Basis swap
A corporate with a floating rate liability that has a view that the longer term (swap) rates will be lower than the forwards are implying can enter into a CMS basis swap in order to benefit from the lower swap rates.

In the previous section we calculated that the CMS structure is worth 29.7 bps per annum. We can incorporate that pricing difference into a basis swap, where the client receives vanilla floating LIBOR and pays the 3-year CMS rate. Not only will the hedger benefit from lower rates (if they do in fact turn out to be lower) but also the interest payment will be subsidised by the 29.7 bps value the CMS structure provides.

CMS basis swap

Term:	5-Years
Client receives:	6 M US$ LIBOR, set in advance paid in arrears
Client pays:	3-year CMS less 29.7 bps, set in advance paid in arrears
NPV:	Zero

CMS cap/floors
Now that we have determined the fair value CMS rates, we can use the same pricing model used the Black '76 equation to price European CMS caps or floors. There are no further adjustments to the price that is required. This would be useful to incorporate in the above basis swap. In fact the hedger can use the value from the CMS structure to buy a CMS cap in order to provide protection in the event that long-term rates increase.

CMS basis swap with a cap

Term:	5-Years
Client receives:	6 M US$ LIBOR, set in advance paid in arrears
Client pays:	3-year CMS rate subject to a Capped rate of 6.50%, set in advance paid in arrears
NPV/Premium:	Zero

The cap is purchased with the 29.7 bps value within the CMS structure. There is no further premium to be paid upfront or on an ongoing basis. In this application the hedger benefits from lower than expected swap rates but has the interest rate protection just in case the rates turn out to be higher.

LIBOR in arrears (LIA)

A LIBOR in arrears swap is similar to a vanilla interest rate swap; the only difference is when the floating rate is fixed. Under a vanilla IRS the floating interest rate is fixed at the beginning of the interest period and paid at maturity (set in advance paid in arrears). For a LIA floating rate coupon the interest rate is fixed at the end of the interest rate period (normally two business days before payment date for settlement purposes) and also paid at the end of the interest rate period (set and paid in arrears).

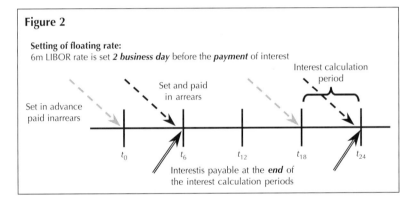

Figure 2

Setting of floating rate:
6m LIBOR rate is set **2 business day** before the **payment** of interest

Interest calculation period

Set and paid in arrears

Set in advance paid in arrears

t_0 t_6 t_{12} t_{18} t_{24}

Interest is payable at the **end** of the interest calculation periods

In order to see how a LIBOR in arrears swap is priced and hedged we compare the LIA cashflows with those of a vanilla swap and a forward starting swap.

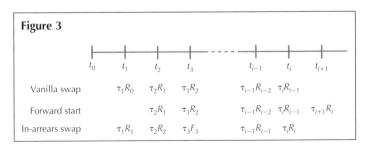

Figure 3

	t_0	t_1	t_2	t_3		t_{i-1}	t_i	t_{i+1}
Vanilla swap		$\tau_1 R_0$	$\tau_2 R_1$	$\tau_3 R_2$		$\tau_{i-1} R_{i-2}$	$\tau_i R_{i-1}$	
Forward start			$\tau_2 R_1$	$\tau_3 R_2$		$\tau_{i-1} R_{i-2}$	$\tau_i R_{i-1}$	$\tau_{i+1} R_i$
In-arrears swap		$\tau_1 R_1$	$\tau_2 R_2$	$\tau_3 F_3$		$\tau_{i-1} R_{i-1}$	$\tau_i R_i$	

where

τ_I time in years between t_{i-1} and t_I, interest calculation period;

R_i LIBOR fixing at time t_i.

If we assume that the interest calculation period (τ) are the same for all period, we notice that the LIA swap is similar to a forward starting vanilla swap. The rate fixings and interest payments will be the same for both legs, unlike a vanilla spot start swap, which has a slightly different set of fixing rates (initial and final rates differ). The only difference between a forward starting vanilla and a LIA swap is the timing of the floating payments. So we can use a forward starting swap to price and hedge an LIA swap, however we will need to make an adjustment to the forward rates given the slight difference in the timing of payments. The adjustment is similar to the timing adjustment we did to the CMS rate using Equation (4). In fact if we assume that the correlation between the two rates is 1 ($\rho = 1$), which is the case since they are the same rate, and thus the vol is the same for each of the rates ($\sigma_R = \sigma_S$), and if we approximate exp(x) as $(1 - x)$ then we can rearrange Equation (4) to get the following equation to calculate the fair value FRA rate given a vanilla FRA (R_i)

$$R_i\_adj = R_i + \frac{R_i^2 \sigma_i^2 t \tau}{1 + R_i \tau} \tag{5}$$

where

R_i unadjusted forward rate;

σ_i volatility of the forward/caplet;

t maturity of the forward/caplet;

τ interest period of R_i.

Adjusted FRA (LIA) rate

Assume that on 19-April-2005 the 6-months rate 3-years forward is 4.5488% and the implied caplet volatility from the market is quoted as 30% we can calculate the adjusted FRA rate for the applicable LIA swap.

R_i 5.5488%

σ_i 30%

t 3-years

τ 0.5-years

$$R_i\_adj = 4.5488\% + \frac{4.5488\% \times 30\%^2 \times 3 \times 0.5}{1 + 4.5488\% \times 0.5}$$

$$R\_adj = 4.5761\%$$

We then adjust all FRA rates within our interest rate swap in order to determine the fair value fixed rate, which provides a swap NPV of zero. We can use the Curveßuilder model to complete all the adjustments to all the applicable forward rates, see Table 2. We notice that the vanilla PAR swap rate for three years is 4.100%, while the forward starting swap rate is 4.2910%, and the adjusted in-arrears swap rate is 4.3059%. Most of the value or difference between a vanilla IRS and a LIA swap rate comes from the forward rates. The magnitude of this difference is a result of the steepness of the yield curve. The steeper the yield curve the higher the forward rates, and the more value the LIA swap structure will have. Generally the yield curve is upward sloping (long-term rates higher than short-term rates) which means the forward swap rate is higher than the spot rate. However, when the curve is inverted (longer-term rates are lower than short-term rates) the forwards are lower than spot and thus the in arrears PAR swap rates will be lower.

Table 2

Curveßuilder: LIBOR in Arrears Calculator — Value date: 15-Apr-05

Start date: 15-Apr-2005
Term (yrs): 3.00
Maturity date: 15-Apr-2008

Curve: USD

Floating Leg Details

Accrual method: 30/360
Floating Cpn Freq: Semi-Annual
FRA Volatiltiy: 30%

Implied Swap Rates

Vanilla	4.1000%
FWD Starting	4.2940%
In Arrears	4.2943%
In Arrears Adjusted	4.3090% 20.9bps difference

Floating Leg

Start Date	DCF	t	t x dcf	FRA	FWD Start	Advance Vanilla FRA	Arrears Unadjusted FRA	Vol	Arrears Adjusted FRA
15-Apr-2005	1.00000			3.4117%					
15-Oct-2005	0.98323	0.500	0.4916	3.9015%		3.4117%	3.9015%	30%	3.9043%
15-Apr-2006	0.96441	0.500	0.4822	4.1858%	3.9015%	3.9015%	4.1858%	30%	4.1935%
15-Oct-2006	0.94464	0.500	0.4723	4.2081%	4.1858%	4.1858%	4.2081%	30%	4.2198%
15-Apr-2007	0.92518	0.500	0.4626	4.3895%	4.2081%	4.2081%	4.3895%	30%	4.4065%
15-Oct-2007	0.90531	0.500	0.4527	4.5803%	4.3895%	4.3895%	4.5803%	30%	4.6093%
15-Apr-2008	0.88504	0.500	0.4425	4.5488%	4.5803%	4.5803%	4.5488%	30%	4.5761%
15-Oct-2008	0.86536	0.500	0.4327	4.5488%					

While the adjusted rate is not significantly different from the forward starting rate the difference does become more pronounced as the volatility of the caplet rates becomes higher, or when the adjustment time periods (maturity date of the FRA) and interest period of the underlying FRA become longer.

IN ARREARS APPLICATIONS

It is common to apply an in arrears structure when the interest rate view is that the realised forward rates will be lower than the implied FRA. If the view is that forward rates will be lower than the current implied rates then an entity should prefer keeping their floating rate liabilities rather than hedging and locking in a fixed rate using a vanilla IRS. In fact an in arrears structure allows the user to pay the FRA an additional 6-months forward, further capitalising on the view that the realised forward rates will be lower than the implied.

Basis swap

A corporate with a floating rate liability that has a view that the short-term rates will be lower than the implied forwards can enter into an in-arrears structure in order to subsidise their floating rate payment.

In the previous section we calculated that the in-arrears structure is worth 20.9 bps per annum (4.309% in arrears fixed PAR rate less 4.10% vanilla PAR fixed rate). We can incorporate that benefit into a basis swap, where the client receives the vanilla floating LIBOR and pays LIBOR in arrears less 20.9 bps. Not only will the hedger benefit from lower rates but the coupon payment will be subsidized by the 20.9 bps value that the in-arrears structure provides.

LIBOR in arrears basis swap
Term: 3-Years
Client receives: 6 M US$ LIBOR
                  set in advance paid in arrears
Client pays: 6 M US$ LIBOR −20.9 bps,
                  set and paid in arrears
NPV: Zero

We see from the following Curveßuilder pricing output that the value of the in-arrears leg with the −20.9 bps spread has the same value as the vanilla floating leg, the NPV of the combined legs is zero.

Table 3

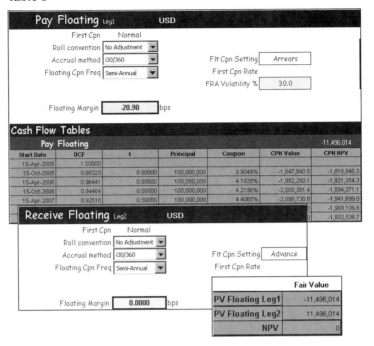

In arrears cap

In the previous example, the view was that interest rates would remain low so the client decides to leave floating rate exposure. The hedger may want to add some protection against interest rates moving higher, just in case they are wrong. In order to do this the hedger can purchase an interest rate cap as described in Chapter 9, but have the price subsidised with an in-arrears structure.

Vanilla cap pricing (in swap form)

Term: 3-Years

Client receives: 6 M US$ LIBOR

Client pays: 6 M US$ LIBOR +33 bps, subject to a cap rate 5.23%

NPV: 0

Table 4

Start date:	19-Apr-2005			Option type	Cap
Term (yrs):	3.0			Cap Stike	4.900%
Maturity date:	19-Apr-2008			Floor Strike	5.000%
Modified Maturity	19-Apr-08			Cap Vol	30.0%
				Floor Vol	17.4%
Notional principal	100,000,000				
Curve	USD				ZeroCost Collar
Flt Rate Setting	Advance			**Option Results**	
Roll convention	No Adjustment				
Accrual method	30/360			Option Price	**922,404**
Floating Cpn Freq	Semi-Annual			Option price / principal	**0.922%**
				per annum bps value	**32.9**
Floating Margin	0.0	bps			

For the vanilla cap the maximum coupon payment is derived from a cap strike rate of 4.90% (which is the cap on the LIBOR fixing not on the coupon payment) plus the floating rate margin of 33 bps, which results in an adjusted cap rate of 5.23%. The 33 bps represent the cost of the cap amortised over the life of the transaction. The premium is paid in swap form rather than as an upfront payment.

In arrears cap pricing (in swap form)

Term: 3-Years
Client receives: 6 M US$ LIBOR
Client pays: 6 M US$ LIBOR +23 bps, subject to a cap rate 5.23% (Assuming 30% vol rate for all caplets)

Table 5

Start date:	19-Apr-2005			Option type	Cap
Term (yrs):	3.0			Cap Stike	5.000%
Maturity date:	19-Apr-2008			Floor Strike	5.000%
Modified Maturity	19-Apr-08			Cap Vol	30.0%
				Floor Vol	17.4%
Notional principal	100,000,000				
Curve	USD				ZeroCost Collar
Flt Rate Setting	Arrears			**Option Results**	
Roll convention	No Adjustment				
Accrual method	30/360			Option Price	**1,219,783**
Floating Cpn Freq	Semi-Annual			Option price / principal	**1.220%**
				per annum bps value	**43.5**
Floating Margin	0.0	bps			

For a cap in arrears structure, the cost of the cap is 43.5 bps pa but the benefit of 20.9 bps as a result of the arrears structure is deducted before adjusting the capped interest rate. The max mum interest payment on a cap in-arrears structure is thus 5.226% (5.00% cap strike + 43.5 bps cost of cap − 20.9 bps arrears benefit).

The hedger essentially enters into a LIBOR *vs.* LIA basis swap and purchases a LIA cap with the extracted value.

Basis swap

Term:	3-Years
Client receives:	6 M US$ LIBOR +0 bp, set in advance paid in arrears
Client pays:	6 M US$ LIBOR +0 bp, set and paid in arrears
NPV:	20.9 bps per annum

The hedger then purchases a LIA cap, with a strike rate of 5.00% which has a cost of 43.5 bps pa. The net cost after deducting the benefit from the basis swap is equal to (approx.) 23 bps per annum. The net payment made by the hedger is therefore:

Client pays:	6 M LIBOR +23 bps, set and paid in arrears, subject to a Max LIBOR fixing of 5.00% or a capped interest payment of 5.23%
NPV:	Zero

The steeper the yield curve the more value is the in-arrears structure and the cheaper the cap will be. If the yield curve was steep enough a hedger could in fact have a free cap, just by paying LIA.

Inverse floating rate note

When an investor has a view that short-term rates will be lower than the implied forwards they can capitalise on this view by buying an inverse floating rate note. The coupon paid will be linked to the actual level of LIBOR and the lower the LIBOR fixings the higher the coupon. While this structure can be structured using conventional LIBOR resets (set in advance paid in arrears) it is normally structured around LIA in order to capture more value from the higher forward rates.

Inverse floating rate note example

Price: 100%
Term: 5-Years
Issuer pays: 6 M LIBOR, set in advance paid in arrears
Issuer receives: 12% less 2 × 6 M LIBOR[4], set and paid in arrears
                    Subject to:
                    Minimum coupon payment of 1.70%
                    Maximum coupon payment of 9.00%

The price is PAR or 100% because the amount of money earned on the funding leg, from the underlying issuer, has the same NPV as the structured coupons. In order to price the underlying hedge for this inverse floating rate note we need to break it down into several different components. Combining the NPV of each component (all figures per 1 million).

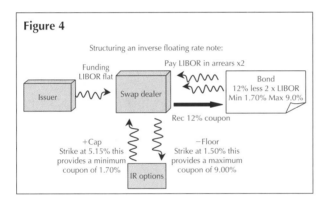

Figure 4

Structuring an inverse floating rate note:

Receive (funding) Leg[5]
    NPV of the interest received from the issuer
    Assuming LIBOR flat funding   +US$193,285
Pay (structured) Leg
    Pay fixed coupon of 12%   −US$536,902
    Rec 2 × LIBOR (in arrears)   +US$402,286
    Long cap;[6] strike 5.15%   −US$58,236
    Short floor; strike 1.50%   +US$768

Net (combined payments)   US$1,201 per US$1 M

In order to ensure the minimum coupon we need to buy an IR cap, to protect against higher rates. The strikes for the long cap are derived from the minimum coupon that the structure pays. The minimum coupon payable is 1.70%, which would occur when LIBOR falls to:

$$1.70\% = 12\% \text{ less } 2 \times \text{LIBOR (in arrears)}$$
$$\text{LIBOR} = 5.15\%$$

We also extract value by structuring in a short IR floor, which provides upfront premium but also limits the upside potential on the coupon we could earn (a floor actually caps the coupon paid). While the floor in this case is not worth very much and probably not worth doing (why cap the coupon when it adds no value to the structure) we have done it here to illustrate how all the components fit together. The strike on the floor required is 1.50% (9.00% = 12% less 2 × LIBOR). We buy a cap to protect the min coupon while we sell a floor to ensure a max coupon regardless of where LIBOR is at the time of fixing.

The net NPV on the combined structure is very close to zero (US$1,201 per US$1 million). The structured bond is therefore priced at PAR (100%). As the value of the components change the swap value will change, as will the price of the underlying bond. This is the initial fair value of the swap, which results in a PAR bond pricing. While the swap is worth PAR, investors may value the structured note differently; the main pricing assumption is that we valued the bond relative to LIBOR flat (which is what we are receiving from the issuer). In other words if we stripped out the optionality from the structured note, the equivalent vanilla floating rate coupon would be LIBOR flat. If the investor thinks a more appropriate credit spread or coupon level for the underlying issuer (given the issuer's credit rating and comparable floating rate debt in the secondary market) was LIBOR plus 50 bps we would need to adjusting our price accordingly, pricing the received (funding) leg assuming a LIBOR +50 bps.

DIFFERENTIAL SWAPS

A differential swap, also known as a diff or quanto swap, is an IRS where one of the legs has an interest payment in one currency while the underlying floating rate interest index is based in another currency. There is no exchange of principal and the swap itself has no exposure to changes in the foreign exchange rate. It allows the user (investor or hedger) to have exposure to a foreign currency interest rate but not the foreign exchange risk. While the user of the diff swap will have no FX risk the swap dealer will need to hedge the FX risk associate with the underlying hedging components of a diff swap.

A hedger or speculator can use a diff swap to take a view on a foreign interest rates but have all payments denominated in a domestic currency, thus no FX risk. For example assume you are the treasurer of a UK corporate with an existing 3-year fixed rate GBP loan. You have the view that GBP interest rates could go higher (hence you decided to lock in the GBP rate with an IRS) you also have the view that US$ LIBOR will be lower over the next 3-years. At the same time you are unclear on the direction of GBP/US$, nor do you want to take any FX risk. You enter into a diff swap where you receive the fixed GBP rate and pay 6-month US$ LIBOR but all payments are denominated in GBP.

As an example

Notional:	GBP10,000,000
Term:	3-Years
Rec fixed rate:	4.08%, semi-annually, 30/360
Pay floating payment:	6-Month US$ LIBOR, 30/360, set in advance paid in arrears
	Payable semi-annually in GBP based on GBP notional
Spot GBP/US$:	1.75 (for reference only)

Assuming that US$ 6 M LIBOR fixes at 3.88% in two years and the FX rate is now GBP/US$ 2.25 then the interest payment on the floating leg is:

$$\text{GBP10 M} \times 180/360 \times 3.88\% = £194,000$$

In fact the GBP/US$ FX rate has nothing to do with the interest payment, there is no FX exposure. The payoff on the floating leg depends on US$ interest rates, so the fixed rate should roughly be equal to the US$ swap rate, rather than the GBP swap rate, even though the payoff is in GBP. The current 3-year US$ swap rate is 4.10%, while the GBP rate is 6.10%.

To hedge the diff swap the trader will enter into a US$ IRS as the primary hedge for the underlying interest rate exposure and then dynamically hedge any FX exposure over the life of the transaction. Since the primary exposure is to changes in US$ rates they enter into a fixed floating US$ IRS. Any gain or loss on the diff swap, as a result of a change in US interest rates will be offset by a loss or a gain on the US$ IRS. But what happens to the hedge over time especially when the FX rate changes.

We examine the FX effects on the underlying hedge by looking at a simplified example. Consider a 6 M US$ FRA quanto into GBP, the 6-month rate 6 months forward (6×6 FRA) is 4.50%, which is hedged with a vanilla US$ FRA. Assume the GBP notional is £1 million, and the initial US$/GBP is 1.75. $t = 0.5$ (6-month).

Payoff on the quanto FRA leg is:
  £1.00 M $\times$ 0.5 $\times$ (R − 4.50%)

Payoff of the vanilla US$ FRA leg is:
  US$1.75 M $\times$ 0.5 $\times$ (R − 4.50%)

Which leg is more valuable? On day one they have the same expected value but the value at maturity depends on the US$ interest rate (R) and the GBP/US$ FX rate at the time of the FRA fixing. If R never moves (R fixes at 4.50%) or if the FX rate never changes from the initial forward rate of 1.75, then the legs will have the same value at fixing.

If $R > 4.50\%$ at fixing then
Quanto leg   = £1 M $\times$ 0.5 $\times$ (5.00% − 4.50%)   = £2,500
US$Vanilla leg = US$1.75 M $\times$ 0.5 (5.00% − 4.50%) = US$4,375
                    Converted to GBP at FX rate on   £1.50 then £2,916
                    fixing date   £2.00 then £2,187

If $R < 4.50\%$ at fixing then
Quanto leg   = £1 M $\times$ 0.5 $\times$ (4.25% − 4.50%) = −£1,250
US$Vanilla leg = US$1.75 M $\times$ 0.5   = −US$2,187
                    (4.25% − 4.50%)
                    Converted to GBP at FX rate £1.50 then −£1,458
                    on fixing date   £2.00 then −£1,094

Assume we are long the quanto leg and short the vanilla leg in the above analysis the following table summarises the results at settlement.

Table 6

GBP/US$	Interest rate		
	4.25%	4.50%	5.00%
1.50	208.3	–	(416.7)
1.75	–	–	–
2.00	(156.3)	–	312.5

The quanto leg is more valuable
  (d) if $R > 4.50\%$ and the GBP have strengthened
  (b) if $R < 4.50\%$ and the GBP has weakened

The vanilla leg is more valuable
  (c) if $R > 4.50\%$ and the GBP has weakened
  (d) if $R < 4.50\%$ and the GBP has strengthened

In order to determine which scenario is most likely to occur we need to know the correlation between the FX rate and the interest rates. If we assume we hedge a long quanto FRA with the vanilla FRA we then will need to adjust the quanto FRA rate to take into account the correlation effect. If there is a positive correlation, we expect a net loss and therefore would want to receive a higher fixed rate in order to compensate for the loss. If the correlation is negative, we would expect to make a net gain and therefore we would be willing to receive a lower fixed rate. The correlation factor used is derived from a historical analysis however it will be the correlation of the rates going forward that affects the hedge effectiveness. It is difficult to hedge the correlation risk therefore traders are careful not to build up significant correlation balances over time.

If US interest rates (R) do not move, there is no effect on the P&L, regardless of what happens to the FX rate. However if the FX rate does move and US rates do not change, then we will need to adjust the notional amount of our original vanilla hedge in order to maintain a valid hedge. If US interest rates (R) do move however, while the FX rate is unchanged, again there is no net impact on the net

P&L, however any further movements in GBP/US$ would cause changes to the net P&L denominated in GBP. We therefore need to neutralise the impact of any further movements in the FX rate on the P&L. The size of the required hedge, equal to the US$ P&L, will keep changing as interest rate and FX rates change therefore dynamic hedging is required.

DIFFERENTIAL SWAP PRICING

In order to take into account the hedging associated with a quanto leg, we need to make an adjustment to the implied FRA rate. As we discussed above the adjustment required is a function of the correlation between the FRA rates and the FX rate. For each FRA, we calculate the quanto adjusted forward rate using the following formula:[7]

$$R_{i\_qadj} = R_i \times \exp(\rho \sigma_{fx} \sigma_i t_i) \qquad (6)$$

where

R_i vanilla unadjusted forward rate;

ρ correlation between the interest rate and FX rate;

σ_{fx} volatility of the underlying FX rate;

σ_i volatility of the underlying FRA rate (caplet vol);

t_i term of the underlying FRA rate.

Quanto adjustment example

Assume that the US$ 6-month FRA rate, 2.5-years forward is 4.5802%. The volatility for the US$ FRAs is 30% while the vol of the GBP/US$ forward rate is 20%. The correlation between US$ interest rates and the GBP/US$ exchange rate is 0.50. The quanto adjusted FRA is therefore:

$$R_i\_qadj = 4.5802\% \times \exp(0.50 \times 0.20 \times 0.30 \times 0.5)$$
$$R_i\_qadj = 4.6494\%$$

We continue the process and derive all the adjusted R_i (FRA$_i$) and then solve for a fair value fixed rate. Table 7 illustrates the all the adjusted FRA rates and then solves for a fair value fixed rate (NPV = 0). The quanto adjusted swap rate comes to 4.083% compared with a vanilla GBP swap rate of 6.10% and a 3-year US$ swap rate is 4.10%.

Table 7

Curveßuilder: Quanto Swap Calculator						Value date:	15-Apr-05		

Start date: 19-Apr-2005
Term (yrs): 3.00
Maturity date: 19-Apr-2008

Base Curve: GBP
FRA Curve: USD

Floating Leg Details   **Fixed Swap Rate: (Base Currency)**

Accrual method: act/360
Floating Cpn Freq: Semi-Annual

Fixed Rate: 4.083%
Fixed Cpn Freq: Semi-Annual

Floating Spread: 0.0 bps
FRA Volatiltiy: 30%

fx Volatiltiy: 20%
Correlation: 0.50

Floating Leg   Advance

	GBP					USD			
Start Date	DCF	t	FRA Vol	fx Vol	Corr	FRA	Adjusted FRA	Fixed	Net NPV
19-Apr-2005	0.99946								
19-Oct-2005	0.97278	0.508	30.0%	20.0%	0.50	3.3682%	3.3682%	-4.083%	-0.70%
19-Apr-2006	0.94464	0.506	30.0%	20.0%	0.50	3.8655%	3.9246%	-4.083%	-0.15%
19-Oct-2006	0.91601	0.508	30.0%	20.0%	0.50	4.1218%	4.1852%	-4.083%	0.09%
19-Apr-2007	0.67348	0.506	30.0%	20.0%	0.50	4.1388%	4.2020%	-4.083%	0.08%
19-Oct-2007	0.86955	0.508	30.0%	20.0%	0.50	4.3175%	4.3839%	-4.083%	0.26%
19-Apr-2008	0.84002	0.508	30.0%	20.0%	0.50	4.5051%	4.5744%	-4.083%	0.41%

While changes in GBP interest rates do have an impact on the pricing, with respect to the discounting of the cashflows, however the effect is minimal and not a significant risk to a trader's overall position. The GBP risk can be measured and managed using the risk analysis model within Curveßuilder, which determines the PV01 risk given the GBP interest rate curve.

Diff in-arrears FRA valuation

We can combine the in-arrears and the quanto adjustment to price and structure a diff-in-arrears swap.

$$R_{i\_qadj\_arrears} = R_{adj} \times \exp(\rho\sigma_{fx}\sigma_i t) \qquad (7)$$

Using the same example as above, rather than paying normal fixing LIBOR the corporate decides to pay US$ LIBOR set and paid in arrears, quantoed into GBP.

As an example

Notional: GBP10,000,000
Term: 3-Years
Fixed rate: 4.291%, semi-annually, 30/360
Floating: 6-Month US$ LIBOR, 30/360,
              set and paid in arrears
              Payable semi-annually in GBP
              based on GBP notional
Spot GBP/US$ 1.75 (for reference only)

The above priced by first making the in arrears adjustment to the implied FRA rates and then applying the quanto adjustment to the arrears adjusted rates. Once the fully adjusted FRA rates are derived we can solve for the fair value fixed rate that provides a zero NPV.

Many interest rate structures can be easily quantoed into another currency using the same hedging and pricing logic discussed above.

SPREAD OPTIONS

A European spread option is an option on the difference between two underlying prices. A spread option on two different interest rates is essentially an option on the shape of the yield curve. Rather than an option on absolute interest rates we can have an option on the spread difference between two points on the yield curve.

The payoff is based on the difference between two rates rather than one: the absolute rate of one point. The following payoff profile diagram shows the payoff for a European spread call option between two rates. In the payoff profile below we have the strike equal to zero, which implied an ATM option when the curve is flat (constant rates).

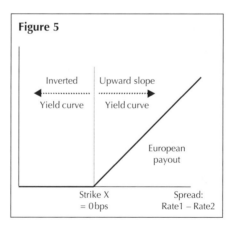

Figure 5

Kirk (1995) formulated an approximation for a European-style spread option, on future rates, based on the original Black's '76 model.

$$\text{Spread}_{\text{Call}} = \text{dcf}_{\text{expiry}} \times (S_A N(d_1) - N(d_2)) \times (S_2 + X) \quad \text{(8)}$$

$$\text{Spread}_{\text{PUT}} = \text{dcf}_{\text{expiry}} \times (-N(-d_2) - S_A N(d_1)) \times (S_2 + X) \quad \text{(9)}$$

where

$$S_A = \frac{S_1}{S_2 + X}$$

$$\sigma = \sqrt{\sigma_1^2 + \left[\sigma_2 \frac{S_2}{S_2 + X}\right]^2 - 2\rho\sigma_1\sigma_2 \frac{S_2}{(S_2 + X)}}$$

ρ Correlation between the two rates
$\sigma_{1,2}$ Volatility of the respective underlying rates
σ Adjusted volatility of the spread, based on the volatility of the underlying

$$d_1 = \frac{\ln(S_A) + \left(\frac{\sigma^2 \times T}{2}\right)}{\sigma\sqrt{T}}$$

$$d_2 = d_1 - \sigma\sqrt{T}$$

where

T is time to expiry in years;
$N(\cdot)$ is the cumulative normal distribution function.

Spread option pricing example
Assume we want to price a 3-year option on the spread between the 5-year swap rate and the 2-year swap rate. If the convexity and time adjusted 5- and 2-year rates are 4.954% and 4.699% respectively. The volatility is the same for both forward rates at 20% and the correlation between the 5- and 2-year rates is 0.8. We want to price an option where the strike is zero. Assume the notional amount is US$100 million and the discount factor to the expiry date of the option (as derived from our zero curve) is 0.88461.

S_{5yr}	4.954%
S_{2yr}	4.699%
X	0 bp
DCF_{expiry}	0.88461

$$S_A = \frac{4.954\%}{4.699\% + 0} = 1.05429$$

$$\sigma = \sqrt{0.2^2 + \left[0.2 \frac{4.699\%}{4.4699\% + 0}\right]^2 - 2 \times 0.8 \times 0.2 \times 0.2 \frac{4.699\%}{(4.699\% + 0)}}$$

$$= 12.649\%$$

$$d_1 = \frac{\ln(1.05429) + \left(\dfrac{0.12649^2 \times 3}{2}\right)}{0.12649\sqrt{3}} = 0.350864$$

$$N(d_1) = 0.637155$$

$$d_2 = 0.350864 - 0.2\sqrt{3} = 0.131775$$

$$N(d_2) = 0.552419$$

$$\text{Spread}_{\text{Call}} = (1.05429 \times 0.637155 - 0.552419) \times (0.04699 + 0)$$
$$\times \text{DCF}_{\text{expiry}} \times \text{Notional}$$

$$\text{Spread}_{\text{Call}} = \text{US\$495,983 or 0.496\% per notional}$$

The value of the option reflects the fact that the option is in the money (ITM) by 25.5 bps (4.954% − 4.699%). The option will be in the money (ITM) when the curve is upward sloping, and is out of the money (OTM) when the curve is downward sloping or inverted.

We can also value a spread option with the Curveßuilder spread option calculator as illustrated in Table 8, which provides the same answers as the manual calculation above.

Table 8

Start Date	19-Apr-05					Currency	USD	
Term	3	Years						
	19-Apr-08							
Spread Option Payoff:		Max((Rate1-Rate2)-Strike,0)						
Call or Put	Call							
Strike	0.00%	bps						
Notional	100,000,000	USD						
								Adjusted
		Term		Freq	Basis	Forward	Forward
Rate1	Swap Rate	5	Years	Semi	30/360	4.904%	4.954%
Rate2	Swap Rate	2	Years	Semi	30/360	4.691%	4.699%
5 Years Swap Rate Volatility	20%						
2 Years Swap Rate Volatility	20%						
Correlation	0.8						
						Risk Parameters	
DCF to Maturity	0.88461					5 Years Vega risk	13,575
Premium	495,983					2 Years Vega risk	9,001
per Notional	0.496%					Combined Vega Risk	20,605
						Correlation Risk	104,388

The volatility and correlation inputs are the derived from the market and are both the "implied" rates (or the expected volatility and correlation). While we can estimate the correlation factor from historical data the implied correlation factor may be different in order to reflect the difficulty in hedging the implied correlation.

We can estimate what the correlation factor should be from historical data. The following analysis calculates the correlation between rates over two different time periods to see how stable the correlation factors are. In the following table shows the historical correlation between US$ swap rates. We see that the correlation between the 5-year and 2-year rate was between 0.952 and 0.969, given historical data from October 1998 to May 2006. (Historic swap rates for other currency are also from the ISDA website.)

Table 9

Historic Data Analysis between Oct-1998 and May-2006

	Y1	Y2	Y5	Y10
Y1	1.000			
Y2	0.991	1.000		
Y5	0.933	0.969	1.000	
Y10	0.842	0.896	0.976	1.000

Historic Data Analysis between June-2000 and May-2006

	Y1	Y2	Y5	Y10	Y30
Y1	1.000				
Y2	0.988	1.000			
Y5	0.900	0.952	1.000		
Y10	0.753	0.829	0.958	1.000	
Y30	0.548	0.639	0.832	0.955	1.000

Source: ISDA http://www.isda.org/fix/historicaldata.html

The effect of a change in the implied correlation has a significant impact on the value of the option so it is important have the proper estimation.

Table 10

5Y *vs.* 2Y CoR	Option value[8]
0.90	US$391,595
0.80	US$495,983
0.70	US$577,240

While the price sensitivity to the implied volatility input (Vega) has less of an impact on the pricing.

Table 11

Increase in volatility input	Option value
Base case	US$495,983
5-year vol only (+1%)	US$509,558
2-year vol only (+1%)	US$504,984
Both vol points (+1%)	US$516,588

The delta of the spread option will have, as expected, varying sensitivities across the interest rate curve. It is important not to look at the NET PV01 figure, as it will not fully reflect the true sensitivity across the curve. In the above example the Net PV01 figure is only US$893 but as you can see from the risk analysis output from our model the exposure is across the curve. The results reflect the fact that the exposure is on 2- and 5-year rates in three years' time (option's expiry date), with the bulk of the exposure at the 5-year (2-year rate 3-years forward) and at 8-years (5-year rate 3-years forward).

Table 12

SWAPS	
2.0 Years	3
3.0 Years	3,927
4.0 Years	28
5.0 Years	-13,027
7.0 Years	6,593
10.0 Years	3,368

DIGITAL SPREAD OPTIONS

A digital option as we have discussed pays a fixed or digital payoff if the option expires in the money and nothing if it expires out of the money. We can price digital spread options using the "call spread" methodology we examined in chapter 9. The payoff profile diagram shows the payoff of a digital spread call option. The strike is set to zero which implies an ATM strike when the curve is flat. A positive fixed payout if the curve is positively sloped and a zero payout if the curve is inverted.

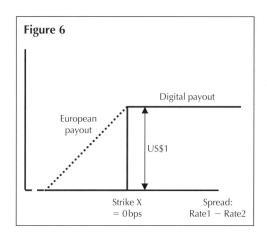

Figure 6

Digital payout

European payout

US$1

Strike X = 0 bps

Spread: Rate1 − Rate2

Example

A common application for a digital spread option is a daily accrual option where the option pays a fixed coupon every day that the curve remains upward sloping and nothing if the curve is inverted. If we assume a daily digital payoff of 10% when the option is in the money and 0% when out of the money we can calculate the required notional and cost for the required call spread.

Calculate the price of a call spread option:[9]

Long call option:
Strike (X):   Spread = −0.10%

Premium: +US$550,530 per US$100 M
Short call option:
Strike (X):   Spread = 0%
Premium: −US$495,983 per US$100 M

Net cost: +US$54,520 per US$100 M
Option payoff: 10 bps or US$100,000 per US$100 M

If on expiry date the curve is upward sloping the call-spread option pays a fixed amount of US$100,000, if inverted it pays US$0. The cost of this digital spread is US$54,520 per US$100 million. But we do not need a payoff of US$100 K; we only need a payoff of:

$$\text{Daily Payoff (required)} = 10\% \times 1\,\text{day}/360 \times$$
$$\text{US}\$100,000,000 = \text{US}\$27,778$$

So we do not have to buy a full amount of the call spread options, but a fraction so that the equivalent payoff is the same:

$$\text{Adjusted option cost} = \frac{\text{Daily payoff (required)}}{\text{Option payoff}} \times \text{Net cost}$$

$$\text{Adjusted option cost} = \frac{\text{US\$27,778}}{\text{US\$100,000}} \times \text{US\$54, 520} = \text{US\$15, 145}$$

And the required notional we would need to purchase:

$$\text{Adjusted option Notional} = \frac{\text{US\$27,778}}{\text{US\$100,000}}$$
$$\times \text{US\$100, 000, 000} = \text{US\$27, 778, 000}$$

The cost of a daily digital option, which pays one day of interest, at 10%, if the curve is upward sloping, would cost US\$15,145. In order to price the full daily range accrual we would need to price the option for each day (260 days a year, Fridays counting as three days) in order to get the full cost of the daily range accrual option. The cost of this option (US\$15,145) compares to receiving one day of interest at 5.45%.

Required Daily Interest Received	= US\$15,145
US\$15,145	= R × 1 day/360 × US\$100,000,000
R	= 5.45%

On a US\$100,000,000 you would need to earn a fixed coupon of 5.45% for 1 day in order to buy the daily call spread that pays a daily digital amount of 10% (on US\$100 M) if the curve is upward sloping and nil interest if the curve was inverted.

1 Source Hull, p 526.
2 See Appendix C.
3 Source Hull, p 528.
4 We have structured this inverse floating rate payoff with 2 times leverage; a fixed rate less 2 × LIBOR. We could use a factor of 1 or increase leverage more than 2 depending on the investors risk profile and the view on the view on underlying rates, any leverage factor other than 2 we would need to adjust the full structure accordingly.
5 All calculations (NPVs) are derived from the Curveßuilder model.
6 Given that the LIBOR leg on the pay side is two times we need to have two times the notional on the cap and floor as an appropriate hedge to protect the minimum and maximum coupon levels, cap and floor priced with 30% volatility.
7 Source Hull, p 601.
8 All other details remain the same as the previous example.
9 All premium calculations are from Curveßuilder calculator.

11

Financial Accounting: IAS39¹ Financial Instruments Recognition and Measurement

INTRODUCTION

Accounting plays a crucial role in applying and trading derivative transactions. This chapter provides an overview of how derivatives are accounted for and how they can affect the end user's decision to apply an applicable hedge or not. The overall objective of the accounting standards is to bring all transactions on to the balance sheet and be fully transparent as to their fair value. Under International Accounting Standards (IAS) 39 all financial transactions must be recognised on the balance sheet and measured at fair value. Any change in fair value is to be passed on to the income statement (P&L). All transactions must be booked under one of the following four portfolios:

❑ Banking;
❑ Held to Maturity (HTM);
❑ Available for Sale (AFS); and
❑ Held for Trading (HFT).

Table 1 outlines each of the portfolios and summarises the characteristics for each.

IAS39 also states that all derivatives, regardless of purpose (hedging or speculating) are to be valued at fair value and any change in fair value is recorded in current P&L. However, IAS39 also allows entities to relax this fair value accounting treatment of derivatives and apply hedge accounting, provided that several conditions are satisfied.

Table 1

Portfolio	Instruments	Characteristics	Accounting method	Restrictions
Banking	Cash instruments, Loans and terms deposits	Unquoted cash instruments	Accrual on an Effective Interest Rate (EIR) basis	Cannot include: Market quoted loans Loans intended to be resold Disposals are not permitted
Held to Maturity (HTM)	Bonds only	Intention and ability to HTM Fixed maturity date Vanilla instruments only	Accrual on an EIR basis	Not allowed to: hedge IR risk dispose items
Available for Sale (AFS)	Bonds and equities	Securities held for non-trading Vanilla instruments only	Fair value changes to reserves, except yield which is amortised to P&L on an EIR basis	Cannot include: Bonds with embedded derivatives short positions
Trading	Bonds, equities, FRAs, Futures, swaps, options, structured products	Held for speculative purposes, or Non-qualifying derivative hedges	Fair value changes to P&L On-balance sheet yield amortised to P&L on an EIR basis	HFT designation is irreversible: not allowed to reclassify

In following chapter when we discuss reserves we are considering the accounts under the equity section of the balance sheet and when we discuss profit and losses (P&L) we are discussing the account entries that effect the current income statement.

Banking

The banking portfolio contains balance sheet transactions such as wholesale and commercial loans and deposits. The banking portfolio should not include loans, which an entity has the intention of reselling, nor should it contain loans, which are quoted in an active market.

Disposals of transactions are also not permitted. These are on balance sheet items, which are accounted for on an accrual on an effective yield (EIR) basis within the current income statement.

Derivatives used to hedge an underlying transaction within the banking portfolio, which qualify as a cash flow hedge can be included in this portfolio. However any change in fair value must be taken to reserve, while any change to the underlying hedged instrument is accounted for on an amortising basis within the current income statement.

Held to Maturity (HTM)

The HTM portfolio contains instruments, which the entity has the intention and ability to hold until maturity. The HTM portfolio is very restrictive and thus has a very limited use. IAS39 does not permit instruments in this portfolio to be hedged for interest rate movements, while hedging is permitted for foreign exchange and credit risk (and qualify for hedge accounting). Generally, only debt instruments can be included in this portfolio, given the requirement that the underlying must have a fixed maturity date (equities would thus not qualify).

Only an immaterial portion of this portfolio is allowed to be sold or reclassified, otherwise the entire portfolio should be moved to either the AFS or trading portfolios. Disposal or transfers from this portfolio are permitted in the following rare circumstances:

❑ credit problems;
❑ adverse changes in tax laws;
❑ change in regulatory requirements including requirement for more capital;

❑ as a result of the underlying issuers' call; or

❑ the result of a merger or acquisition.

HTM instruments are accounted for on an accrual on an effective yield (EIR) basis. The amortisation cost includes any premium or discount on purchase as well as any costs upon acquisition (such as upfront fees). Derivatives that are used to hedge the interest rate expose do not qualify under hedge accounting and therefore must be accounted for on a fair value basis with any changes in fair value recorded in P&L.

Available for Sale (AFS)

This portfolio consists of both debt and equity instruments held for non-trading purposes. AFS instruments should not include bonds with embedded derivatives, with the exception of callable or putable bonds, nor should the portfolio include short positions of securities. Transactions that involve the funding of the AFS portfolio can also be included within the portfolio and accounted for on an accrual basis. Accounting for instruments within this portfolio is done as follows:

❑ accrual on an effective yield (EIR) basis to P&L;

❑ change in FX translation to P&L; and

❑ fair value changes, as a result of movements in interest rates and credit spreads, and accounted for in reserves.

When the fair value of an instrument is considered more significant and longer term it is classified as impaired. Rather than account for fair value changes in reserves, there must be a provision in current P&L for the *impairment*, which is accounted for by reversing the fair value out of reserve and accounted for in current P&L. The impairment of an asset may be the result of:

❑ a significant financial difficulty of the underlying issuer;

❑ a significant probability of default or financial restructuring; and

❑ no longer an active market for underlying asset.

Disposal of instruments from the AFS portfolio should be rare but not as restrictive as the HTM portfolio. Disposals are acceptable for the following reasons:

❑ liquidity requirements;

❑ strategic decisions such as, portfolio's size and duration;

❑ credit problems with the underlying issuer;

❑ adverse changes in tax and regulatory requirements;

❑ as a result of the underlying issuer's call; or

❑ the result of a merger or acquisition.

If the disposal of an AFS asset is a hedged item then the underlying hedging instrument must be either terminated or revert to fair value accounting.

Held for Trading (HFT or Fair value portfolio)

This portfolio includes all items acquired or held with the intention for resale. Most financial assets and liabilities can be classified under this category, with the exception of unquoted loans and deposits (they are included in the banking portfolio). All instruments classified within this portfolio must be designated to HFT at acquisition and is consistent across the entire product group. Once an instrument is classified to the HFT portfolio it is irreversible, you cannot reclassify an instrument out of HFT to another portfolio.

All instruments (both hedged and hedging items) in this portfolio are recorded at their fair value with any changes passed to P&L.

EFFECTIVE INTEREST RATE (EIR)

IAS39 requires that all interest income or yield revenue to be calculated and reported using the effective interest rate (EIR). The EIR can be defined as the underlying coupon or interest rate plus the amortisation of any premium or discount on the purchase price at inception (plus any costs or fees paid or received at inception). The impact of using the EIR method to account for interest income *vs.* using the simple straight line amortisation method previously used by most entities, is that there may be a difference in timing in the recognition of the income. This timing difference is illustrated in column G in Table 2.

Example

Assume an entity purchases a fixed rate debt security, US$10,000,000 notional, at an all in discount price (total proceeds) of 98.88%. The debt pays a fixed annual coupon of 3.00%. The entity decides to classify the debt security under the hold to maturity portfolio.

Table 2

	Nominal (USD)	10,000,000						
	Value Date	22-Apr-06						
	Maturity Date	22-Apr-11						
	Purchase Price	98.88%						
	Coupon Rate	3.00% Annual						
		3.25%	EIR					
Year	Amortizing Cost at beginning A	Cashflows Received B	Yield Income $C = A \times EIR$	Amortization of Debt $D = C - B$	Amortizing Cost at End E	Straight Line Amortization F	Timing Difference $G = D - F$
2007	9,888,000	300,000	320,992	20,992	9,908,992	22,400	-1,408
2008	9,908,992	300,000	321,674	21,674	9,930,666	22,400	-726
2009	9,930,666	300,000	322,377	22,377	9,953,043	22,400	-23
2010	9,953,043	300,000	323,104	23,104	9,976,146	22,400	704
2011	9,976,146	300,000	323,854	23,854	10,000,000	22,400	1,454
						-	0

In this example we solve for an effective interest rate (EIR) where the final amortising cost (column E within Table 2) is equal to the nominal value of the underlying asset. In the following example we determined that the effective interest rate (EIR) is 3.25%. Yield income (column C in Table 2) which is derived from the EIR *vs.* the outstanding amortising cost at the beginning of the interest period (Column C = Column A × EIR). This yield income is what is reported as income, which includes coupon and the amortisation of any premium or discount.

FAIR VALUE VS. HEDGE ACCOUNTING
Fair value

From an accounting perspective fair value is defined as "the amount for which an asset could be sold or a liability settled between knowledgeable and willing counterparties in an arm's length transaction. It is not the amount that an entity would receive or pay in a distressed sale". Fair value is determined from one of two sources:

❑ price quoted in an active market; and
❑ valuation technique commonly used in the market and incorporating only observable market date (eg an IRS).

Where "observable data" is defined as readily and regularly available quotes from multiple independent sources.

Long positions are to be valued at the market bid while short positions are valued at the market offer. A portfolio of the same instrument can apply this bid-offer rule to the net position.

Where fair value is uncertain, as a result of an inactive underlying market or uncertainty within the valuation techniques, an adjustment is required to cover the possible uncertainty. IAS39 states that at inception the fair value is the transaction price. Valuation uncertainty may arise from either:

❑ Modelling uncertainty, as a result of:
   ❑ no market standard model has been established;
   ❑ where the valuation may rely on a number of market data inputs which may not be readily observable (such as correlation factors); or
❑ Market data uncertainty, as a result of:
   ❑ illiquid or undeveloped markets;
   ❑ parameters estimated based on historical or forward projections, for example historic or long-term volatility.

Generally when non-optionality derivatives such as forwards and interest rate swaps are transacted at current market rates, their initial fair value is zero.

Hedge accounting

IAS39 requires that all derivative contracts (hedging items) be recorded on the balance sheet at fair value and any change in fair value to be reflected in the P&L. The result of this requirement would be an increase in the volatility of earnings. In order to reduce the volatility of earnings the accounting standards allow the application of "*Hedge accounting*". Hedge accounting can be used to relax the usual accounting standards in order to efficiently (reduce the volatility of earnings) match the cashflows or fair values of an underlying hedged item (an asset or liability) with that of a hedging instrument (derivative). All derivative contracts with an external counterparty may be designated as a hedging instrument, with the exception of net written options. A hedged item, as defined under IAS39.78, can be:

❑ a single recognised asset or liability, firm commitment, highly probable transaction, or a net investment in a foreign operation;

❑ a group of assets, liabilities, firm commitments, highly probable forecast transactions, or net investments in foreign operations with similar risk characteristics;

❑ a held-to-maturity investment for foreign currency or credit risk;

❑ a portion of the cash flows or fair value of a financial asset or financial liability; and

❑ a portfolio hedge of interest rate risk (macro hedge only), a portion of the portfolio of financial assets or financial liabilities that share the risk being hedged.

When an entity has multiple financial assets or liabilities with the same underlying counterparty (same legal entity) they can offset the balances and account for the net balances. *Netting* can be done provided that the netting is legally enforceable and there is intention to settle net.

Hedge accounting can only be applied where the underlying hedging relationship satisfies several requirements:

❑ formal documentation of the hedged and hedging item;

❑ apply and pass effectiveness testing, retrospective and prospectively;

❑ derivative is done with a third party; and

❑ the underlying hedged item is not an intra-group transaction.

Hedge accounting attempts to match the timing of the P&L recognition between an underlying hedged item with that of the hedging or derivative transaction in order to minimise P&L fluctuations. Hedge accounting involves a process, which includes identifying the hedged and hedging items, calculating the fair value of the instruments and performing hedge effectiveness tests.

The administration and infrastructure required to comply with the hedge accounting standards is onerous and may not always be appropriate or cost effective to apply. In such a case an entity may elect to value and account for many of their financial instruments at fair value. The application of fair value accounting may not have a significant impact on current earnings volatility so the benefits of hedge account is minimal and may not be worth the effort. Also, many valid hedging applications may not satisfy the accounting standards definition of a "qualified hedge" and again fair value accounting may be applied. While it is advantageous and preferable to use hedge accounting, it should not prevent an entity from applying the most appropriate hedging alternative available. Even if hedge accounting cannot be applied, certain derivative hedges or strategies may be the most appropriate alternative given the entities' views on market rates and the long-term economics of an underlying (unqualified) hedging relationship.

In order to qualify as a hedging relationship, and thus able to apply hedge accounting, an entity must, at inception of the hedge formally document the hedging relationship and the entity's risk management objective and strategy for undertaking the hedge. The formal hedge document must include the following points:

- ❑ risk management objective and strategy (eg hedge exchange rate risk);
- ❑ identification of the hedging instrument and hedging item or transaction;
- ❑ type of hedge accounting relationship (eg FVH, CFH, NIH);
- ❑ the specific risk being hedged (eg interest rate or foreign exchange exposure); and
- ❑ how hedging effectiveness will be assessed and demonstrate that the hedge will be highly effective in reducing risk exposures.

Not only does the hedging relationship need to be formally documented the entity must also provide quantitative testing that shows that the underlying hedge is effective.

HEDGE EFFECTIVENESS TESTING
In order to qualify for hedge accounting IAS39 requires the underlying hedge to be "highly effective". An entity must provide quantitative tests, initially and on an ongoing basis, which proves the effectiveness of hedging relationship between the hedged and hedging item. Effectiveness testing requires two stages of testing:

Prospective effectiveness testing
A prospective (anticipated) effectiveness test is a forward-looking test, examining how the hedging relationship is expected to be highly effective in future periods. This test is required at the inception of the hedge, and on each subsequent reporting dates during the life of the hedging relationship. This test should demonstrate

that the change in the fair value or cash flows from the hedged instrument is to be almost fully offset by the change in the fair value or cash flows of the hedging instrument.

For interest rate hedges the prospective effectiveness testing is performed initially and on an ongoing basis by examining how the fair value or cash flows of the derivative and the hedged item change as interest rates change. The test can be performed by shifting the yield curve (which is used to MTM the hedge and hedging items) up or down by 25, 50 and/or 100 basis and/or time shifting the curves to examine how changes in interest rates and time effects the hedging relationship. Normally at least three different interest rate scenarios should be used to test the effectiveness of the hedge.

Retrospective effectiveness testing

A retrospective (actual) effectiveness test is a backward looking test, which examines whether the hedging relationship has been actually effective. A retrospective test must be performed at each reporting period. In order for a hedge to be considered effective and thus allow an entity to apply hedge accounting the actual results of the hedge must be within a critical range of 80% to 125%. That is the change in the fair value of the hedged item must be offset by the hedging item by at least 80% (4/5) but no more than 125% (5/4).

The hedge effectiveness can be improved through careful risk designation. For example by designating an interest rate swap as a hedge to only the interest rate risk of a bond and excludes the change in value as a result of changing credit spreads. If we allow any fluctuations in fair value as a result of changes in credit spreads to flow directly to the P&L then the underlying hedge may have a much more significant hedge effectiveness result. Another way to improve the effectiveness results is to designate that the hedged item is greater than the hedging instrument. The designation of an "under hedged" relationship should also help improve effectiveness test results which will fall within the required critical value range. With an under hedge relationship there will be no ineffectiveness to be recognised in the P&L, however any changes in value of the unhedged portion is then fully reflected in the P&L.

No hedge is 100% perfect or effective, so any hedge ineffectiveness is passed directly to the income statement (P&L). At expiry, sale or termination of the hedge relationship, the hedging instrument will be measured at fair value with changes going directly through to the income statement.

The method of proving effectiveness must be documented at the inception of the hedge and must be consistently applied across all similar hedges, and consistent for each period.

EFFECTIVENESS TESTING METHODOLOGIES

While IAS39 does not specify which effectiveness test to apply however the most common methods for testing the effectiveness of the hedging relationship are:

❑ critical terms comparison (short cut method);
❑ dollar offset method;
❑ regression analysis method; and
❑ variance reduction method.

Generally the more sophisticated the method the better the overall effectiveness results.

Critical terms comparison

This short cut method compares the critical terms of the hedged item with those of the hedging item. The hedge is assumed to be highly effective if all the critical terms match exactly. The critical terms include the notional amount, term, payment or re-pricing dates, coupon basis, currency of cashflows, and there is no optionality embedded that would alter the critical characteristics of either the hedged or hedging item. This method does not require any prospective testing, however, retrospective testing is still required to show that the actual hedge was highly effective.

As an example, when an entity obtains a floating rate loan and then hedges it with an interest rate swap, receive floating paying fixed. When all the critical terms of the floating leg of the IRS match that of the loan the hedge is said to be effective and no prospective testing is required, however a retrospective test is still required.

Dollar offset method

The dollar-offset method is the most common method to apply, which compares the change in fair value or cash flows of the hedge item to that of the hedging item (derivative). The change in value of one item should be equally offset by the change in fair value of the other item. Assessment can be performed on a period to period or on a cumulative basis. For the hedge to be deemed highly effective the test results must be within the −80% and −125% effectiveness.

Discrete dollar offset method

$$DOM_{dis} = \frac{\Delta HedgeItemValue}{\Delta DerivativeValue} \qquad (1)$$

The test can also be performed on a cumulative basis where results from one period to another are summed in order to demonstrate effectiveness over a longer term.

While the methodology is simple to apply the actual effectiveness results are sensitive to small changes in fair value. The results tend to focus on period to period comparisons rather than a reduction in the fair value volatility. The effectiveness tends to break down which leads to the conclusion that hedge accounting cannot be applied whereas other testing methods do pass the hedge effectiveness criteria.

One of the positive results from this method is that it provides the quantifiable ineffectiveness of the hedge, which must be passed to P&L.

Regression analysis method

The regression analysis method measures the "statistical relationship" between the hedged item and the hedging item. A regression analysis is performed in order to determine the "line (or equation) of best fit". This line is then assessed to determine how well the given relationship holds, also known as "goodness of fit". The method and results are based on the standard linear regression model:

$$Y = \alpha + \beta X + \varepsilon$$

The equation states that the value of the hedged item (Y, which is the dependent variable) is dependent on the hedging (derivative) item (X, which is the independent variable). The slope represents the variance minimising hedge ratio, or in simple terms the best hedge ratio for a given relationship between the hedged and hedging item. The slope therefore demonstrates the correlation between the independent and the dependent variable. A beta of −1 means the hedged item and hedging item are perfectly (inversely) correlated,[2] and would also demonstrate a perfect hedge. We then test the strength of the regression model using the R^2 test statistic (correlation of determination). The R^2 test statistic effectively determines how much of the dependent's change in fair value can be explained using the regression's equation. If the equation can predict 100% of the dependent variable's fair value changes then the R^2 test statistic would be 100%. Under a perfect hedge R^2 would be 100%, which means that the change in the derivative value 'explains' 100% of the change in the hedge items value.

There are 2 critical statistical measurements used to test hedging effectiveness:

❏ slope (β) should negative and between −0.80 and −1.25;
❏ R^2 test statistic should be greater than 0.90.

Variance or variability-reduction method
This method compares the variance or standard deviation of the unhedged item's fair value to that of the combined (hedge plus hedging instrument) fair value variance. For the hedge to be effective the overall variance should be significantly reduced. We can calculate the effectiveness of the hedge by measuring how much the variance has been reduced using the following equation:

$$VRM = 1 - \frac{\text{Var}(x_1 + y_1)}{\text{Var}(y_1)} \qquad (2)$$

where

VRM	Variance reduction method;
	y_1 is the change in fair value of the hedged item;
	$x_1 + y_1$ is the change in the fair value of the combined hedge and hedging item;
Var(…)	Variance of the variable [using excel use the formula = var(*dataset*)].

A perfect hedge would produce a result of 1 ($VRM = 1$), meaning that the fair value variability is reduced by 100%. The variability of the hedged item combined with the hedging item is zero, which represents 100% effective hedging. For this method to pass the hedging effectiveness test the result must be between 80% and 125%

While the last two methods for testing for hedging effectiveness does prove how effective the hedging is, it does not calculate the amount (dollar value) of any ineffectiveness. We will need to quantify any ineffectiveness and pass this amount to P&L.

Hedge effectiveness example

Table 3 is an example of the various tests for effectiveness of a fair value hedge, between a hedged item (fixed rate bond) and that of the hedging item (interest rate swap). We examine the fair value of the bond and swap at the end of each month over a 12-month period. The results show that if we were to apply the dollar offset method (period on period or cumulative) there would be many cases when the critical test fails (see shaded results) and thus the entity would not be allowed to apply hedge accounting for this particular hedging relationship.

When we use the second method, the regression analysis, we calculate the correlation between the bond and swap's fair value (as measured at the end of each month). The results show that the correlation coefficient of the bond and swap's fair value is -0.991 with an R^2 of 98.1%, which means the results pass the effectiveness test. As an alternative method, rather than compare the absolute fair values we can also test the effectiveness by calculating the correlation between the *change* in the bond and swaps fair value. The results show a correlation coefficient of -0.966 but a lower R^2 score of 93.3%, which again both results pass our minimum criteria for testing hedge effectiveness.

The last test is the variance reduction method, the results show that the variance of the bond's value when combined with the

Table 3

Effectiveness Test Results								
Bond Details	Fixed Rate Bond, $20M Notional, 5Y Term					Results		
Swap Details	Rec Fixed pay Floating 6M LIBOR Interest Rate Swap							
						Variance reduction		97%
						Correlation Price		-99%
						R2 Price		98%
Variance	232,337,087,040	175,621,782,622	7,747,685,088			Correlation value Change		-97%
						R2 Value Change		-97%
	Bond	Swap	Combined	Change	Change	Change	Dollar Offset	
Month	FV	FV	FV	FV Bond	FV Swap	FV Combine	Period	Cum.
Month1	20,200,000	438,114	20,638,114					
Month2	20,304,819	325,467	20,630,286	104,819	(112,646)	(7,827)	-93%	-93%
Month3	20,207,218	414,523	20,621,741	(97,601)	89,056	(16,373)	-110%	-31%
Month4	20,500,881	42,978	20,543,859	293,663	(371,545)	(94,255)	-79%	-76%
Month5	21,323,517	(483,154)	20,840,363	822,636	(526,132)	202,249	-156%	-122%
Month6	20,955,518	(188,465)	20,767,053	(367,999)	294,689	128,939	-125%	-121%
Month7	20,837,338	(70,642)	20,766,696	(118,180)	117,823	128,582	-100%	-125%
Month8	20,488,473	138,585	20,627,058	(348,865)	209,227	(11,056)	-167%	-96%
Month9	20,267,324	324,601	20,591,925	(221,148)	186,016	(46,188)	-119%	-59%
Month10	19,930,011	660,804	20,590,814	(337,314)	336,203	(47,299)	-100%	-121%
Month11	19,841,234	763,604	20,604,838	(88,777)	102,801	(33,276)	-86%	-110%
Month12	19,655,043	990,501	20,645,545	(186,190)	226,897	7,431	-82%	-99%
							Failed	Pass

hedge (IRS) is reduced significantly by 96.7%. This again passes the minimum criteria required for the hedge to qualify as effective.

In our example we notice that at the end of the report there is a change in the combined fair value (bond plus swap value) which results in a (hedge ineffectiveness) net gain of US$7,431 which is passed to the income statement at the end of the period.

The method applied is important in achieving a suitable level of effectiveness. While the dollar-offset method is simple to apply, the results may prevent the application of hedge accounting in the first place. Remember you cannot change the effectiveness method from one period to another.

HEDGING RELATIONSHIP

There are three types of hedging relationships that qualify for hedge accounting, these are:

❑ Fair value hedges (FVH);
❑ cashflow hedges (CFH); and
❑ net investment hedges (NIH).

Fair value hedge (FV Hedge)

A fair value hedge provides protection from a change in the fair value of the underlying hedged item. A derivative qualifies as an FV hedge if the change in the derivative's fair value (as a result of changes in underlying market rates) offsets, in an equal but opposite amount, the change in the fair value of a designated hedge item. A typically FV hedge is an interest rate swap hedging the fair value of a fixed rate bond (hedged item); where the fair value of the liability is at risk to changes in interest rates. An entity can hedge the fair value of the bond with an interest rate swap, any change in the fair value of the hedged item, as a result of changes in interest rates, will be offset by a change in fair value of the hedging instrument (IRS). Practically speaking a corporate treasurer enters into an FV hedge on a fixed rate liability in order to convert from a fixed rate into a floating rate liability. This allows the corporate to take advantage of their view that short-term rates will be lower than the forwards imply. Therefore, the FV hedge of the fixed rate liability is more of a strategic decision, given a specific outlook on interest rate rather than a concern about the fair value of their liability.

An entity can apply more than one derivative as a hedging instrument in a fair value hedge. For example if an entity issues a fixed rate bond, and as a hedge enters into a vanilla IRS (receive fixed pay floating) in combination with an interest rate cap (or collar) to protect themselves against higher interest rates.

Accounting for FVH

Within a qualified FV hedge the hedging and hedged instruments are recognised at their fair values, with changes in fair value reported in the P&L. For hedged items within an AFS portfolio this means that the fair value changes are reversed from reserves and posted to current P&L. For hedged items in the banking or HTM portfolios, the accrual of the underlying designated risk is reversed and the fair value change is posted to P&L, along with changes in fair value of the hedging item.

Cash flow (CF) hedge

The risk associated with variable cash flows, such as floating interest rate payments, can be hedged using a cashflow (CF) hedge. A typical example is an interest rate swap (receive floating pay fixed) as a hedge to a floating rate liability. The IRS hedges the risk of the variable payment by effectively fixing the interest payments.

Accounting for CF hedge

The accounting for the underlying hedged item does not change under a CF hedge relationship. The derivative is recognised as an on balance sheet item and is accounted for at its fair value. The effective portion of the fair value gain or loss from the derivative is passed through to reserves, while the ineffective portion is recorded in the current P&L. Any interest (from the derivative) is accrued through the net interest income in P&L.

Micro vs. macro hedges

IAS39 allows the FV and CF hedge to be applied to a portfolio of instruments (macro hedge) as well as on an individual basis (micro hedge). For example an entity can use interest rate swaps to manage the interest rate exposure on a portfolio of floating rate liabilities (loans and bonds). IAS39 also allows the designation of more than one derivative as part of a macro hedge. While a macro hedge is applicable there are stringent guidelines which need to be followed in order to satisfy the standards definitions of a "qualified macro hedge".

Net investment hedge

The last hedge category allows an entity to apply hedge accounting to the hedging of its foreign operations (subsidiaries). Entities that have exchange risk arising from highly probable gains or losses as a result of changes in FX rates are able to hedge the risk and apply hedge accounting. While an entity is permitted to hedge the foreign exchange risk it cannot hedge the value of the underlying invest- ment itself. A typical example is when an entity uses FX forward con- tracts to hedge regular (reliable) profits generated by a subsidiary.

As with a CF hedge any gains or losses are accounted for in reserves, and these gains or losses are then recycled when the for- eign currency investment is realised or disposed.

Table 4 illustrates common examples of transactions for an entity, the portfolio they have designated for each and if the associ- ated hedging instrument qualifies as a hedging relationship. The example is of a US based corporate with a subsidiary in Japan.

Table 4

Trans Ref	Description	Notional	Coupon	Maturity	Intent	Hedge Account
Banking Portfolio (BK)						
BK010	**Bond Issuance**	(JPY10Bil)	-1.00% FXD Ann	13-Apr-10	Funding Requirements	
BK011	HSBC - CCIRS	JPY10Bil	1.00% FXD Ann	13-Apr-08	Hedge FX and JPY Int Rates	FVH [1]
BK012	HSBC - CCIRS	(US$90M)	-4.50% FXD Semi	13-Apr-08		
BK020	**Intra Group Loan**	US$100M	6M LIBOR +100bps	2-Jun-12	Funding of a Sub	
BK021	UBS - IRS	(US$100M)	-6M LIBOR +100bps	2-Jun-12	Hedge Interest rate Risk	Not applicable [2]
BK022	UBS - IRS	US$100M	5.00% FXD Semi	2-Jun-12		
BK030	**Bank Loan**	(US$30M)	-6M LIBOR +25bps	22-May-07	Funding Requirements	
BK031	CSFB - IRS	US$30M	6M LIBOR +25bps	22-May-07	Hedge Int rate risk	CFH
BK032	CSFB - IRS	(US$30M)	3.75% QRT	22-May-07		
Hold to Maturity Portfolio (HM)						
HM010	**FRN "AA" Bond**	US$5M	3M LIBOR +35	10-Sep-08	Hold to Maturity	
HM011	DB - Long Floor	(US$5M)	Min (3.00%, 3ML)	10-Sep-08	Hedge interest rate risk	Not applicable [3]
Asset for Sale Portfolio (AS)						
AS010	**FRN "A" CD**	US$3M	6M Libor +75bps	20-May-09	Held for liquidity reasons	
AS011	CSFB - IRS	(US$3M)	-6M Libor +75bps	20-May-09	Hedge Int rate risk	CFH
AS012	CSFB - IRS	US$3M	4.88% Semi	20-May-09		
Trading Portfolio (TP)						
TP010	**Fixed "AA" CD**	US$3M	4.88% Ann	4-Apr-14	Short term holding- to be sold	
TP011	ABN - IRS	(US$3M)	4.88% Ann	4-Apr-14	Hedge	Not applicable [4]
TP012	ABN - IRS	US$3M	6M Libor +25bps	4-Apr-14		

[1] FVH: exposure hedged to 2008 only, which is allowed.
[2] Not a qualified hedge as the item is an intra group loan.
[3] Not a qualified hedge as item is in the HM portfolio.
[4] Not a qualified hedge as items are in the TP: fair value accounting applies.

Note: Move item to Asset for Sale so that hedge accounting qualifies

Accounting and the use of options

An entity can use interest rate and foreign exchange options as part of a qualified hedge. As long as the options fit the required qualifying criteria and they are net long options. Interest rate options such as caps and floors can be qualified hedges under either a fair value or cash flow hedge, depending on the underlying hedging application. For cash flow hedges where the critical terms of the asset or liability match the cap and or floor it normally will be considered a qualified hedge. A cap or floor can also be a qualified fair value hedge, however it may be more difficult to satisfy the pass the effectiveness testing. One way to improve the hedge effectiveness results is to designate only the option's intrinsic value as the hedge while any changes to the underlying time value is recorded to P&L.

For example

An entity has a floating rate liability, and hedges the variable interest rate risk with an IR (long) cap. The cap has the same fixing/payment dates, and is fixed against the same 6-month US$ LIBOR fixing rate as the underlying liability. The entity is thus protected against variable interest rates fixing above the cap's strike rate. Any increase in rates above the strike rate is compensated by the payoff on the cap. This hedging relationship would qualify as a qualified cash flow hedge, since the critical terms match and would be booked under the banking portfolio.

An entity can also use an interest rate collar to hedge the interest rate risk on a floating rate liability. The collar may be a qualified fair value hedge provided that the critical terms match and collar is purchased from only one external counterparty. An entity cannot buy a cap from one counterparty and then sell the floor to another; the collar must be purchased as a package (in one transaction).

An entity can apply cap spreads, knock in or knock out caps as a hedging instrument, however it would be unlikely given the characteristics of the derivative that any of the effectiveness tests would be satisfied nor would the critical terms match. While these interest rate options can still be used as hedges to an underlying asset or liability, hedge accounting would not apply and any change in fair value to the derivatives would flow directly to P&L.

Discontinuation of hedge accounting

Hedge accounting must be discontinued if:

❑ the hedging instrument expires or is sold, terminated, or exercised;
❑ the hedge fails the effectiveness test;
❑ for cash flow hedges, the forecasted transaction is no longer expected to occur; or
❑ the entity revokes the hedge designation and reverts to fair value accounting.

If hedge accounting is discontinued for a cash flow hedge relationship because the forecast transaction is no longer expected to occur (hedging item is no longer expected to occur), gains and losses which were deferred into reserves must be taken to the income statement immediately. If the transaction is still expected to occur and the hedge relationship ceases, the amounts accumulated in reserves will be retained in reserves until the hedged item affects profit or loss.

If a hedged instrument, which is measured at amortised cost, has been adjusted for the gain or loss attributable to the hedged risk in a fair value hedge, this adjustment is amortised to profit or loss based on a recalculated effective interest rate on this date such that the adjustment is fully amortised by the maturity of the instrument. Amortisation may begin as soon as an adjustment exists and must begin no later than when the hedged item ceases to be adjusted for changes in its fair value attributable to the risks being hedged.

ISDA DOCUMENTATION AND DERIVATIVE CREDIT

The International Swaps Dealers Association (ISDA) is an independent trade association founded in 1985 to streamline derivatives transaction. Generally ISDA covers over-the-counter (OTC) contracts as opposed to exchange traded derivative contracts. Transactions covered under ISDA include swaps (and related products), options and forwards. Where the underlying asset class include:

❑ interest rates;
❑ equity;
❑ foreign exchange;
❑ commodity;
❑ credit; and
❑ weather.

There are various categories of members under the association. *Primary* members are financial institutions and large corporations, which regularly deal (trade) in derivative contracts. Members categorised as a *Subscriber* are non-dealing financial institutions and corporates as well as government entities. *Associate* members are those service providers such as lawyers and accountants.

The purpose of ISDA is to help streamline the process of dealing derivatives by standardising the documentation of transactions. Rather than negotiate the detailed terms and economic conditions for each transaction an ISDA agreement allows two counterparties to enter into a transaction and only the economic terms of any transaction needs to be agreed. Both parties can then rely on the pre-agreed definitions and framework of the ISDA to provide full details if required. ISDA allows participants to agree upon the ongoing legal and credit issues between parties and have only the economics of individual transaction to be negotiated.

An ISDA is structured in modules or building blocks. The primary document is the master agreement and then there are other documents, which are "added on" as and when required. The individual documents are amended and updated from time to time to reflect the development of the underlying derivative markets. For example the current master agreement is the version adopted in 2002, which updates the previous (1992) version. The main ISDA agreement is divided into two parts, the Master Agreement and the Schedule.

ISDA Agreement Structure

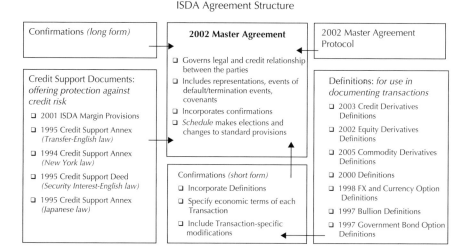

Part 1

The ISDA master agreement (multi-currency cross border agreement) is agreed and signed by both parties without amendments. It includes provisions relating to payments and deliveries under each individual transaction, which is to be governed by the agreement. The master agreement also covers payment netting, events of default and termination events of the agreement, withholding tax and various other definitions and standard contractual terms, including governing law and jurisdiction.

Part 2

The second part of the agreement is the schedule attached to the master agreement, which is negotiated between parties and contains elections to be made in relation to the main agreement itself, plus any additional terms or details agreed between parties. Any credit support agreements (CSA) are included in this section.

The ISDA master agreement (MA) contains 14 sections, which is to be agreed and signed by both parties without any amendments. We highlight the main sections and details below.

Section 1: Interpretation

Section 1 states in the case of any inconsistency between the master agreement, the schedule and the specific confirmation, the schedule takes precedence over the main body of the MA. For individual transaction the specific confirmation takes precedent over the MA and schedule.

Section 2: Obligations

Section 2 of the MA states that each party will make a payment as specified in each confirmation, subject to other terms in the agreement and confirmation. Failure to pay on the due date attracts interest and if payment not made within the allowable one local business day grace period (three days under 1992 agreement) it will constitute an event of default.

Section 2(c) covers payment netting.[3] Payment netting covers the settlement of cash payments from one party to another. When payments are to be made between counterparties in the same currency, on the same day and with respect to the same transaction, then only the net amount needs to be paid by one of the counterparties. Payment netting helps reduce payment or settlement risk. Within the agreement the parties can select to net within individual transactions or across all transactions (multiple transaction payment netting). The ability to select multiple transaction netting, while preferable, depends on the operations of the individual parties.

Section 2(d) MA deals with issues relating to withholding tax. Both parties enter into the MA under the assumption that there is no withholding tax payable. Each party's tax representation is made in the schedule which is intended to establish the necessary legal and factual framework so that no withholding tax is required. All payments will be made without any deduction or withholding on account of tax, UNLESS such deductions or withholding tax is required by any applicable law, in which case the payer is required to gross up the payment.

Section 3: Representation and covenants

In Section 3 both parties make representation that they have capacity and authority to enter into the MA, and that the schedule and any credit support documentation are factually true, legally valid and binding. Each party also states that there are no events (or potential) events of default and no litigation against either party, which may effect the legality of the MA:

Section 4: Agreement

Section 4 states that each counterparty must provide any required documentation or information as specified in the agreement, schedule or any credit support documentation. Both parties agree to maintain authorisation (to enter into transactions), comply with all applicable laws, and inform each other of any adverse changes in withholding tax or stamp duties. Section 4 is a generic outline of what each party is responsible for, while any specific document requirements are listed within the schedule (see schedule Part 3).

Section 5: Events of default and termination events

Section 5 of the master agreement outlines two classes of default; an event of default and a termination event, which can lead to the termination of all or specific transactions under the master agreement.

Events of default, which are fault based events, where all transactions under the MA are terminated. An example of an event of default is when either party fails to pay a required payment as specified on an individual contract. Once the non-defaulting counterparty has given notice to the defaulted party they normally have one local business day to remedy the defaulted payment.[4]

Other events of default as outlined in Section 5 of the MA include:

❑ breach of agreement, where one party fails to comply with the agreement or its specified obligations;
❑ credit support default;
❑ misrepresentation, within the agreement;
❑ cross-default, is an optional or elective event of default which allows an event to cover "any obligation in respect of borrowed money", with a specified threshold amount;
❑ default under specified transaction, similar to cross-default but more specific to other derivative transactions – generally this does not include transactions with third parties but it can be agreed to include "specific transactions" which will include third party derivative transactions;
❑ bankruptcy, by either party or their respective credit support providers; and

❑ merger (without assumption), where either counterparty or credit support provider transfers the assets to another entity but leaves the derivative transaction behind under the MA.

Events of default do exclude defaults caused by a technical failure or good faith disputes.

The second class of defaults are "termination events" which are non-fault events outside the control of either counterparty and generally lead to the termination of the transactions affected by the termination event. An example is when specific laws are amended that effects the requirement of withholding tax, in such a case only the specific transactions effect by the changes are terminated.

It is also common to include, as additional termination events (which are to be listed in the schedule):

❑ if an entity's parent owns less than a certain percentage as a result of selling its shareholdings or following a significant group restructuring;
❑ if a credit rating agency downgrades the party's debt obligations, below a specified threshold; or
❑ if there is a significant adverse change in the party's financial condition, which is common to include for weaker credits.

Section 6: Early termination (close out netting)

When there is an early termination, as specified under Section 5, Section 6 outlines how the payment is measured and the method of payment. Under the 2002 MA the amount is determined on the basis of quotes from reference market makers or from reliable third parties or an amount determined in good faith by a party as its total losses and costs. The amount of loss may be determined separately for each transaction or on a portfolio basis for a group of transactions. The net close out amount includes the settlement amount plus any unpaid amounts owed less any unpaid amounts to be received.

Close out payments are to be done on a net basis on all transactions (for events of default) or on all affected transactions (for termination events). Under close out netting, when contracts are terminated, the counterparties set off (or net off) payments in order to avoid "cherry picking" by liquidators and to provide a relief on the amount of capital required as it is applied on a net amount of exposure only.

Section 7: Transfer

In Section 7 the parties agree that neither may transfer any transaction governed by the agreement without the consent of the other party. While transfers are generally prohibited, the two exceptions are:

❑ pursuant to a merger or a transfer of substantially all a entity's assets; and
❑ payment due to a party on early termination.

Section 10: Offices: multi-branch parties

Section 10 allows for parties, who may transact through an office other than its head office, to add additional (optional) representation. Entities are classified as a multi-branch party if more than one office (residing in another jurisdiction) is allowed to transact under the same master agreement but with ultimate recourse to the head or home office. Regardless of where the transaction is booked, the liability and obligations are the same as if the transactions had been entered into with the head office directly. Any additional representation is specified in detail in the schedule.

Section 14: Definitions

Section 14 provides definitions and details of meaning to terms and clauses used in the agreement. Additional terms or further clarification of the definitions can be included in the schedule.

Other sections within the agreement

Section 8   Contractual currency
Section 9   Miscellaneous
Section 11   Expenses: generally expenses incurred as a result of one party defaulting
Section 12   Notices: when and how notices are to be sent from one party to another
Section 13   Governing laws and jurisdictions: specify either English or New York in the schedule.

While the master agreement is to be agreed and signed without any amendments, any additional conditions, which are agreed between parties with respect to the agreement are documented in the "master agreement schedule". The schedule also allows parties to elect on how certain provisions are to be applied, for example netting on an individual or multi transactional basis. The schedule to the master agreement is divided into five parts.

Part 1: Termination provisions
❏ Specifies entities related to events of default and termination.
❏ Specifies selections in the case of default or early termination.

These additional selections or provisions are generally related to Section 5 of the master agreement.

Part 2: Tax representation
❏ Both counterparties claim tax representation, which normally states that neither entity is liable to withholding tax (neither as a payer or receiver of payments).
❏ For US entities, they must provide regular confirmation of their status.

Part 3: Agreement to deliver documents
Part 3 may include any of the following:

❏ taxation documents (often nothing to deliver other than for a US counterparty which may be required to deliver a W8-BRN form (to claim US status);
❏ financial statements and representation;
❏ legal opinions; or
❏ verification of agreement authorisation by an entity's board of directors, plus any authority to specific persons allowed to transact under the agreement.

Part 4: Miscellaneous
❏ Address/contact details for notices, agents, offices, and multi-branch offices; and
❏ details of credit support provide (if any).

Part 5: Other
Part 5 includes any amendments to the body of the MA or extra credit related provisions.

CONFIRMATIONS

Once two counterparties have entered into an ISDA master agreement, any specific transaction that is made verbally, is then agreed and documented with a written confirmation.

Confirmations govern the economic terms of each individual transaction. Each confirmation is governed by the provisions of the signed MA and schedule, but as specified above, any inconsistencies between the confirmation and MA, the confirmation shall prevail. The confirmation relies on details of the agreement, the schedule and may rely on one or more sets of ISDA definitions.

Confirms can come in two forms:

❑ *Long form confirmation* contains in full all the terms necessary to document the economic terms of an individual transaction. Long form confirmations are not common for most established markets.

❑ *Short form confirmation* does not contain *all* the terms necessary to document the economic terms of a transaction. It relies on the standard terms and provisions that are contained within the other agreed documents such as the MA, schedule and ISDA definitions. For a sample confirmation of a cross currency interest rate swap refer to the end of this chapter.

ISDA DEFINITIONS

There are various sets of definitions or booklets, which provide the standard definitions, which the short form confirmation relies on for details and clarification, the ISDA definitions include:

2000 ISDA definitions: interest rate and currency swaps
2005 Commodity derivative definitions
2003 Credit derivative definitions
2002 Equity derivative definitions
1998 FX and currency option definitions
1997 Government bond definitions
1997 Bullion definitions

CREDIT: EXPOSURE, COLLATERAL AND CREDIT SUPPORT

When counterparties enter into derivative transactions, at market rates, the initial fair value of most (non-optionality) derivative contracts are normally zero. However, as we have discussed, when interest rates and foreign exchange rates move, the value of the underlying derivative contract can have a positive or negative value. If the contract has a positive value and the underlying counterparty defaults the non-defaulting party faces a real loss, as they will need to replace the contract at current market rates. For derivatives we call this credit risk "contingent risk", that is the amount of risk is contingent on movements in underlying market rates, unlike a vanilla loan where the credit is fixed upfront at the notional amount.

Most entities monitor the contingent credit risk they have with another counterparty using the following methodology.

$$\text{Credit risk} = \text{Current MTM} + \text{potential exposure} \qquad (3)$$

The current MTM is the fair value of the contract valued at current market rates, at any given point in time. The potential exposure is an estimate of what the contract's value can be at anytime between now until maturity. This potential is calculated by estimating how rates (interest rate and FX) can move over time, which is based on an underlying assumption of an instrument's volatility over time. For example we can estimate the dispersion of the EUR/US$ FX rate over time, based on a flat volatility (standard deviation of EUR/US$ rate) of 10%. We calculate the *potential* spot rate at any time (t) in the future ($Spot_{fut}$) using the following formula:

$$Spot_{fut} = Fe^{k\sigma\sqrt{t}} \qquad (4)$$

where

- F the current forward rate (which for this example is flat to the current spot rate);
- k the number of standard deviations up ($+$) or down ($-$);
- σ the standard deviation or volatility of the underlying currency pair;
- t the time in years.

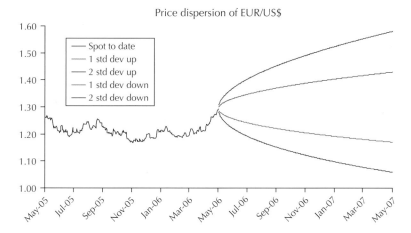

Price dispersion of EUR/US$

The confidence of our FX rate estimate is determined by the number of standard deviation we use in our calculation:

±1 standard deviation provides a confidence interval of 68.2%
±2 standard deviation provides a confidence interval of 95.4%
±3 standard deviation provides a confidence interval of 99.7%

The same analysis can be used to estimate the potential movement in forward interest rates over time. Once we have the estimated movement in the FX and interest rates over time we can then estimate the value of our derivative contract over time, applying these potential adverse changes in rates.

An example of the potential credit exposure from an interest rate swap is illustrated in Figure 1, which shows the potential movement in the MTM over one year, with one year to maturity.

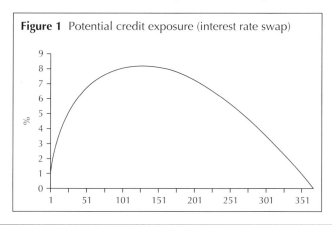

Figure 1 Potential credit exposure (interest rate swap)

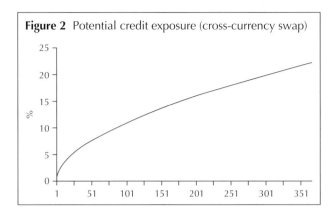

Figure 2 Potential credit exposure (cross-currency swap)

Exposure increases initially as interest rates increase and then starts to decrease as rates continue to increase but the number of coupon payments remaining decreases. In this example the estimated maximum potential credit exposure is 8.24%, based on a 95% confidence interval. This example only illustrated the situation when we have a positive credit exposure and ignores the possibility that the counterparty owes the customer on any given date (you cannot have negative exposure). If there is negative exposure and the counterparty defaults the contract can be replaced at current market rates, which will be in our favour.

An example of the potential credit exposure for a cross-currency swap is illustrated in Figure 2, which again shows how the potential MTM can move over the one year life of the swap. Unlike an IRS, the CCIRS has significant exposure at maturity, as a result of the exchange of principal at maturity. Given this FX exposure, cross-currency swap have significantly more potential credit risk compared to a vanilla IRS. In this example we have calculated a maximum potential credit exposure of 22.2%.

The maximum credit exposure is not how much the counterparty would owe you, if and when they default, it is an estimate of how much the replacement hedge could be worth given an adverse movement in rates (between valuation and termination date), within a 95% certainty. As a general rule the longer the term the more credit risk and in particular credit exposure is significant for cross-currency transactions. Therefore it is imperative that solid counterparties are used for long dated cross currency swaps in order to minimise the contingent credit risk. In order to get a true representation of the contingent credit risk, we also need to consider the credit rating of our counterparty. The credit rating determines the probability of default while the above numerical analysis provides the potential MTM value, combined we can determine the expected loss on an individual transaction for any given counterparty. Where netting is applicable we must also consider the net exposure to a counterparty.

Bilateral collateral

While netting of payments is one way of reducing the potential credit risk associated with derivative transactions between counterparties another method which can significantly reduce the credit exposure is the use of collateral. A collateral agreement between counterparties, as part of the overall ISDA agreement, allows one party to pledge collateral (such as government bond) when the net MTM of outstanding contracts reaches a specified threshold amount. The collateral acts as security in the case of default. The use of collateral reduces the maximum credit risk to the amount of the threshold or the potential amount that the mark to market can move between calculation dates.

ISDA publishes standard credit support documentation, which provides the mechanism for the parties to post collateral against their exposure to each other. The current credit support documentation is the 2001 ISDA margin provision, which encompasses all of the following older documents:

1994 Credit support annex (bilateral form) New York law
1995 Credit support annex (bilateral form – transfer) English law
1995 Credit support deed (bilateral form – securities interest) English law
1995 Credit support annex (bilateral form – securities interest) Japanese law

The use of collateral agreements is an efficient means of reducing credit exposure which in turn provides regulatory capital benefits. However, depending on the jurisdiction of an individual counterparty, (close out) netting and/or collateral agreements may not be enforceable under local laws. ISDA obtains and updates legal opinions on the validity and enforceability of the netting provisions and collateral agreements, which enables institutions to reduce credit risk and consequently capital requirements in jurisdictions subject to BIS capital regulations.

While collateral reduces credit exposure it normally incurs additional costs to the counterparty posting the collateral as a result of the negative spread between the cost of funding the collateral and what the collateral earns.

Mark to market structures/re-couponing

Applying a mark to market structure or agreeing to re-coupon a transaction if a certain valuation threshold is reached can also reduce credit exposure. In this case, when the MTM of an existing transaction breaches a specified threshold, the transaction's specific cashflows are re-set to reduce the current exposure. For example under a typical interest rate swap the fixed coupon paid is amended in order to reduce the current MTM. When the cashflows are amended a cash payment will be made from one counterparty to another. This effectively reduces the credit exposure to the level of the threshold or to the maximum potential exposure between calculation dates.

This technique and mechanism is very similar to bilateral collateralisation, however in jurisdictions where there is uncertainty of the legal enforceability of a collateral agreement re-couponing is a preferred method.

While effective in reducing credit exposure for some firms it may become a liquidity issue to obtain, fund and deliver cash.

Break clauses/mutual termination

The use a mutual break clauses within a transaction can also significantly reduce the potential credit exposure. A break clause (also refereed to as a mutual termination or mutual put) allows either counterparty to close out an existing transaction on an agreed break date or dates. For example a counterparty may enter into a 15-year transaction, where both counterparties have the right to close out and cash settle the transaction after every 5-years (at years 5 and 10). If the transaction is terminated, a cash settlement is made from one party to another in the amount of the outstanding MTM of the transaction. While the mutual put option has no economic value it does effectively reduces the term of the credit exposure from 15-years to a maximum of 5-years, which will significantly reduce the potential exposure, particularly on cross currency swaps.

Sample Cross Currency Swap Confirmation (Short Form)

The UKCO Company
London, England
020 7888 8888

Attention: Steven Brown   8 Aug 2005

Cross-currency Interest Rate Swap Transaction Confirmation
Reference: UKC/8/8/05

Dear Sirs

The purpose of this fax (this "Confirmation") is to confirm the terms and conditions of the Swap Transaction entered into between us on the Trade Date specified below.

The definitions and provisions contained in the 2000 ISDA Definitions as published by the International Swaps and Derivatives Association, Inc., are incorporated into this Confirmation. In the event of any inconsistency between those definitions and provisions and this Confirmation, this Confirmation will govern.

This Confirmation constitutes a "Confirmation" as referred to in, and supplements, forms part of and is subject to, the ISDA Master Agreement dated as of 2 November 2003, as amended and supplemented from time to time (the "Agreement"), between ABC Bank ("Party A") and UKCO Company ("Party B"). All provisions contained in the Agreement govern this Confirmation except as expressly modified below.

The Terms of the Swap Transaction are as follows:

The terms of the particular Swap Transaction to which this Confirmation relates are as follows:

Trade date:	8 August 2005
Effective date:	10 August 2005
Termination date:	10 August 2010

Fixed amounts:

Fixed rate payer:	Party A
Fixed rate payer currency amount:	GBP 100,000,000
Fixed rate payer payment dates:	10 August and 10 February in each year, commencing on 10 August 2005 and ending on 10 August 2010 subject to adjustment in accordance with the Following Business Day Convention
Fixed rate:	5.25 per cent per annum
Fixed rate day count fraction:	Actual/Actual

Floating amounts:

Floating rate payer:	Party B
Floating rate payer currency amount:	US$175,000,000
Floating rate payer payment dates:	10 August and 10 February in each year, commencing on 10 August 2005 and ending on 10 August 2010 subject to adjustment in accordance with the Following Business Day Convention

Floating rate option:	US$-LIBOR-Telerate
Designated maturity:	6 months
Spread:	−0.10 per cent per annum
Floating rate day count fraction:	Actual/360
Reset dates:	2 business days prior to each calculation period
Business days:	London and New York Settlement Days
Calculation agent:	Party A

Initial exchange:

Initial exchange date:	10 August 2005 subject to adjustment in accordance with the Preceding Business Day Convention
Party A initial exchange amount:	GBP 100,000,000
Party B initial exchange amount:	US$175,000,000

Final exchange:

Final exchange date:	10 August 2010 subject to adjustment in accordance with the Preceding Business Day Convention
Party A final exchange amount:	US$175,000,000
Party B final exchange amount:	GBP 100,000,000

Account details:

Account(s) for payments to Party A:	Account Number 123000 at A Bank Plc
Account(s) for payments to Party B:	Account Number 456000 at B Bank Plc

Offices:

(a) The office of Party A for the swap transaction is: London
(b) The office of Party B for the swap transaction is: London

This Confirmation will be governed by and construed in accordance with English Law.

Please confirm that the foregoing correctly sets forth the terms of our agreement by executing the copy of this confirmation enclosed for that purpose and returning it to us or by sending to us a letter substantially similar to this letter, which letter sets forth the material terms of the swap transaction to which this confirmation relates and indicates your agreement to these terms.

Yours faithfully,

ABC Bank

Confirmed as of the
date first above written:

UKCO Company

By: _____

1   Similar accounting standards are under the US accounting standard FAS133.
2   Perfect correlation would be positive 1 but since we are long one instrument and short the other we want the positions to be perfectly inversely correlated, where their values move in opposite directions but by the same absolute amounts, in such a situation beta would be −1.
3   Payment netting deals with regular payments on existing transactions and not "close out netting" which is a result of a default or termination events which force a termination of a transaction. Close out netting is covered in more detail in a later section on defaults.
4   Normally parties agree to extend this grace period given that 1 day is too short to solve technical operational problems.

Appendix A:
Quotation Basis for Interest Rate Swaps

Currency	Basis for Floating Interest			Basis for Fixed Interest	
	FLT basis	Payment freq	Index	FXD basis	Payment freq
US$	Act/360	3M	LIBOR	Act/360 30/360	Annual Semi-Ann
GBP	Act/365	1M for 1 year then 3M	LIBOR	Act/365	Annual
EUR	Act/360	3M for 1 year then 6M	EURIBOR	30/360	Annual
JPY	Act/360	3M	LIBOR or TIBOR	Act/365	Semi-Ann
CAD	Act/360	6M	90D BAs compounded to 6 Month payments	Act/365	Semi-Ann
AUD	Act/365	90D	Bank Bills	Act/365	Quarterly out to 3 years then Semi-Annual
CHF	Act/360	3M for 1 year then 6M	LIBOR	30/360	Annual
DKK	Act/360	6M	CIBOR	30/360	Annual

Currency	Basis for Floating Interest			Basis for Fixed Interest	
	FLT basis	Payment freq	Index	FXD basis	Payment freq
HKD	Act/365	3M	HIBOR	Act/365	Quarterly
KRW	Act/365	91D	CD	Act/365	Quarterly
NOK	Act/360	6M	NIBOR	30/360	Annual
NZD	Act/365	90D	Bank Bills	Act/365	Quarterly out to 3 years then Semi-Annual
PLN	Act/360	3M for 1 year then 6M	WIBOR	Act/365	Annual
SAR	Act/365	3M	JIBAR	Act/360	Quarterly
SEK	Act/360	3M	STIBOR	30/360	Annual
SGD	Act/365	6M	SOR	30/360	Semi-Ann

Source:Tullut & Tokyo, Bloomberg.

Appendix B:
Interpolation Methods

In our example we have constructed our zero curve using DCFs, some practitioners convert these DCFs to zero coupon interest rates and then use the zero rates to interpolate the FRAs and DCFs to non grid dates. If the compound interest discount factor for an interest rate that is compounded over multiple payment periods equals:

$$dcf = \frac{1}{\left(1+\dfrac{r}{p}\right)^{tp}}$$ **(B.1)**

We can then derive the zero rates by rearranging Formula (B.1) and solving for r.

$$r_{zero} = \left[\frac{1}{dcf^{(1/tp)}} - 1\right] \times p$$ **(B.2)**

where

> p = number of payments per annum (payment frequency);
> t is time in years to maturity.

Whenever a DCF or swap rate needs to be interpolated we have several alternatives on how we interpolate the rate. While in our construction and examples we have used linear interpolation there are several alternatives, of which there is no absolute correct method.

❑ linear interpolation of discount factors
❑ linear interpolation of the zero coupon rates
❑ linear interpolation of the logarithm of discount factors
❑ Other methods commonly used try to "fit" a curve to the DCFs or zero rates such as the cubic spline technique.

If we assume the following data as of 15-April-2005:
If we know the following DCFs and calculate the zero IR using B.2:

Date	DCF	t	Zero Rate (ZR) (%)
21-Sept-05	0.985541	0.4356	3.400
21-Dec-05	0.976030	0.6849	3.606
19-Apr-14	0.658588	9.016	4.741
19-Oct-14	0.641174	9.518	4.780

Linear Interpolation:
We can use linear interpolation to derive the DCF or zero rate using the following formula:

$$Rate_{datei} = Rate_1 + (Rate_2 - Rate_1) \times \frac{(Date_i - Date_1)}{(Date_2 - Date_1)} \qquad \textbf{(B.3)}$$

where

$Rate_{datei}$ = interpolated rate to date i;
$Rate_1$ = near number;
$Date_1$ = near date;
$Rate_2$ = far number;
$Date_2$ = far date.

Log-linear Interpolation
We can use log-linear interpolation to derive the DCF or zero rate using the following formula:

$$Rate_{datei} = Rate_1 \times \left[\frac{Rate_2}{Rate_1} \right]^{\frac{Date_i - Date_1}{Date_2 - Date_1}} \qquad \textbf{(B.4)}$$

In practice it is more common to use the log linear interpolation of the discount factors and to use linear interpolation on the interest rates. While there is a great debate on which method of interpolation is the most accurate the difference in pricing is not significant.

Interpolate to date$_i$	DCF Interpolation		Zero Rate Interpolation	
	linear	log-linear	linear	log-linear
15-Oct-05	0.983267	0.983258	3.4095%	3.4088%
1-Aug-14	0.648692	0.648634	4.7635%	4.7634%

Curveßuilder also has a build in interpolation function, which allows you to interpolate a rate between any 2 dates. The parameters shown illustrated below (output from excel function =interp( )) should be self-explanatory given the formula above.

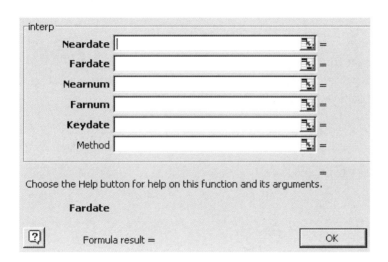

The interpolation [=interp( )] function allows you to use three different methods to interpolate a rate (DCF or zero rate)

Method

1	or Omitted	Linear interpolation
2		Log linear interpolation
3		Cubic spline interpolation[1]

CUBIC SPLINE[2]

A number of zero curve models interpolate using a polynomial function to model and create a "fitted zero curve". A series of linked cubic polynomial (cubic splines) are generated to fit a curve through a given series of data points (either DCF or interest rates). The objective of a cubic spline curve is to fit a smooth curve given the grid points, which we have already extracted from our boot-strapping method.

The most common method and easiest to implement is the piece-wise cubic spline technique. A complete "fitted" yield curve is generated as follows:

❑ Generate a zero curve in terms of grid points (specific dates), which in effect divides the data into a series of sections.
❑ Each section is then defined as a unique polynomial function.
❑ Each polynomial defines the individual section of the zerocurve and is dependent to the adjacent polynomials. The two splines meet at a common grid point where the slope (first derivative) and the rate of change of the slope (second derivative) are both equal.

The problem with the cubic spline methodology is that the fitted curve's result can be effected by all the curve inputs. So if we want to calculate a 1-year swap the pricing maybe sensitive to our 5-year swap rate, which we included in our curve construction.

The curve is divided into two separate sections, which are linked by discount factors (DCF) as at time t_1, t_2, and t_3 using two cubic splines as shown in the graph below.

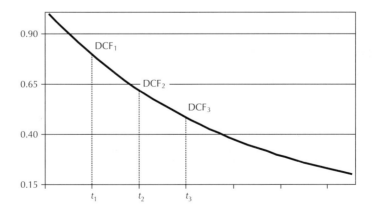

Where the section between t_1 and t_2 is defined by:

$$DCF_1 = a + bt_1 + ct_1^2 + dt_1^3 \qquad\qquad \text{(B.5)}$$

And the section between t_2 and t_3 is defined by:

$$DCF_3 = e + ft_3 + gt_3^2 + ht_3^3 \qquad\qquad \text{(B.6)}$$

There are eight parameters to be determined (four from each polynomial). By having the two polynomials go through a common grid point and having the first and second derivative of each of the polynomial equal where they meet. We can calculate DCF_2 where the two cubic splines meet and are equal:

$$DCF_2 = a + bt_2 + ct_2^2 + dt_2^3 \quad \text{and} \quad DCF_2 = e + ft_2 + gt_2^2 + ht_2^3 \quad \text{(B.7)}$$

If section t_2 can be described by the combined polynomials above, then the first and second derivative at t_2 must be equal:

$$b + 2ct_2 + 3dt_2^2 = f + 2gt_2 + 3ht_2^2 \qquad\qquad \text{(B.8)}$$

$$2c + 6dt_2 = 2g + 6ht_2 \qquad\qquad \text{(B.9)}$$

We then require two extra equations in order to solve for the coefficients in the above equations. We therefore need to have the second derivatives of each equation equal and both set to zero:

$$2c + 6dt_2 = 2g + 6ht_2 = 0 \qquad\qquad \text{(B.10)}$$

We now have the required six equations in order to solve for the six coefficients (six unknowns). Once we have this fitted curve we can then interpolate a DCF for any given date. The following table compares the results of the spline method with the linear and log linear methods.

Interpolate to date$_i$	DCF interpolation		
	linear	log-linear	Spline
15-Oct-05	0.983267	0.983258	0.983324
1-Aug-14	0.648692	0.648634	0.648663

Apart from the function above [=interp( )], there are two further functions within Curveßuilder which allow you to interpolate using the cubic spline method.

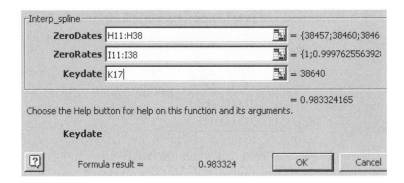

The generic function [=Interp_spline( )] inputs a range of zero dates (or grid points) along with a range of corresponding zero rates (or discount factors) which calculates an interpolated DCF to a given date (*Keydate*).

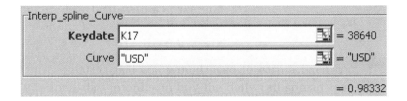

We can also use the more specific function, which uses the derived zerocurve. The function [=Interp_spline_Curve( )], calculates an interpolated DCF to a given date (*Keydate*) from a given named curve, for example "USD". If no curve is included then by default USD (first curve) is used by default.

1   Not recommended using the spline method in this function as it only uses the 2 data points to 'fit' the curve. It is more appropriate to use the full curve as outlined in the next section and use the separate spline interpolation function, which uses the full zerocurve.

2   See Cox, David "Yield curves and how to build them", 1995 Capital markets strategies 4 pages 29–33. For further information on alternative interpolation techniques see Hagan, P., West, G. "Interpolation methods for curve construction", June 2005, Bloomberg.

Appendix C:
Convexity Adjustment

The following appendix examines the convexity adjustment equation 10.1, which we applied in chapter 10. We compare the results of the full valuation technique, which involves calculating the first and second partial derivative with that of the approximation we use in equation 10.2. We use equation 10.2 in order to minimise the computational process time within our models.

The convexity adjustment for the forward rate has been proven to be worth:

$$S\_cvx = -\frac{1}{2}\sigma^2 S^2 t \frac{P''(S)}{P'(S)} \tag{10.1}$$

where

S = Forward swap rate;
σ_S = volatility of the forward swap rate;
t = time to payment date (in years);
$P'(S)$ = First derivative of swap price with respect to the swap rate (S);
$P''(S)$ = Second derivative of swap price with respect to the swap rate (S).

A swap with a coupon of S, a payment frequency of f, and a yield to maturity of y, has a price $P(S)$ of

$$P(S) = \Sigma \frac{S/f}{\left(1+\dfrac{y}{f}\right)^{ft}} + \frac{1}{\left(1+\dfrac{y}{f}\right)^{fT}}$$

$P(S)$ is the price of the forward starting swap which is a function of the forward rate S, $P'(S)$ is the first partial derivative, while $P''(S)$ is the second partial of price relative to swap rates.

Consider a constant maturity swap that provides a payoff in three years, which is equal to the 3-year swap rate, at that time. What is the convexity adjusted forward swap rate if the implied forward rate is 8.00% (annual basis)? Assuming that the zero rate for all maturities is 8.00% pa (annual basis), the volatility rate for the 3-year forward starting swap rate is 20% (derived from the swaption vols.). If the annual swap rate and the yield to maturity (y) is equal to 8.00% (annual basis) then the price of the underlying swap is:

$$P(S) = \frac{0.08}{(1+0.08)^1} + \frac{0.08}{(1+0.08)^2} + \frac{1.08}{(1+0.08)^3}$$

and $P'(S)$ and $P''(S)$ equate to:

$$P'(S) = -\frac{0.08}{(1+0.08)^2} - \frac{0.16}{(1+0.08)^3} - \frac{3.24}{(1+0.08)^4} = -2.5771$$

$$P''(S) = \frac{0.24}{(1+0.12)^3} + \frac{0.72}{(1+0.12)^4} + \frac{13.44}{(1+0.12)^5} = 9.3002$$

We can approximate the convexity adjustment using formula 10.1:

S	8.00%
σ_S	20%
T	3 years
t	3 years

$$S\_cvx = -\frac{1}{2} \times 0.20 \times 0.08^2 \times 3 \times \frac{9.3002}{-2.5771} = 0.001386$$

The convexity adjustment is thus 13.86 bps (0.1386%) and therefore the convexity adjusted forward rate is 8.1386%.

Using short cut formula 10.2 we can approximate the convexity adjustment for the above example.

$$-\frac{1}{2}\sigma S^2 t \times \frac{P''(S)}{P'(S)} = -S\sigma^2 t \left(\frac{ST}{\left(1+\dfrac{S}{f}\right)^{(fT+1)} - \left(1+\dfrac{S}{f}\right)} - 1 \right) \tag{10.2}$$

Therefore the convexity adjusted forward rate is the implied forward rate plus the convexity adjustment.

$$-0.08 \times 0.20^2 \times 3 \times \left(\frac{0.08 \times 3}{(1+0.08)^4 - (1+0.08)} - 1 \right) = 0.001386$$

The convexity adjustment is thus 13.86 bps (0.1386%) and therefore the convexity adjusted forward rate is 8.1386%. Which provides the same result as above.

Appendix D: Curveßuilder: Installation and Overview

The excel model on the CD contains one file which has several different spreadsheets that price various interest rate derivative products and applications.

While the model works without the need for further installation many users have found that installing the built in excel add-ins has provided many useful functions.

To install the Analysis ToolPak and Analysis ToolPak – VBA

(1) On the Tools menu, click Add-Ins.
   If Analysis ToolPak (Analysis TookPak – VBA) is not listed in the Add-Ins dialog box, click Browse and locate the drive, folder name, and file name for the Analysis ToolPak add-in, Analys32.xll (ATPVBEAN.xla) – usually located in the Microsoft Office\Office\Library\Analysis folder – or run the Setup program if it isn't installed.
(2) Select the Analysis ToolPak (Analysis ToolPak – VBA) check box.

If you do encounter a problem send an email to mail@ curvebuilder.com.

Curveßuilder.xls has many models over several worksheets which we have described and implemented throughout this book:

Worksheet	Description
Zerocurve	This includes all the yield curve inputs, and generates the required zero curve. The results of which are then used in all the models. The zerocurve needs to be generated anytime the inputs or data changes by clicking the Curveßuilder button. There is a time and date stamp at the top of the page to tell you the last time the curve was updated. DO NOT CHANGE THE NAME OF THIS WORKSHEET
Zerocurve2	The alternative currency so that we can price cross currency and quanto swaps. DO NOT CHANGE THE NAME OF THIS WORKSHEET
Risk	This worksheet runs the delta or PV01 analysis. By simply linking the valuation from any of the models to the NPV cell on this worksheet and then running the Risk simulation (click the Run Risk button), the interest rate sensitivity (PV01) is given. There is a timer at the top of the worksheet which indicates how long it takes to run the analysis. It should take between 30 and 90 seconds to run, depending on your system. In order to speed it up you can close down other programs or other worksheets you may have open. If it is still too slow you can delete unused worksheets within the Curveßuilder.xls (this reduces the number of calculations the system has to run. DO NOT CHANGE THE NAME OF THIS WORKSHEET
Swap Calculator	This is the main cashflow or swap calculator. This worksheet can price new or existing interest rate and cross currency swaps including: ❏ Fixed for Floating IRS and cross currency swaps ❏ Floating for floating (cross currency) basis swaps

Worksheet	Description

❏ Either leg can be floating where fixing is
  ❏ set in advance paid in arrears
  ❏ set and paid in arrears (LIBOR in arrears swap)
❏ Amortising (straight line) swaps
  ❏ Straight line amortisation schedule is automatic but the frequency for both legs must be the same, can manually override the principal schedule if frequency is different.
❏ Include varying principal amounts
❏ Include any fees to be paid or received (on leg one only)
❏ The second leg can also be used to price various floating legs, as shown in diagram 1 below.
  ❏ Constant Maturity Swaps
  ❏ Quanto or Diff Swaps

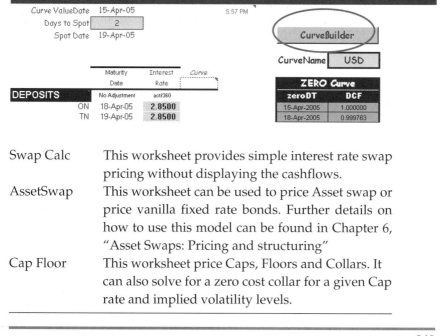

Swap Calc	This worksheet provides simple interest rate swap pricing without displaying the cashflows.
AssetSwap	This worksheet can be used to price Asset swap or price vanilla fixed rate bonds. Further details on how to use this model can be found in Chapter 6, "Asset Swaps: Pricing and structuring"
Cap Floor	This worksheet price Caps, Floors and Collars. It can also solve for a zero cost collar for a given Cap rate and implied volatility levels.

Worksheet	Description
Swaption	This worksheet prices swaptions: ❑ Payer or Receiver Swaptions ❑ European or Bermudan
Swaption Full	This spreadsheet allows you to price the swaption combined with an underlying swap, which is useful if you want to price a callable bond.
Portfolio	This allows you to manage a portfolio of interest rate sensitivity instruments, in order to manage the interest rate exposure on a portfolio rather than on one underlying security. In the current version interest rate swaps, fixed rate bonds and short term (Eurodollar) futures can be included.
SpreadOption	This model allows you to price a European spread option on different floating interest rates. The spread payoff and option pricing can be based on either a short term rate (*Floating Index*) or a longer term CMS swap rate (*Swap rate*).

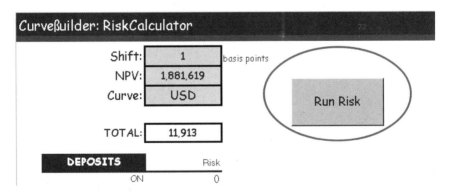

Many electives are available from hidden pull down menus. In order to help provide further info and support we have included many hidden comments throughout the spreadsheet which are indicated by a red comment flag. An example of the hidden menus and comments are illustrated in the following diagram.

While many hours of testing have been done on the models there will inevitably be a few bugs which have not been discovered. If you find any bugs or have any suggestions for improvements please email us so we can improve the system, anyone that submits comments will receive an updated version of the models as and when it becomes available. Send an email, and a short description of the error or improvement suggestion to mail@curvebuilder.com.

While the spreadsheets provide the structure and framework to price all the interest rate derivative products covered in this book there are also some useful and key functions which are also available to the user in their own spreadsheets. Users can access these functions under the user defined functions within the insert-function application within excel.

Function	Description
Black Scholes	A simple Black and Scholes option calculator. Call or Put
CapFloor	Prices a European cap or floor
CMS_adj	Calculates a time and convexity adjusted fair value forward swap rate, as outlined in Chapter 10
DCF	Calculates (interpolates) a discount factor to a given date using a specified zero curve
FixedRate	Calculates a Fixed Par Swap rate for a given set of parameters provided. Assumes the floating leg has no margin
FRA	More complex FRA calculation method, taking into account long or short stubs, in arrears fixings and different daycount basis
FRAs	Simple FRA calculation, determines the fair value FRA rates based on the underlying zero curve, start and end dates and the daycount basis
Interp	See Appendix B
Interp_spline	See Appendix B
QuantoFRA	Calculates the fair value FRA valuation for a floating FRA rate, which is derived in another currency. Provides an adjusted rate based on the methodology outlined in Chapter 10
SpreadOption	Provides a calculation for a European Spread option, where the payoff is based on the difference between two interest rates. Either short term floating rates or long term swap rates. Pricing methodology and inputs based on the material covered in Chapter 10
SwaptionEUR	Calculates the fair value price of a European swaptions, based on the methodology and inputs described in Chapter 9

You can also register your spreadsheet in order to be included in our updates mailing list by sending an email with your name, date of purchase, city of residence and email address to mail@ curvebuilder.com. You will only be sent updated Curveßuilder.xls no other mailings will be done on the back of this registration.

You can also email the author directly at todd@curvebuilder.com.

Bibliography

Black, F., 1976, "The Pricing of Commodity Contracts" *Journal of Financial Economics*, **3** January–March.

Black, F. and M. Scholes, 1973, "The Pricing of Options & Corporate Liabilities", *The Journal of Political Economy*, May.

Burghardt G. and B. Hoskins, 1995, "A Question of Bias", *Risk*, March.

Hagen, P. and G. West, 2005, "Interpolation Methods for Curve Construction".

Das, S., 2004, "Swap/Financial Derivatives: Products, Pricing, Application and Risk Management", Third Edition Wiley Finance.

Fabozzi, F., 1998, "Handbook of Fixed Income Securities", 6th Edition, McGraw-Hill New York.

Grannan, L., "Strips: Arbitraging the Eurodollar Cash and Futures Market", Chicago Mercantile Exchange.

Hagan, P., 2003, "Convexity Conundrums: Pricing CMS Swaps, Caps and Floors", *Wilmott* magazine, March, pp 38–44.

Cox, D. 1995, "Yield Curves and How to Build Them", *Capital Markets Strategies* **4**.

Hagan, P., "Accrual Swaps and Range Notes", unpublished Bloomberg paper.

Haug, E., 1998, "Complete Guide to Option Pricing Formulas", McGraw-Hill New York.

Hull, J., 2002, "Options, Futures and Other Derivatives", 5th Edition, Pearson.

Kirk, E., and J. Aron, 1995, "Correlation in the Energy Markets" *Managing Energy Price Risk, Risk Books.*

PricewaterhouseCoopers, 2005, "International Financial Reporting Standards: IAS 39 – Achieving hedge accounting in practice", PWC, December.

Reiner, E. and M. Rubinstein, 1991, "Breaking Down the Barriers", *Risk*, **4(8)** pp 28–35, September.

Reiner, E. and M. Rubinstein, 1991, "Unscrambling the Binary Code", *Risk*, **4**, October.

Rubinstein, M., 1994, "Return to Oz", *Risk*, **7(11)**.

Rubinstein M., 1991, "Two-Color Rainbow Options", *Risk*, November.

Smith, D., 1990, "By the Bootstraps", *Risk*, **3(6)**, June.

Steiner, R., 1998, "Mastering Financial Calculations", Prentice Hall.

Martin, J., 1996, "Derivatives Math: A user's Guide to the valuation of financial derivative instruments." IFR.

Miron, P. and P. Swannell, 1990, "Pricing and Hedging Swaps", Euromoney Books.

From Black-Scholes to Black Holes, 1994, Risk Books.

Chicago Board of Trade, "CBOT Treasury Futures: A simple treasury duration adjustment".

Barclays, "Repo and Securities lending product guide".

Wikipedia "Volatility" www.wilkipedia.com

Wikipedia "Standard deviation" www.wilkipedia.com

www.global-derivatives.com

www.isda.org

www.risklatte.com

Index